Reviewers' comments about the author's previous books

"It takes a pro to teach Final Cut Pro, and Tom Wolsky delivers. His years of TV and film experience make him uniquely qualified to demystify Final Cut Pro and teach good editing techniques. Every editor needs this book."

 — Jim Heid, Avondale Media

"If you want to learn editing with Final Cut Pro, look no further. Tom Wolsky brings a depth of experience to digital editing that few others share. He has proven himself an excellent teacher at Stanford University's Academy for New Media, and I will encourage, if not require, future students of the Academy to read this book."

 — Phil Gibson, president, Digital Media Academy

"Tom Wolsky's longtime professional career with ABC News in London — and his later teaching position and full-time studio work in California — takes this work far beyond the simple "how to" books that address Final Cut. In Tom's hands, the subject becomes a look into the process of professional editing and project management as well. Because of this, we believe that he knows Final Cut in many ways better than the people that write the program."

 — Ron and Kathlyn Lindeboom, founders, creativecow.net

"*Final Cut Pro 3 Editing Workshop* shows off both Tom's complete expertise with FCP and his skill as a writer. He has always written in a clean, understandable manner with the ability to demystify his subject matter."

 — Ken Stone, www.kenstone.net

FINAL CUT EXPRESS 2
EDITING WORKSHOP

Tom Wolsky

CMP**Books**

Published by CMP Books, an imprint of CMP Media LLC
600 Harrison Street, San Francisco, CA 94107 USA
Tel: 415-947-6615; fax: 415-947-6015
www.cmpbooks.com
email: books@cmp.com

Managing Editor:	Gail Saari
Copyeditor:	Hastings Hart
Layout Design:	Madeleine Reardon Dimond
Cover Layout Design:	Damien Castaneda

Distributed in the U.S. by:
Publishers Group West
1700 Fourth Street   **distributed in Canada through Jaguar Book Group**
Berkeley, CA 94710
1-800-788-3123

Library of Congress Cataloging-in-Publication Data

Wolsky, Tom.
Final cut express 2 editing workshop / Tom Wolsky.
    p. cm. — (DV expert series)
Includes bibliographical references and index.
ISBN 1-57820-256-6 (alk. paper)
1. Digital video—Editing--Data processing. 2. Motion pictures—Editing—Data Processing. 3. Final cut (Electronic resource) I. Title. II. Series.
TR899.W65967 2004
778.59'6'0285536--dc22

                                    2004010455

For individual orders and for information on special discounts for quantity orders, please contact:
CMP Books Distribution Center, 6600 Silacci Way, Gilroy, CA 95020
Tel: 1-800-500-6875 or 408-848-3854; fax: 408-848-5784
email: cmp@rushorder.com; Web: www.cmpbooks.com

ISBN: 1-57820-256-6

CMP Books

*For Michael Horton, who has done so much
to help and foster the community of Final Cut users*

Contents

Introduction

What Is Editing?

Video or film production is based on the notion of time, usually linear time of a fixed length. Whether it is 10 minutes, 30 minutes, one hour, two hours, or more, the film is seen as a single event of fixed duration. On the other hand, time within the film itself is infinitely malleable. Events can happen quickly: we fly from one side of the world to another, from one era to a different century, in the blink of an eye. Or every detail and every angle can be slowed down to add up to a far greater amount than the true expanse of time—or seen again and again.

Because film and video production are based on the notion of time, the process of editing, controlling time and space within the story, is of paramount importance. This process of editing, however, does not begin after the film is shot. It begins when the idea is conceived. As soon as you are thinking of your production as a series of shots or scenes, you are mentally editing the movie, arranging the order of the material, juxtaposing one element against another.

The first movies were single, static shots of everyday events. The Lumière brothers' screening in Paris of a train pulling into the La Ciotat train station caused a sensation. Silent, black and white, it still conveyed a gripping reality for the audience. The brothers followed this with a staged comic scene. Georges Méliès expanded this into staging complex tableaux.

Nonlinear Movies?

The notion of nonlinear presentation of films and videos that DVD offers is antithetical to the idea of film as a progression in time. Over the years there have been many attempts to make films nonlinear or with variable structures and outcomes, much like a game. None have been really successful. I think the reason is that the movies are about storytelling, and that requires a linear presentation. If variability is introduced to the movie, or if the scenes can be seen in any order, then its ethos as a story disappears. We will all see a different story. We'll no longer be able to say, "Did you like Casablanca?" The question would then be, "How was your version of Casablanca?" It's not quite the same thing and probably doesn't provide the same sense of satisfaction and fulfillment, which is why I think the attempts at nonlinearity or variability have largely failed except in games.

It wasn't until Edwin H. Porter and D. W. Griffith in the United States discovered the power of editing one shot next to another that the movies were really born. Griffith also introduced such innovations as the flashback, the first real use of film to manipulate time. Close-ups were used to emphasize the moment of impact and wide shots to establish context. Parallel action was introduced, and other story devices were born, but the real discovery was that the shot is the fundamental building block of film and that the film is built one shot at a time, one after the other.

Editing is about three things: selection, arrangement, and timing—selecting which shot to use, determining where that shot should be placed, and deciding how long the shot should be on the screen. The first of these, selection, begins in the process of capturing your material. For many editors the process of logging and capturing material is part of the selection process. In days when hard drives were small and very expensive, this was a critical step in the digital editing process. Now, because drives have become relatively cheap and much, much larger and faster, the pressure to capture selectively has been greatly reduced.

The moment of the edit is dictated by rhythm: sometimes by an internal rhythm the visuals present, sometimes by a musical track, more often than not by the rhythm of language. All language, whether it's dialog or narration, has a rhythm, a cadence or pattern, dictated by the words and based on grammar. Grammar marks language with punctuation: commas are short pauses; semicolons are slightly longer pauses; periods are the end of an idea. The new sentence begins a new idea, a new thought, and it is natural that as the new thought begins, a new image is introduced to illustrate that idea. The shot comes, not on the end of the sentence, not in the pause, but on the beginning of the new thought. This is the natural place to cut, and it's this rhythm of language that drives the rhythm of film and video.

Films and videos are made in the moments when one shot changes into another, when one image is replaced by the next, when one point of view becomes someone else's point of view. Without the image changing, you just have moving pictures. The idea of changing from one angle to another or from one scene to another quickly leads to the concept of juxtaposing one idea against another. It soon becomes apparent that the impact of storytelling lies in the way in which the shots are ordered. Editing is about selection, arrangement, and timing. Editing creates the visual and aural juxtaposition between shots. That's what this book is about, how to put together those pieces of picture and sound.

Who Am I To Write This Book?

I have been working in film and video production for longer than I like to admit, nearly 40 years. A few years ago I left ABC News, for whom I'd worked as an operations manager and producer for many years, first in London and then in New York, to take up teaching—video production, of course—at a small high school in rural northern California. I also have written curriculum for Apple's Video Journalism program as well as teaching training sessions for them, and in the summers I have had the pleasure of teaching Final Cut at the Digital Media Academy on the beautiful Stanford University campus.

The structure of this book follows that of my Final Cut Pro Editing Workshop books. It is organized as a series of tutorials and lessons that I hope have been written in a logical order to lead the reader from one topic to a more advanced topic. The nature of your work with Final Cut Express, however, may require the information in Lesson 6, for example, right away. You can read that lesson by itself and edit your sound. There may, however, be elements in Lesson 6 that presuppose that you know something about using the **Viewer** in conjunction with the **Canvas**.

Who Is This Book For?

This editing workshop is intended for all FCE users. So the broader question should really be, Who is FCE itself intended for? It appeals, I think, to serious hobbyists, the so-called prosumer market, event producers, and even small companies with video production requirements. I also think it's a great product for education, fully featured, far beyond the frustration many students find in iMovie, but without the professional features in its older brother Final Cut Pro. Institutional education pricing makes it affordable for schools even in penny-pinching times. Final Cut is not a simple application to use. It's not plug-and-play. It requires learning your way around the interface, its tools, and its enormous capabilities.

What's on the DVD?

The DVD included with this book is a hybrid DVD. It contains an introduction to Final Cut aimed at the iMovie user. If you have been using iMovie, I urge you to watch it. It will explain, compare, and contrast the two applications. I hope it will make the transition easier for you. The DVD also has a DVD-ROM portion that contains some of the lessons, projects, and clips used in the book. Not all of the lessons require materials from the DVD. For some, such as Lesson 2, you don't need any at all. For others you may want to substitute your own material, clips you want to work with or are more familiar with. I hope you find this book useful, informative, and fun. I think it's a good way to learn this kind of application.

Acknowledgments

First, as always, my gratitude to all the people at CMP Books who make this book-writing process relatively painless, particularly Paul Temme, associate publisher, for his thoughtful advice and guidance; Dorothy Cox, senior editor, and Gail Saari, for organizing the files I needed. Many thanks as always are due to Madeleine Reardon Dimond for her work on the layout, and to Hastings Hart for his meticulous copyediting. My thanks again to Damien Castaneda for his wonderful work on the covers, and to Gary Adcock of the Chicago Final Cut Pro Users Group, for his help in looking over some of the chapters. Any errors or omissions that remain are the results of my oversights or misunderstandings, not his.

Special thanks to Patty Montesion for her help and continued support.

So many helped in making this book possible: Sidney Kramer for his expert advice, Anne Renehan of BorisFX for her excellent suggestions for Calligraphy, Rich Corwin and Anita Lupattelli for their gracious cooperation, Toby Malina of Avondale Media for her gracious help. To the creative software engineers who allowed me to put samples of their work on the DVD, especially Graeme Nattress, Christoph Vonrhein, John Wainwright, and Klaus Eiperle; and Eric Fry, for his Timecode Calculator.

A great many thanks are due to my partner, B. T. Corwin, for her insights, her endless encouragement, her engineering technical support, and her patience with me. Without her, none of this would have been possible. Finally, again my thanks the wonderful people of Damine, Japan, who welcomed us into their homes and whose lives provided the source material for many of these lessons.

Want to receive e-mail news updates for Final Cut Express 2 Editing Workshop?

Send a blank e-mail to:
fce2@news. cmpbooks.com.

We will do our best to keep you informed of software updates and enhancements, new tips, and other FCE-related resources.

Lesson 1

Installing Final Cut Express 2

Welcome to Final Cut Express 2, the latest version of Apple's video editing software for DV users. Although the first version of Final Cut Express was based on Apple's older editing software, version 3 of Final Cut Pro, this version of Final Cut Express, version 2, is wholly based on Final Cut Pro 4. This brings many changes and substantially more complexity to the application, together with a great deal more real-time capabilities, including many more real-time transitions, filters, and motion effects.

Many Mac users working in video have been frustrated by the limitations of iMovie, despite its improvements since it was first introduced. There are a few similarities between iMovie and FCE, but there are many, many distinct differences, not only on the surface, but also in the very format that the applications work in.

For more information about making the step from iMovie to Final Cut Express, see the DVD that comes with this book. It is a hybrid DVD, including a section that will play with your Mac's DVD Player. There I'll explain a little about the differences between the two applications and moving from one to the other.

I'm sure you want to dive right into it, but Final Cut Express 2 first must be installed properly on a properly functioning system. Video editing software is not simple shareware but a complex, system-integrated piece of software that requires your system to be running in optimal condition. This means that you have to have all the correct system software installed, and have it installed on hardware, computer and hard drives that can support digital video. Your hard drives must be fast, clean, and running properly, ready for moving large amounts of data at high speed.

What You Really Need

Final Cut Express 2 will work only with Apple's OS X 10.2.5 (Jaguar) or with 10.3 Panther or higher. Unlike the earlier version of the application, this version will run only on a G4 Mac 350MHz or higher with AGP graphics. It will no longer run on a G3-based computer. It will run on a G4 iBook, PowerBook, iMac, or an eMac, and of course it will run beautifully on a top-of-the-line Power Mac G5 tower. To achieve real-time preview capabilities, you'll need 500MHz or faster single- or any dual-processor Power Mac G4 or G5 or at least a 667MHz Power-Book G4. Final Cut Express allows processor-based real-time transitions, graphics, and motion. The ability to see transitions and graphics in real time is a great boon, and much greater real-time capabilities have been added to the new version of the application.

Memory: How Much and What Kind

In addition to the computer, you will need at least 384MB of RAM, with 512MB required for real-time preview. The more you can put in, the better, allowing you to have multiple applications open with ease. You'll also need 40MB of storage space available for installation. See the sidebar on RAM and drive space on page 3.

Your finances almost invariably dictate which computer you purchase for editing video. My recommendation is always to get the biggest, fastest, most powerful computer you can afford. If you have budget constraints, get started on an iMac. If you need to be on the road a lot, get a PowerBook. If you have a larger budget, go for it: a multiprocessor G5 loaded with lots of RAM.

Multiple Drives

Storage is an essential part of any video system. DV consumes about 3.6MB per second of storage space. That translates to 216MB a minute, approximately 1GB for five minutes, and

RAM and Storage

Applications have to deal with two distinct types of memory: RAM and storage. They perform quite distinct functions. RAM (random access memory) are the chips that hold the system and applications while they are running. FCE is stored in RAM while it's open, as is the operating system.

The other type of memory is storage. The platters of the hard drive store your data. In the case of media drives for your video, these are often very big—and very fast—hard drives. They can store huge quantities of data and access them very quickly. In Figure 1.1 the hard drives are on the left, and the three strips of RAM are circled on the right.

1.1 Hard drives and RAM

Mac OS X also works with Virtual Memory, which allows it to have many applications open at the same time, swapping the inactive ones out to your hard drive space when they are not in use or when the RAM is overloaded. FCE does not work well in virtual memory, so it is preferable to get more RAM rather than relying on this operating system feature.

almost 13GB for an hour. Fortunately, cheap hard drives are available in ever-increasing sizes, with platter speeds, seek times, and caches ample for working with DV-quality material.

Because a digital video editing system needs to move large amounts of data at high speed, you should use separate drives purely for storing video data. You should have one internal hard drive dedicated to your operating system and applications, such as Final Cut Express, Photoshop or Photoshop Elements, your iLife applications, iTunes, iDVD, etc., and everything else from Internet access software to word processing and spreadsheets. All of these should be on one drive. Unlike video media, they usually don't take up that much space, so this drive doesn't need to be either exceptionally large or even exceptionally fast. You should also have at least one other hard drive, one that's large and fast. This drive—better still, drives—should carry only your media.

A separate drive is much more efficient at moving large amounts of data at high speed. The media drive needs to get that data off the drive very quickly and play it back. In addition, it needs to play back multiple tracks of audio from various places on the drive simultaneously. That's quite enough work for any one drive to be doing at any one time. To then have it be accessing the application and the operating system as well is often the straw that breaks the camel's back. You are much less likely to have video playback or capture failure through dropped frames and other issues if you have the media on a separate, dedicated hard drive. This drive should run at 7,200rpm and have at least an 8MB cache. For PowerBook, iMac, or eMac users, external FireWire drives are a good solution, such as those from LaCie or WiebeTech or boxes from Granite Digital in which you can put a number of different fast, bare drives.

Many new computers are capable of connecting to FireWire 800 drives. These give great performance and should be the drive of choice if you want to use an external FireWire drive, if you have a computer that can support it and the budget to purchase it.

Optimizing Your Computer for FCE

There are things you can do in **System Preferences** to optimize your computer for video editing with Final Cut Express, mostly switching off things that might interfere with its operations while it's running.

- Make sure **Software Update** is not set to check for updates automatically. That way there is no chance it will take off and try to run while you're working in FCE.

- The **Displays** should be set so that your computer monitor is running in **Millions of colors** and at the resolution settings the system recommends for your display.

- The **Energy Saver** should be set so that the system never goes to sleep. It's less critical that the monitor doesn't go to sleep. I usually set it around 10 minutes, but the system and the hard drive should never shut down. This can cause havoc with slow renders.

- One last step I recommend is to switch off **AppleTalk**. This is simplest to do in OS X by going to **Network Preferences** and creating a new location called **None**. Set up your **None** location without any active connections—no internal modem, no Airport, no Ethernet—everything unavailable and shut off. To reconnect to the network, simply change back to a location from the **Apple** menu that allows access to whatever connection you want to use.

Monitors

In addition to your computer display, you should have also a video monitor. A video monitor reproduces images differently than a computer monitor, which has much greater color depth, resolution, and contrast range, and does not have the interlaced scan lines that a television set or video monitor has. These are all critical to how your video will finally look. If your project will be shown on a television set, you must edit with a video monitor that shows true color output. You may also want a second computer display for the large number of windows that video editing applications need.

To get the video out of your computer and onto the video monitor or TV set, you're going to need to use some kind of digital-to-analog conversion device. The simplest one for most people is a camcorder. The video and audio comes out of the computer's FireWire port, which gets connected to the camcorder, or DV deck, or DV converter box, such as the Canopus ADVC100. The output of the camcorder in turn is connected to the video monitor. That's the best place to watch your movie while you work. The audio from the camera or from the video monitor is fed into speakers. Figure 1.2 shows a typical connection layout. The camera on top of the monitor is the hub that passes the digital signal back and forth to the analog video monitor and speakers.

1.2   Typical connection layout

If you are using an external FireWire hard drive, in most cases the system works best by daisy-chaining the FireWire connection. A six-pin to six-pin FireWire cable connects the computer to the hard drive. Then a six-pin to four-pin cable connects the hard drive to the camcorder or converter box, and then standard video cables connect the camcorder to your television set or video monitor.

Speakers

Good-quality speakers are very important. They should be connected to the same source as the video you're monitoring. The rule of thumb here is that audio follows video, so if you are looking at your video on a television monitor, you should listen to your audio from the same source. So if you have a deck or a DV camera that is feeding the signal from your computer to your TV monitor, then that should also be feeding your audio speakers. Switchable speakers would be ideal, with two inputs to monitor either the video source or the computer output.

Note

Updates: After installing the software it's probably a good idea to check the Apple Final Cut Express web page http://www.apple.com/finalcutexpress to see if there have been any updates to the application. Applications are constantly being refined and updated to fix problems or to accommodate developments in hardware or the operating system. You can also do this by choosing **Software Update** in the **System Preferences**. Also, don't forget to register your new software and get your free copy of Joe Maller's Color Glow filter.

1.3   Final Cut Express icon

Firing Up the Application

Now it's time to launch that program. Double-click on the icon in the *Applications* folder, or better yet make an alias in the **Dock** and click on that (see Figure 1.3). After you start up the application, the first window that greets you is one asking you to enter your name, organization, and serial number.

After a new installation or after you have trashed your *Final Cut Preferences* file, you will next be greeted with the setup preferences screen. The default setting is **DV-NTSC** with audio at 48kHz, and you have a number of settings available to you for NTSC as well as PAL, as shown in Figure 1.4. If you are working with 12-bit, also called 32kHz audio, more choices are available. If you click on the little **Show All** checkbox in the upper right of the window, you will have the option to select from a longer list of options (see Figure 1.5). For now, choose **DV-NTSC**. That's the format we'll be working in.

The second pop-up makes you choose your primary scratch disk. The pop-up defaults to your system partition, setting the scratch disk inside the user's *Documents* folder. It also offers you the choice of any hard drives attached to your system. You should set this to your dedicated media drive whenever possible.

1.4   Choose Setup dialog box

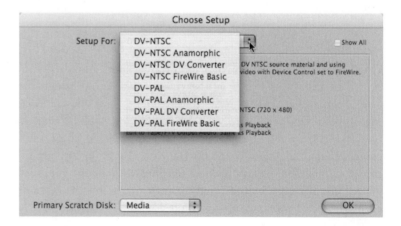

If you do not have a camcorder or DV deck connected to your computer you will get the warning dialog in Figure 1.6. If you'll be working consistently without a deck or camera connected, notice the little checkbox in the lower left that allows you to switch off this warning. You can turn it back on in the **User Preferences**.

Understanding the Interface

Launching a new application for the first time is always an adventure, especially when it's as complex as Final Cut Express. Some software can be intimidating; some can be downright headscratching. When FCE launches it fills your screen with lots of windows, buttons, and tools to explore. Figure 1.7 shows you the default arrangement.

The Primary Windows

The screen is divided into four primary windows, with two large empty screens as your principal monitors:

- The **Browser** is the first window at the top left of the screen, a new location in FCE2 and the opposite of the **Clips** pane in iMovie.
- The **Viewer**, the empty black window in the middle of the screen, allows you to look at individual video clips, either from the **Browser** or from the **Timeline**.
- The **Canvas**, the empty monitor on the right, displays the output of your material as you edit it. The **Canvas** is linked directly to the **Timeline**.
- The **Timeline** for your video is the window with the horizontal sections in the bottom half of the screen. This is where you lay out your video and audio material in the order you want it.

Though the **Viewer** is your primary editor in traditional editing, you can also edit in the **Timeline** window, as well as control transitions and other effects.

The project materials are listed in the **Browser**. Think of the **Browser** as a giant folder. You can nest folders within folders, just like you can on the **Desktop**. This is not where your clips are stored; it is only a list. Your clips are physically stored on your media hard drives. In the **Browser** you can have a variety of different types of files: not only video files but also audio files, graphics, and still images.

DV–NTSC
DV–NTSC 32 kHz
DV–NTSC 32 kHz Anamorphic
DV–NTSC 32 kHz Anamorphic Basic
DV–NTSC 32 kHz FireWire Basic
DV–NTSC Anamorphic
DV–NTSC Anamorphic Basic
DV–NTSC DV Converter
DV–NTSC FireWire Basic
DV–PAL
DV–PAL 32 kHz
DV–PAL 32 kHz Anamorphic
DV–PAL 32 kHz Anamorphic Basic
DV–PAL 32 kHz FireWire Basic
DV–PAL Anamorphic
DV–PAL Anamorphic Basic
DV–PAL DV Converter
DV–PAL FireWire Basic

1.5   FCE presets

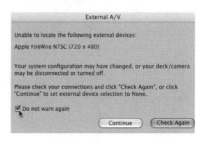

1.6   External A/V warning

1.7   The Final Cut Express 2 interface

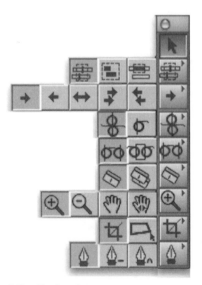

1.8   Tools palette

You'll also notice small vertical bars to the right of the **Timeline** that contain the **Tools** and **Audio Meters**. Some of the tools are hidden, nested inside the **Tools** palette. Figure 1.8 shows all the tools displayed. There is a **Selection** tool, the arrow at the top. There are **Edit** and **Range Selection** tools; **Track Selection** tools; editing tools such as **Roll**, **Ripple**, **Slip**, and **Slide**; **Blade** tools; **Zoom** and **Hand** tools; **Crop** and **Distort** tools; and various **Pen** tools for creating and editing keyframes. Figure 1.7 shows the default configuration, called **Standard**.

➢**Tip**

Open Sequence: Should your project ever open and you don't see a Canvas or Timeline, it means that there is no sequence open. There needs to be at least one sequence in a project. Double-click the sequence icon in the **Browser**, and it will open the **Timeline** with its Canvas.

1.9   Long Browser arrangement

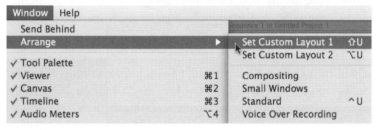

1.10   Window > Arrange > Set
Custom Arrangement

Many people like to work with larger screens, particularly when working on a PowerBook, where the computer screen is more likely to be your primary monitor. In FCE2 you can create new window arrangements by moving the screens into new positions such as in Figure 1.9 with a long tall **Browser** on the left. You can save this, or any other window arrangement, by holding down the **Option** key and selecting from the **Window** menu, **Arrange>Set Custom Layout** (see Figure 1.10). Here there are a few other presets available to you.

Once the arrangement has been set, it can be called up at any time from the **Window>Arrange** menu or by using the listed keyboard shortcut. You can always return to the **Standard** window arrangement from the **Window** menu or using the keyboard shortcut **Control-U**.

New to FCE2 is the ability to resize windows dynamically by grabbing the edges where the cursor changes to a **Resizing** tool (see Figure 1.11). When you pull with the **Resizing** tool, the windows will move proportionately, expanding and contracting as needed to fill the available space.

1.11   Resizing tool for window
arrangements

🐾 Note_____

Sequence: You'll notice that the Browser is not empty. When you create a new project, FCE creates a new sequence called *Sequence 1*. You can rename sequences just as you would any file in the **Finder**. Click on the name to highlight it, and type in a new name. You can have as many sequences as you want in a project, and you can place, or nest, sequences within sequences. We'll look at nesting later (page 172 in Lesson 7).

Tabbed Palettes

You've probably also noticed that most of these windows have tabs with other windows behind them. Let's take a quick look at what's back there. Tabbed in the **Browser** is the **Effects** window. Video and audio effects, transitions, and generators are stored here, including any favorites you want to access frequently.

The **Viewer** has tabs behind it as well:

- **Stereo (a1a2)** or **Mono (a1) and Mono (a2)**, which hold the two channels of audio associated with a video clip. This is where you can see a video clip's audio waveform and manipulate the sound by raising and lowering the levels or panning the tracks from left to right.
- **Filters** is where you control effects applied to clips.
- **Motion** lets you view and change settings for properties such as **Scale, Rotation, Center, Crop,** and others.

Most of these properties can be animated. You can also change the image's **Opacity**, making it more transparent. At zero opacity it will be invisible. You can add a **Drop Shadow** that will appear on any underlying layers, and you can add **Motion Blur,** which simulates the amount of smearing, creating by a fast movement across the screen. We will look at these **Motion** tools in later lessons (see Lessons 7 and 8, which start on pages 153 and 185, respectively).

The **Canvas** and the **Timeline** window also have tabs. If you have more than one sequence open at a time, they will appear as tabs in the **Timeline** window and in the **Canvas.**

Browser

Now let's bring some material into the project so that we can look at each window in greater detail. We'll begin by opening a project I have already created for you.

If you have a project open, close it by clicking the red **Close** button in the upper left of corner of the **Browser.** FCE allows you to have more than one project open at a time, which is very useful because it allows you to easily move elements from one project to another. However, you may get confused with which window belongs to which project, so I normally don't have more than one project open at a time unless I need to.

Let's begin by loading the book's DVD into your DVD drive. When you begin any lesson that needs material from the DVD, you should first drag the needed folders onto the media drive of your computer. The sound and video clips included in those folders will play much better and more smoothly from your computer's high-speed media drive than from any DVD drive. This is a hybrid DVD, and it will probably start up your DVD Player application when you mount the disk. The DVD portion contains a short introduction to FCE aimed at iMovie users, but if you double-click on the DVD icon in the Finder you will find a folder called *Hybrid DVD-ROM Contents*. Inside that folder are a number of other folders. For this lesson you'll need the folder called *Media 1* and also a project file that is inside the *Projects* folder on the DVD.

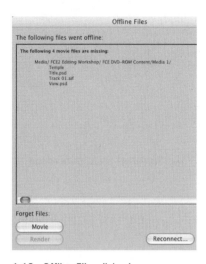

1.12 Offline Files dialog box

1. Drag the *Projects* folder onto your internal system drive. It's not very large. Probably the best place to put it is inside your home *Documents* folder.

2. Drag the *Media 1* folder into your media drive.

3. Before doing anything else, eject the DVD.

4. Open the *Projects* folder on your hard drive, and double-click the project file *Lesson 1* to open the project.

When the project finishes loading, you'll be greeted with the dialog box in Figure 1.12.

Do not click the **Movie** button underneath **Forget Files**, because the application will do exactly that: forget that it needs the media. Nor should you press **Return** or click the **OK** button.

5. Instead, click the **Reconnect** button.

6. After you click **Reconnect**, you will get the **Reconnect Options** dialog box in Figure 1.13.

1.13 Reconnect Options dialog box

7. Click **OK**.

The computer will now search through your hard drives looking for *Temple*. When the file is found, you'll get a dialog box similar to the one in Figure 1.14.

8. If this is the correct file on your media drive, make sure the **Reconnect All Files in Relative Path** box is checked and click the **Select** button.

Final Cut will now reconnect all the material for the project, and then you're ready to go.

1.14 Reconnect Selection window

Importing Files

This project comes with material already in it. If it had been a new project you could have imported the various pieces that are on your hard drive. You can import QuickTime movies, sound files, still images, and more.

There are a couple of different ways to import material. You could use **Command-I** to import a single item or groups of items from one folder, or the **File** menu under **Import>Folder** to bring a folder full of clips or other material. Another way is to move the **Canvas** to the left grabbing it with the bar at the top and sliding it out of the way to access your **Desktop**. You can drag and drop folders and files from anywhere on your drives directly into the **Browser**. This is the simplest, quickest way to bring lots of material into your project.

You can also **Control**-click (or right-click with a two-button mouse) in the **Browser** window and choose **Import>Files** or **Folder** from the shortcut menu.

Importing Music

Importing music either from a CD or in other formats (such as MP3) is slightly different from importing video. Final Cut can work with audio CD files, but they do raise some problems. Audio CDs use a audio sample rate of 44.1kHz. This is not the sampling rate used by the DV format, which uses either 32kHz or, most commonly, 48kHz. MP3s should also be converted to the AIFF format while being resampled and having their compression removed. Although FCE can deal with resampling the audio while it plays it back, it doesn't do it very well, and it requires processor power, which may limit your ability to do real-time effects or to play back video or multiple tracks of audio without dropping frames, i.e., the audio or video stuttering. To avoid this, I always recommend resampling the audio to the correct sampling rate you want to use before importing it into FCE. There are a number of different ways to do this.

> **➤Tip**
>
> **Shortcut Menus:** There are shortcut menus throughout FCE that can be accessed by **Control**-clicking or right-clicking in the application. These are context-sensitive menus that change, depending on where the cursor is. These shortcut menus provide powerful tools for working with the application.

✎ Note

Item-Level Rendering: We'll look at *rendering* in greater detail later, but FCE2 has introduced a new feature that is worth mentioning here. There are new render settings in the application that include the ability to render audio at the item level. This means that you can render a piece of audio such as an MP3 file or a piece of 44.1kHz CD music into the correct sampling rate as a separate item. If you place an audio clip in the **Timeline** and render it out, that render file will stay with the clip wherever you place that audio in your **Timeline.** It will remain fully rendered to the correct settings. It will have a blue indicator bar on the clip to tell you it's been rendered as an item and will not need to be re-rendered. Unfortunately as of this time, item-level rendering of MP3 audio files does not produce the best quality and should be avoided.

I think that the best way to do this is to use the QuickTime Pro Player. The standard QT player will not be sufficient, but by upgrading to the pro version you will get the ability to change file into a number of different formats. You can also do basic video and audio editing in the QT Pro Player. It's a great value and can easily be purchased from Apple at http://www.apple.com /quicktime.

To resample the audio of a CD track or an MP3 file, drag the track or tracks from the CD onto the QuickTime icon that is probably in your **Dock** (see Figure 1.15). This will launch the QT Pro Player and open the files into it.

1.15   QuickTime icon

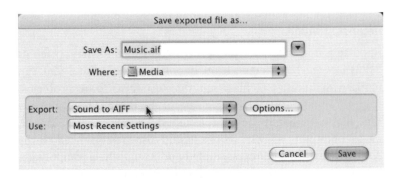

1.16   Export > Sound to AIFF

1. Once the files are open choose **File>Export** (Command-E).

2. From the **Export** pop-up menu select **Sound to AIFF** (see Figure 1.16).

3. Click on the **Options** button and choose the correct settings: **None** for **Compressor, 16-bit, Stereo** and either **48,000Hz**, which is most commonly used in DV, or **32,000Hz**, if that's the setting the rest of your material uses (see Figure 1.17).

4. Give the new file a name, such as *SongName48k*, and save it onto your media drive.

The file will be copied from the audio CD onto your hard drive, converted and resampled to the correct sampling rate. This is the file you should import into and work with in FCE.

Another way to do this if the QuickTime Pro Player is not available to you is to use iTunes. To do this you have to set up your iTunes preferences.

1. Under the **iTunes** menu, go to **Preferences**, select the **Importing** tab, and change the settings to those in Figure 1.18.

2. From the **Import Using** pop-up menu, select **AIFF Encoding**.

3. From the second pop-up menu, select **Custom**.

4. Set the sampling rate to **48,000Hz** or whatever sampling rate you're working with.

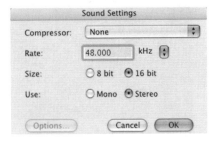

1.17   Sound Settings dialog box

1.18   iTunes Importing preferences

5. Set the **Channels** to **Stereo** and the **Sample Size** to 16-bit, as in Figure 1.19.

Now you're ready to import the music.

6. In the **iTunes** window, **Command**-click on one of the checked track boxes. This will deselect all the tracks.

7. Check the tracks you want, and click the **Import** button on the upper-right corner of the window (see Figure 1.20).

iTunes will copy the track from the CD to your iTunes library, which can be a pretty labyrinthine place to find a track. You want to find the track because you want to move it from your iTunes library, which is on the internal system drive of your computer, onto your media drive. The simplest way to find it is to **Control**-click on the track in your iTunes library and from the contextual menu choose **Show Song File** (see Figure 1.21). This will open a **Finder** window for the folder that holds the file and select the file for you. Copy it, or by holding down the **Command** key, move it to your media drive, and you're ready to import it into FCE2.

1.19   iTunes Custom Settings

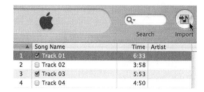

1.20   iTunes window

Browser Views and Buttons

When you start the **Browser**, the project called *Lesson 1* should look like Figure 1.22.

The default view for the **Browser** in Final Cut Express is a medium-size icon view. You'll see icons for video clips—notice the small speaker to indicate that the clip has audio. You'll see an audio track with its speaker icon, and you'll see a couple of folders. Although it uses a folder icon, in Final Cut-speak this folder is called a *bin*, an old film term. Think of long bits of processed film hanging from pins into a large, cloth-lined bin. Whatever you call it, it behaves like a folder.

1.21   Show Song File

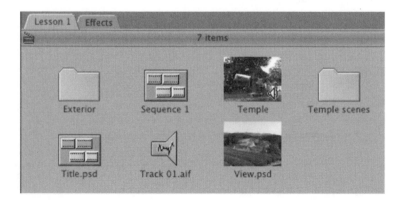

1.22   Lesson 1 Browser window in Medium Icon view

1.23 Browser buttons

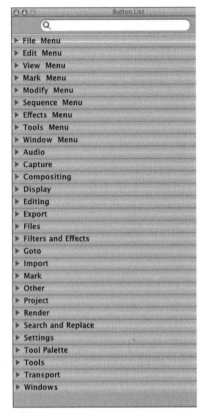

1.24 Button List

1.25 Button holder shortcut menu

You can change the **Browser** view by clicking one of the tiny buttons in the upper-right corner of the window (see Figure 1.23). These are new to FCE2 and let you choose **List** view or three different icon views, **Small**, **Medium**, and **Large**. Small is pretty useless, and the large icons take up a lot of screen space. You can also change views by selecting **View>Browser Items**. Finally, as in much else in FCE, there is a keyboard shortcut you can use. **Shift-H** will cycle through the four **Browser** options.

FCE2 has the ability to create buttons that you can place in the various windows of the interface. To create a new button, open the **Button List** from the **Tools** menu (or use the keyboard shortcut **Option-J**). This calls up the **Button List** in Figure 1.24. To find a function for which you want to create a button, start typing in the find window at the top of the list, and all the functions that have that word will appear in the list below.

To make a button for **Export to QuickTime Movie**, for instance, type *export,* and five items will appear. Drag the item you want to any one of the little coffee bean-like holders in the upper-right corner of any of FCE's windows. The buttons can be further customized by adding colors to the buttons and spacers to group them into sections. You can even color the spacers by using the shortcut menu, with which you can also save your button configurations for all your windows (see Figure 1.25). To remove a button, drag it out of the bean. It will disappear, like an item from the **Dock**, in a puff of smoke.

In the *Extras* folder on the DVD that came with this book is a **Button List** called *Editing Workshop Button Bars*. Using the **Load Button Main Button Bars** function and navigating to that file on the DVD, you can load a group of buttons that I find useful to have. There aren't many of them, because I'm not a great advocate of mousing around the desktop and clicking buttons, but of course you can add your own favorites to any of the button holders.

Let's change the **Browser** to List view. To see the contents of the bins:

* Click the twirly disclosure triangle to expand the folder view or
* Double-click on the folder icon

If you double-click the icon, the folder will open in a new window. To close the window, click on the little red **X** button in the upper-left corner of the window or use the keyboard shortcut **Command-W**.

There are two sequences in the **Browser**; one called *Sequence 1* and another called *Title.psd*. A sequence is a **Timeline** window in which you lay out your video, audio, and graphics clips. A sequence can have multiple tracks of video and audio. You can also place sequences within sequences, as we shall see later. Whenever you create a new project, FCE always creates a default empty sequence called *Sequence 1*. The *Title.psd* also has a sequence icon because FCE imports Photoshop files as layered sequences, with each of the layers in the PSD file appearing as a separate video layer in the Final Cut sequence, one stacked on top of the other. The other PSD file, *View.psd*, is a single-layer file and imports as single-layer graphic and has a different icon. We'll look at working with graphics in Lesson 7 on page 153.

➤**Tip**

Tabbed Bins: You can open a bin tabbed into the project window by holding down the **Option** key as you double-click to open it. To close a tab, **Control**-click on the tab and select **Close Tab**.

Browser Details

With the **Browser** in List view and the window arrangements set to **Standard**, stretch out the **Browser** window to the right, and you'll see just some of the many things the **Browser** displays in List mode (see Figure 1.26).

Name	Duration	Comment 1	Comment 2	Master Clip	Film Safe	In	Out	Tracks	Good	Log Note	Audio
▼ 🗀 Courtyard											
🎞 Hut	00:00:08;14			✔		Not Set	Not Set	1V, 2A			A1 + A2
🎞 LS temple bell	00:00:09;08			✔		Not Set	Not Set	1V, 2A			A1 + A2
🎞 Memorials	00:00:10;16			✔		Not Set	Not Set	1V, 2A			A1 + A2
▦ Sequence 1	00:00:00;00					Not Set	Not Set	2V, 4A			Stereo
🎞 Temple	00:01:39;24			✔		Not Set	Not Set	1V, 2A			A1 + A2
▼ 🗀 Temple scenes											
🎞 LS incense at the altar	00:00:13;17			✔		Not Set	Not Set	1V, 2A			A1 + A2
🎞 LS incense up steps	00:00:15;09			✔		Not Set	Not Set	1V, 2A			A1 + A2
🎞 man praying	00:00:10;10			✔		Not Set	Not Set	1V, 2A			A1 + A2
🎞 woman praying	00:00:14;15			✔		Not Set	Not Set	1V, 2A			A1 + A2
🎞 woman with incense	00:00:17;23			✔		Not Set	Not Set	1V, 2A			A1 + A2
▦ Title.psd	00:00:10;00			✔		Not Set	Not Set	1V			Stereo
◁ Track 01.aif	00:00:17;27			✔		Not Set	Not Set	2A			Stereo
▦ View.psd	00:00:10;00			✔		00:01:00:00	00:01:09:29	1V			

1.26 Browser List View

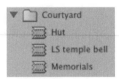

1.27 Subclips in the Browser

1.28 List of available Browser items

The **Browser** shows the duration of clips, the In and Out points, which are probably marked **Not Set** at this stage. You also see track types (whether video and/or audio) and how many audio tracks. Note that the Photoshop sequences tell you how many layers there are in the sequence. Also notice that *Sequence 1* by default has two video tracks and four audio tracks.

Notice the column **Master Clip** and items that are checked. This is a new feature in FCE2, which will substantially affect the way you have to work with the application. We'll look at this more closely in Lesson 3 on page 58.

Notice in Figure 1.27 that the clips in the bin **Courtyard** have torn edges on the left and right. These are subclips. We'll look at subclips and how to use and create them in Lesson 3 starting on page 58.

The **Browser** also shows the type of audio, frame size, and frame rate (in the case of these clips, 29.97 frames per second, the standard frame rate for all NTSC video).

Other information displayed in the **Browser** is:

- Type of video compression used
- Data rate
- Audio sampling rate
- And much, much information that you'll probably never need to look at

Only the **Name** column cannot be moved. It stays displayed on the left side of the window. You can move any of the other columns by grabbing the header at the top of the column and pulling it to wherever you want the column to appear.

>**Tip**

Ordering: You can arrange the order in which clips are shown in List view by selecting the column header. By clicking the little triangle that appears in the header, you can change the order from descending to ascending. Also, if you **Shift**-click on the header of other columns, another triangle will appear and will be added as secondary ordering lists. Secondary sorting allows you to organize and arrange your material to suit your workflow. To clear secondary sort orders, choose a new primary sort, click on an unsorted column header without the **Shift** key.

The FCE Facade

FCE and its entire interface is a facade. What you're bringing into the FCE project, the media your importing into your **Browser**, is the equivalent of aliases of your media (see Figure 1.29). While you're working with these aliases, you're using them to pass instructions to the computer about which pieces of video and audio to play when and what to do with them. The conveniences created for you in the application are a very elaborate way of telling the computer what to do with the media on your hard drives and how to play it back. All the clips in the project, whether in the **Browser** or the **Viewer** or in the **Timeline**, are simply pointers to the media on the hard drive. This is a nondestructive, completely nonlinear, random-access artifice. This means that your media is not modified by anything you do in the application; it means you can arrange the media and work on any portion of your project at any time; and it means that you can access any piece of media from anywhere on your hard drive at any time. The clips are not brought into the **Browser** or placed in the **Timeline**. They never leave their place on the hard drives. They're never in the project at all except as a list. You can change the names in the list to anything more convenient, and it has no effect at all on the data stored on your hard drive. All you're doing is changing how you give instructions to the data; you're not changing the data at all. On the other hand, if you change the names of the clips on your hard drive, that will throw FCE into confusion, and you'll have to reconnect each clip to establish the links between the two.

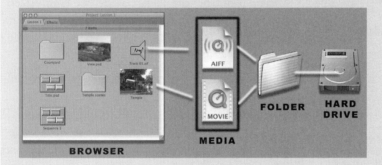

1.29 Media and FCE workflow

If your cursor is over the column headers in the **Browser** and you press the **Control** key while clicking the mouse, you get a shortcut menu. Figure 1.28 shows the list of available categories, except for **Name** and **Duration**, which are active columns in the **Browser**.

The **Comments** columns can be renamed by clicking in the **Comments** column header and choosing **Edit Heading** from the shortcut menu. These are the only columns you can rename.

One of the important items you can call up here is **Source**. This tells you the file path to a clip's location on your hard drive.

Another item hidden in the shortcut menu is **Show Thumbnail**. This cool feature brings up a thumbnail that shows the first frame of the video. Grab the thumbnail and drag the mouse. This is called *scrubbing*, and what you're doing is dragging through the video clip itself so you can see what's in it. Viewing media in the **Browser** can save time. You can quickly scan through a shot to see if it's the one you're looking for.

You can also change the Poster frame, the frame that appears in the thumbnail. The default is the first frame of the video (or the In point), but if you scrub through the video and find a new frame you would like to set as the thumbnail, press the **Control** key and release the mouse. A new Poster frame has been set. If you change the Poster frame for a clip here or in any other **Browser** window, the poster will change for each instance of that clip anywhere in the **Browser** and will also display as the poster when the **Browser** is set to Icon view.

When the **Browser** is in Icon view, the clips are shown with their Poster frame. Like the thumbnails we saw earlier in List view, these icons have the same scrubbable property. To do this you have select the **Scrub** tool from the **Tools** palette (see Figure 1.30). Or, if you hold down **Control-Shift**, the cursor will change to the **Scrub** tool, which is the **Hand** tool with forward and reverse arrows that will let you scrub the icons.

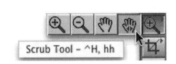

1.30   Scrub Tool

As everywhere in the application, **Control**-clicking in the **Browser** will call up a number of useful items, allowing you to make new bins and sequences, as well as importing and arranging material. The clips themselves hold a shortcut menu that can do a variety of useful things including the ability to **Merge Clips** (see Figure 1.31). This is a neat new feature of FCE2 that gives you the ability to merge up to 24 tracks of audio with a single track of video. Select the material, video and audio, that you want to merge, **Control**-click (or right-click) on one of the selected items and from the shortcut menu choose **Merge Clips**. This will bring up the dialog box in Figure 1.32. Here you can select how the clips will be merged, based on timecode, if they have the same timecode, or more commonly their selected In or Out points.

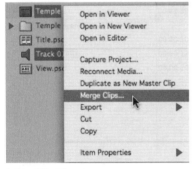

1.31   Clip Shortcut menu

1.32   Merge Clips dialog box

Audio and video do not have to be the same duration or the same start or end times. The application will create a merged clip long enough to cover the duration of the media, beginning with the one that starts first, video or audio, and ending with whichever is longer.

Item Properties: Temple

Format				
	Clip	V1	A1	A2
Name	Temple	Temple	Temple	Temple
Type	Clip			
Source	Media: FCE2 Editing Wor	Media: FCE2 Editing Wor	Media: FCE2 Editing Wor	Media: FCE2 Editing Wor
Offline				
Size	360.8 MB	360.8 MB	360.8 MB	360.8 MB
Last Modified	Tue, Aug 12, 2003, 6:46	Tue, Aug 12, 2003, 6:46	Tue, Aug 12, 2003, 6:46	Tue, Aug 12, 2003, 6:46
Tracks	1V, 2A			
Vid Rate	29.97 fps	29.97 fps		
Frame Size	720 x 480	720 x 480		
Compressor	DV/DVCPRO – NTSC	DV/DVCPRO – NTSC		
Data Rate	3.6 MB/sec	3.6 MB/sec	3.6 MB/sec	3.6 MB/sec
Pixel Aspect	NTSC – CCIR 601	NTSC – CCIR 601		
Anamorphic				
Field Dominance	Not Set	Not Set		
Alpha	None/Ignore	None/Ignore		
Reverse Alpha				
Composite	Normal	Normal		
Audio	A1 + A2		Mono Mix	Mono Mix
Aud Rate	48.0 KHz		48.0 KHz	48.0 KHz
Aud Format	16–bit Integer		16–bit Integer	16–bit Integer

1.33 Item Properties format panel

Another very useful option in the clip's shortcut menu is **Item Properties**.

Item Properties, which can also be called up by using the keyboard shortcut **Command-9**, calls up an information window that tells you everything about a clip (see Figure 1.33). You can rename a clip here, as well as see technical information about the clip and its specifications.

In the previous version of the application there were two more very important panels behind the **Format** panel, one for **Timing** and, even more importantly, one for **Logging Info**. **Logging Info** was particularly useful because you could enter searchable descriptions and comments and other information about the clip in different windows. Unfortunately Apple chose to remove this functionality, which is extensively described with screenshots in the application's documentation. Fortunately the descriptive

1.34 Browser comments

Temple scenes								
Name	▼	Camera	Sound	Comment 1	Comment 2	Comment 3	Comment 4	Log Note
LS incense at the altar		wide angle	quiet	nice shot	LS at altar	from behind	incense smoke	
LS incense up steps		blue		walks up steps	LS to altar	from behind	"	
man praying								NG
woman praying		exposure change	OK	LS push	good for MS	from the side		
woman with incense				bowing at incense				

capabilities are still available in FCE, just a little more awkward to access. The descriptive information and comments can still be entered in the **Browser** columns (see Figure 1.34). To get from one comment field to the next, press the **Tab** key, and the cursor will move to the next editable window.

Notice that two of the column headers have been renamed *Camera* and *Sound* to add information about the technical quality of the material. Except for *Comments 1* and *Comments 2* the other comments columns can have their names changed by **Control**-clicking in the column header and choose **Edit Heading** from the shortcut menu (see Figure 1.35).

1.35 Editing a column heading

✎ Note_____

Updates: For some reason **Comments** 1 and **Comments** 2 cannot be renamed in the **Browser** at the project level, but the same columns can be renamed inside a bin that's in List view.

_____

➤ Tip_____

Shortcut Menus: Using shortcut menus in List view lets you change items for multiple clips with a few clicks of the mouse. For instance, to add a comment to the **Log Note,** I select a number of clips. Then I use the shortcut menu in the same column, the **Log Note** column. This will bring up a list with all my recent notes in that column. I select the one I want, and all the selected clips will have their log notes changed (see Figure 1.36).

_____

1.36 Log Note shortcut menu

Viewer

The **Viewer** is one of the primary editing places in Final Cut Express. This is where you manipulate your clips, mark where they start and end, and prepare them for your timeline. To load a clip into the **Viewer**, double-click on it or select it and press the **Return** key. Start by double-clicking on the clip *Temple* to open it into the **Viewer** (see Figure 1.37).

Viewer Buttons

Let's take a look at that array of buttons clustered around the bottom of the **Viewer** so that you are familiar with them and what they do (see Figure 1.38).

1.37 The Viewer *(left)*

1.38 Viewer buttons *(below)*

The **Shuttle** tab, on the left just below the video display in the **Viewer**, lets you shuttle the clip forwards and backwards. Grab it with the mouse and move right and left. The farther from the default center position you go, the faster the video will play.

The **Jog** wheel on the right, opposite the **Shuttle** tab, will let you roll back and forth through the frames slowly.

The central button in the middle is, of course, the **Play** button. Starting from the left in the group around the **Play** button, the first button is **Go to Previous Edit** (**Up** arrow). The next button is quite useful—it lets you play from your In point to your Out point. The keyboard shortcut is **Shift-**.

The next button to the right of the central **Play** button is **Play Around Current Point** (****). The default is for playback to start five seconds before where the playhead is and play for two seconds past where the playhead is. We'll look at how to use these functions in later lessons.

The last button is **Go to Next Edit** (**Down** arrow).

Another cluster of smaller buttons sits at the bottom left of **Viewer**. From the left, the first button is **Match Frame** (**F**). This is a very useful tool, although it won't work for you at the moment.

1.39 Top of the Viewer

> **Tip**_____
>
> **Match Frame Variations:** Another useful tool to remember is **Command-Option-F.** This is a variation of **Match Frame.** This matches back to the same frame from a new clip of the original piece of media taken from the clip on your hard drive. Another useful shortcut is **Shift-F,** which doesn't open the clip into the **Viewer,** but finds it and selects it in the **Browser.** This can be very handy if you have lots of bins and even bins within bins.

If you open a clip that's in a timeline, it allows you to match back to the same frame in the **Canvas.**

The next button is **Mark Clip (X),** which selects as the In and Out points the entire length of the clip.

The next button, the diamond shape, adds a keyframe, which you need when creating animation.

The next button adds a marker to the clip (**M**). Markers are useful. They let you set visible marks on clips that appear in the **Timeline** window. You can mark the beat of a piece of music, where a phrase appears in dialog, where a pan or zoom starts or ends. Practically anything you can imagine noting about a clip can be made to appear on the screen. Think of them as on screen Post-It notes for video editor.

Next to the **Marker** button is a group of two buttons, **Mark In (I)** and **Mark Out (O).**

There are two more buttons at the bottom right of the **Viewer.** The one with the **Clip** icon lets you load recently opened clips. Next to that is a button with a large **A.** This opens a menu that accesses the **Generators,** such as **Bars and Tone, Render Gradients, Color Mattes, Slug, Text, Title 3D,** and the **Title Crawl** tool. We'll delve into this button in later lessons.

Put your cursor in the white bar directly below the video image. As you mouse down, the playhead will jump to where you are. The playhead is the little yellow triangle with a line hanging from it. There are other playheads in Final Cut Express. In addition to the **Viewer,** they're in the **Canvas** and the **Timeline,** every place where you can play video.

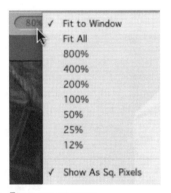

1.40 Zoom pop-up menu

Top of the Viewer

Let's look at the top portion of the **Viewer** for a moment (see Figure 1.39). In the center are two buttons, actually pop-up menus. The one on the left, the **Zoom** pop-up menu (see Figure 1.40), adjusts the size of the image displayed in the **Viewer.** You can set to **Fit to Window (Shift-Z),** or to a percentage from very small to so large that you can see all the pixels at their blocky best.

1.41 View pop-up menu

The other button, the **View** pop-up menu, changes the view from **Image** mode to **Image+Wireframe** (see Figure 1.41). You need this mode especially for compositing in the **Canvas** when you're combining and animating multiple layers of video. The pop-up also lets you turn on overlays, including the **Title Safe** overlay.

Viewer Time Displays

At the top of the **Viewer** are two sets of numbers. The time display on the left is the duration of the clip from its marked In point to its marked Out point. If the In and Out are not set, it will show the duration of the media from start to finish.

The time display on the right shows the current time for the frame where its playhead is sitting. This is not the timecode for the clip, which FCE does not display; but timecode is crucial to accurate editing, and FCE does keep track of the timecode internally, although it is not viewable. Like all time displays in Final Cut Express, it's addressable. Click in it to type a new number, or add and subtract a value. When you change the time in the current time display, the playhead immediately jumps to that time.

Playing Clips

There are a number of different ways of playing a clip to look at your video. The most apparent is the big **Play** button in the middle of the **Viewer** controls. If you like working with the mouse, this will be for you, but it is not the most efficient way to work by any means.

There are other ways to view your video besides at real speed. The buttons on the **Viewer** do this, but learn the keyboard. It's your friend, and it's really a much simpler, easier way to control your editing than the mouse.

Spacebar

Press the spacebar to play the clip. To pause, press the spacebar again. Spacebar to start, spacebar to stop. To play the clip backwards, press **Shift**-spacebar. This method is much quicker and keeps your hands on the keyboard and off the mouse. You can play and manipulate clips in the **Viewer** with great efficiency using only the keyboard.

What Is Timecode?

Timecode is a frame-counting system that is almost universal to video cameras. A number is assigned to every frame of video and is physically recorded on the tape. We'll look at working with timecode more closely on page 45 in the next lesson on capturing.

Timecode is a series of numbers that are written on your videotape whenever you make a DV recording. The numbers represent time and on most consumer cameras begin at 00:00:00:00, zero hours, zero minutes, zero seconds, and zero frames. On professional and some prosumer cameras the start number can be set to anything you like. A timecode number is assigned to every frame of video—25 frames per second in the European PAL system and 30 frames per second in the North American and Japanese NTSC system.

For NTSC this is a problem, because the true frame rate of all NSTC video isn't 30fps but 29.97fps. Because of this NTSC has created two ways of counting timecode called Drop Frame and Non-Drop Frame.

Non-Drop Frame displays the numbers based on a simple 30fps frame rate. The problem with this is that when your timecode gets to the one-hour mark, one hour of real world time hasn't passed yet. It's still almost four seconds from completing the hour.

Drop Frame uses a complex method of counting that compensates for the difference between 29.97fps and 30fps. No frames of video are dropped. DF drops two frames a minute in its count except every 10th minute. This means that at the one-minute mark, your DF video will go from 59;29 to 1:00;02. There is no 1:00;00 or 1:00;01. Notice the semicolons. The convention is to write DF timecode with semicolons, or at least one semicolon, but NDF is written only with colons.

The DV standard uses Drop Frame timecode as its counting method, though some prosumer and all professional cameras can be switched between the two.

Some consumer cameras, particularly inexpensive Canon cameras, are dependent on having their date/time clock set so that they can generate timecode. It is crucial that the clock on your camera be set to some date or time; otherwise every time you press **Record**, the camera will restart the timecode at 0:00:00;00, which will create a break in what should be continuous timecode.

Keyboard Shortcuts

Another common way to play the clip is with the L key.

- L is play forward.
- K is pause.
- J is play backwards.

On your keyboard they're clustered together, but you're probably thinking, Why not comma, period, and slash? There is reason to the madness. **J**, **K**, and **L** were chosen because they're directly below **I** and **O**. **I** and **O** are used to mark the In and Out points on clips and in sequences. They are probably the most commonly used keys on the editing keyboard. Hence **J**, **K**, and **L**, positioned conveniently for the fingers of your right hand with the **I** and **O** keys directly above them.

You can view your video at other speeds. You can fast forward by repeatedly pressing the **L** key. The more times you press **L**, the faster the clip will play. Similarly, hitting the **J** key a few times will make the clip play backwards at high speed.

> **Tip**

Shortcut Help: If trying to remember all the keyboard shortcuts is shorting out your brain, you can get color-coded special keyboards with keys that display the shortcuts. A great tool is Loren Miller's KeyGuide. No FCE editor should be without one. He makes them for a number of applications as well as FCE. You can find out more about them and order them from http://www.neotrondesign.com.

To play a clip one frame at a time, press the **Right** arrow key. To play it slowly, hold down the key. To play slowly backwards, hold down the **Left** arrow key. To jump forward or backward one second, use **Shift** with the **Left** or **Right** arrow keys. Pressing **K** and **L** together will give you slow forward, and **K** and **J** together, slow backwards. To go back to the previous edit—the cut prior to the point where you are currently—use the **Up** arrow key. To go to the next edit event, use the **Down** arrow key. To go to the beginning of the clip, press the **Home** key; to go to the end, press the **End** key.

Table 1.1   Some Principal Keyboard Shortcuts

Play	L
Pause	K
Play backwards	J
Fast forward	Repeat L
Slow forward	L + K
Fast backwards	Repeat J
Slow backwards	J + K
Forward one frame	Right arrow
Backward one frame	Left arrow

Table 1.1   Some Principal Keyboard Shortcuts (Continued)

Forward one second	Shift-Right arrow
Backward one second	Shift-Left arrow
Go to previous edit	Up arrow
Go to next edit	Down arrow
Go to beginning	Home
Go to end	End
Mark the In point	I
Mark the Out point	O
Go to In point	Shift-I
Go to Out point	Shift-O
Play Around Current Point	\
Play from In point to Out point	Shift-\
Match Frame	F
Mark Clip	X
Add Marker	M

This is just the surface of the **Viewer.** We'll be visiting it again and again in the lessons to come, especially the tabbed windows behind the video window.

Exploring the Canvas

You'll probably first notice that the **Canvas** window (see Figure 1.42) is similar to the **Viewer.**

Most controls are duplicated. Some have been placed in mirrored positions, such as the cluster in the lower right corner, which mirrors the cluster in the lower left of the **Viewer.** The **Shuttle** and the **Jog** are also in mirrored positions in **Canvas,** but they function the same.

The time displays at the top function the same as in the **Viewer.** The two pop-up menus in the top center are the same also.

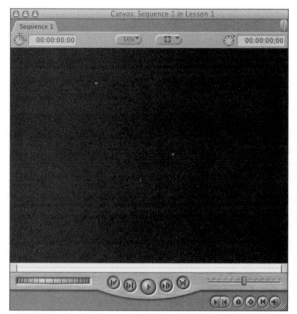

1.42 The Canvas window *(left)*

1.43 The Timeline window *(below)*

The **Canvas** is missing the **Recent** and **Generators** pop-ups, but there are hidden features in the **Canvas** window that we'll look at in later lessons.

Timeline Window

Let's look at the **Timeline** window, which, being empty at this stage, isn't much to look at (see Figure 1.43). This is one of the few windows in FCE2 that has changed substantially from the first version of the application.

The Patch Panel

The **Timeline** window made up of tracks. Above the horizontal central double bar are the video tracks. FCE defaults to two video tracks visible, marked **V1** and **V2**. You can change this in **Preferences**, which we'll look at in the next lesson on page 34. An FCE sequence can have up to 99 tracks of video and 99 tracks of audio.

One of the video tracks has a small **v1** attached to it. This is the source button and indicates what selected destination track the source video will be sent to. This area, which sets the source video and audio to the destination video and audio tracks, is called the *patch panel*. We'll talk about the patch panel more in later lessons.

Shortcuts: There are simple keyboard shortcuts to select each of
FCE's windows. The principal windows are shown in Table 1.2.

Table 1.2   Principal FCE2 Windows and Shortcuts

Window	Shortcut
Viewer	Command-1
Canvas	Command-2
Timeline	Command-3
Browser	Command-4
Toggle between Viewer and Canvas	Q

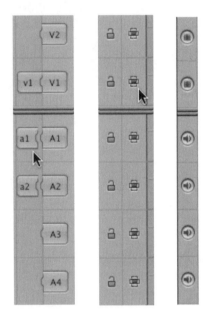

1.44   Setting destination tracks in the
       Patch panel *(left above)*

1.45   Tracks locks and Auto Select
       features *(center above)*

1.46   Visibility and Audibility buttons
       (right above)

Below the horizontal bar are the audio tracks. There are four
showing. **A1** and **A2** are set as destination tracks, awaiting a stereo pair of audio clips. **A3** and **A4** are ready for additional sound
tracks. You can separate the source button from the destination
track by clicking the small source button, separating it from the
track icon as in Figure 1.44. You can reset the destination track
by clicking the link together. You can also reassign source buttons
to destination tracks by pulling the patch to the desired track.

More Timeline Functions

To the right of the patch panel are track locks, which let you lock
and unlock specific tracks as you need to (see Figure 1.45).

Just to the right of that, next to the tracks themselves, is FCE2's
new **Auto Select** feature. **Auto Select** is used to perform copy, lift,
add edit, and some paste functions to specific tracks. It also controls FCE's matchframe function, which is no longer controlled
by destination track settings as in the first version.

To the left of the patch panel are new **Visibility** and **Audibility**
buttons, which can be toggled on and off as needed. We'll look at
those in later lessons (see Figure 1.46).

There are more controls for the **Timeline** windows along the bottom and the left edge of the window (see Figure 1.47). Again this
is a new configuration of buttons in FCE2.

The slider on the far right lets you change the horizontal scale at
which your clips are displayed in the **Timeline** window. Drag the
clip *Temple* from the **Browser** into the **Timeline**. You don't have
to be very precise; just drop it anywhere. It's a pretty long clip, so

use the slider to adjust the scale of the **Timeline** to see how it functions.

The triangle to right of the slider is a pop-up menu that lets you set different displays in the **Timeline** window (see Figure 1.48), audio waveforms or filmstrip display.

The buttons to the left of that set the track height. There are four settings of track height, which can be toggled with the keyboard shortcut **Shift-T**. Choose whichever is comfortable for you and your monitor's resolution. You can also set individual track heights by putting the cursor between the tracks and dragging up or down to resize the track height (see Figure 1.49).

The second button from the left displays **Clip Overlays**, which allow you to adjust the clip's audio levels and video opacity.

On the far left edge of the **Timeline** window is a new button to FCE2. Clicking the little speaker opens up the **Mute/Solo** buttons on the left edge of the window (see Figure 1.50). These buttons allow you to selectively mute tracks or solo a track so that you hear only the selected tracks. The difference between muting and switching off audibility is that a muted track will still export or record to tape, while a track with audibility switched off will not export nor be heard during recording to tape.

The **Track Mover** tool lets you change the proportions of the video and audio panels by moving the **Static Display Line** (see Figure 1.51). This can also be split to show different sections of the video and audio panels simultaneously, which can be very useful when you're working with multiple tracks of video or audio. By pulling the tabs on the right edge, you can pull the **Static Display Line** apart (see Figure 1.52). Much like word-processing software, this lets you keep a number of tracks displayed while scrolling through the rest of the tracks independently.

In the upper right corner of the **Timeline** window are two tiny icons that tell you whether **Snapping** and **Linked Selection** are turned on (see Figure 1.53). When these are turned on, the buttons are green; when they're switched off, the buttons are black.

If **Snapping** is on, the playhead, clips, and anything you move in the **Timeline** will automatically want to butt up against each other as though they had magnetic attraction.

1.47 Timeline buttons

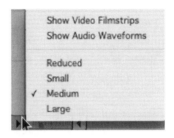

1.48 Timeline pop-up menu

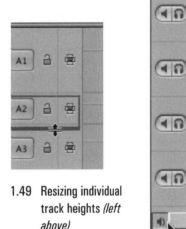

1.49 Resizing individual
      track heights *(left
      above)*

1.50 Mute/Solo buttons *(right above)*

1.51 Track Mover and Static Display
      Line closed *(left above)*

1.52 Track Mover and Static Display
      Line split *(center above)*

1.53 Snapping and Linked Selection on
      (right above)

Turn on **Linked Selection** if you want the sound and the picture together when you grab a sync clip. With **Linked Selection** on, they'll move in unison. With it off, the two elements can be moved separately. I recommend leaving **Linked Selection** on at all times, bypassing it only when necessary.

Summary

So ends Lesson 1. We've covered a lot of ground, made sure our system is properly set up, started up the software, and seen just the tip of the iceberg that lies under deep waters. Spend some time clicking around in the Final Cut Express windows. You can't hurt anything. And remember to try the **Control** key to bring up shortcut menus.

In the next lesson you'll to learn how to set up your preferences and how to get your own material into the Final Cut Express 2 edit suite.

➢**Tip**

Help: If you have problems with your computer or with Final Cut Express specifically, there are two useful places you can go to for help. One is the Apple Final Cut Express discussion forum, which you can link to from http://discussions.info. apple.com. The other is the oldest Final Cut discussion forum at 2-pop.com, which can now be reached at http://www.uemforums.com/2pop/ubbthreads/ubbthreads.php.

Lesson 2

Getting Material into FCE2

Digital video editing is divided into three phases:

- Getting your material into the computer

- Editing it, which is the fun part

- Getting it back out of your computer

This lesson is about the first part, getting your material into your computer. First you have to set up your application correctly. In Final Cut Express 2, as in most video editing programs, that means setting up your preferences—a number of choices for video and audio and system settings.

After setting preferences, we'll go into capturing your media. These fundamentals are absolutely necessary for Final Cut Express to function properly. Set it up right, get your material into your project properly, and you're halfway home. You cannot overestimate how important this is.

Setting Up a New Project

Let's begin by creating a new project.

1. Start by double-clicking the **Final Cut Express** icon in the *Applications* folder. Or better yet, if you've created a **Dock** alias for FCE, click on the icon in the **Dock**.

➤**Tip**
Adding Items to the Dock:

Remember that you can add any application to the **Dock** by dragging the application icon there. After you've launched an application, you can also add it permanently to the **Dock** by mousing down on the icon and from the shortcut menu selecting **Keep in Dock**.

FCE will launch the last project that was open. If a previous project does open, close the **Browser**, which will close the project.

2.   Go up to **File>New Project (Command-Shift-N)**.

You get a new project called **Untitled Project** with the empty sequence in the **Browser** called *Sequence 1*.

Because FCE uses your project name to create folders that organize your material inside designated folders such as the *Capture Scratch and Render* folders, it's a good idea to give your project a name right away. At this stage you can't save the project because there's nothing to save. However, you can use **Save Project As** to save it with a name. FCE will use that name to create files in designated places on your hard drive.

3.   Give the project a name and save it inside your *Documents* folder.

User Preferences

Final Cut Express 2 has three separate preferences settings:

- **User Preferences**, which sets up how you want to work with the application

- **System Settings**, which sets preferences that control your computer

- **Easy Setup**, which is for audio/video preferences and deals with how you get your material in and out of your computer

The first is the **User Preferences**. To access these go up to the **Final Cut Express** menu and select **User Preferences (Option-Q)**.

As soon as you open **User Preferences**, you see the pane in Figure 2.1.

General Preferences

This is the **General Preferences** panel.

The **User Preferences** may seem daunting because it's made up of three tabbed windows. We'll work through it, starting with **General**, the first window. Fortunately, most of the items here can be left at their default setting.

General \ Timeline Options \ Render Control \

Levels of Undo: `10` actions	☑ Show ToolTips
List Recent Clips: `10` entries	☑ Bring all windows to the front on activation
Multi-Frame Trim Size: `5` frames	☐ Dynamic Trimming
Real-time Audio Mixing: `8` tracks	☑ Trim with Sequence Audio
Audio Playback Quality: `Low (faster)` ⬍	☑ Warn if visibility change deletes render file
☐ Record Audio Keyframes	☐ Prompt for settings on New Sequence
	☐ Pen tools can edit locked item overlays
Still/Freeze Duration: `00:00:10:00`	
Preview Pre-roll: `00:00:05:00`	☑ Report dropped frames during playback
Preview Post-roll: `00:00:02:00`	☑ Abort capture on dropped frames
☑ Autosave Vault	☑ Auto Render
Save a copy every: `30` minutes	Start Render after: `45` minutes
Keep at most: `40` copies per project	Which Sequences: `Open Sequences` ⬍
Maximum of: `25` projects	☑ Render RT Segments

☑ Do not show External A/V Device Warning when device not found on launch

2.1   User Preferences General tab

Levels of Undo defaults to 10 actions, which seems to me to be a pretty good number. You can increase the number of actions up to 32, but the higher you make it, the slower your system will get. The application will have to keep more stored in memory, making its performance sluggish. On a fast computer with plenty of RAM, I'd set it to 32.

For **List of Recent Clips**, 10 seems like a good number. This is the number of clips retained for the pop-up at the bottom of the **Viewer** (see Figure 2.2). Again, a higher number means slower performance. The limit is 20.

Multi-Frame Trim Size sets the number of frames that can be trimmed in the **Trim Edit** window or the **Timeline**. Five is the default. I prefer two. Pick what suits you. We'll look at items such as multiframe trimming in closer detail in later lessons.

Real-time Audio Mixing determines how many tracks the application will try to play back in real time before it requires rendering. This is no guarantee that it will be able to do it, but it will try. The default is fine.

The default setting for the **Audio Playback Quality** pop-up menu is **Low**. It's fine to work in **Low**; it will allow a greater number of real-time tracks for playback. When you're outputting to tape, exporting, or doing an audio mixdown, these are automatically done at **High** quality. You don't need to reset this. Changing this item will also reduce the number of audio tracks that you can preview without rendering.

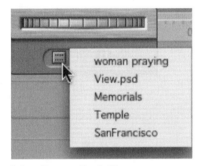

2.2   Recent clips in Viewer pop-up menu

The **Record Audio Keyframes** checkbox lets you adjust and record audio levels in real time while you control the levels of a clip in the **Viewer**. It's a new feature in FCE2 that we'll look at in Lesson 6 on page 144.

Still Image Duration sets the length of imported single-frame graphics and freeze frames made in FCE. You can change them once they're in FCE, but they'll appear at this length in the **Browser**. The default setting of 10 seconds seems long to me, so I set it to five seconds, a reasonable length for most stills or graphics from applications such as Photoshop. If you're doing training or other videos that require many full-screen graphics, leaving it at 10 seconds might be better for you. Although stills and freeze frames have a default duration of 10 seconds, they're actually two minutes and 10 seconds long when they're imported. The duration can be changed to any length you want. You have to set the maximum duration for the still inside the **Browser** before it is placed inside a sequence. After that, the still cannot be extended beyond its designated duration unless you use the **Fit to Fill** edit function, which we'll see in the next lesson. It can be made shorter, but not longer. There is also a sequence time limit of four hours that you cannot exceed.

In the previous lesson we talked about playing around the current time. If you hit the **Play Around** button or use the keyboard shortcut \, playback will begin a defined amount of time before the playhead and play for a defined amount of time past it. You define those times here. The default preview preroll is five seconds, a traditional preroll time for VTR machines. The default preview postroll is two seconds. Five seconds for a preroll always feels long to me, so I set it to two seconds. I leave the postroll at two seconds. Play with it and see what feels right for you.

In the lower left are the *Autosave Vault* preferences. Autosaving saves your project incrementally with a date and time stamp. Here you can assign how often you want the project saved, how many copies to keep, and how many projects you want to be held. Saving a project to disk can take a moment or two. The larger the project gets, the greater the number of clips and sequences, and the longer the save will take. So interrupting your workflow by setting the **Save a copy** box too small might be counterproductive.

I find the default of 30 minutes a good number. You probably won't lose too much if the application does crash, plus you'll save a couple of days' worth of work in the vault. If you make the save time too quick—say 10 minutes or less—you may want to increase the copies per project that's saved. The saved files can be called up from the *Autosave Vault* from the **File** menu by selecting **Restore Project**. You'll be given a dialog that offers you a list of time-stamped copies of that project (see Figure 2.3).

2.3   Restore Project dialog box

You can save up to 100 copies of each project, with a maximum of 100 projects. It works on a first-in/first-out basis. The oldest project saved is dumped into the **Trash** as new autosaves are added. Because it's not deleted from your hard drive, you can still retrieve an autosaved project from the **Trash** if you haven't emptied it.

✎ Note_____

Restoring Project: When you restore a project, the application first gives you a warning. The project then opens with the project name, and when you save it, it saves in the location of the original project.

You can also use **Revert Project** that, as in other applications, will take you back to the last saved state. Note that neither **Restore** nor **Revert** will bring back arrangements. These are in your preferences and will not be restored.

On the right side of this window is a list of checkboxes. The default settings for the first six are probably best left the way they are.

The next pair affects playback and capturing your material. It's probably wise to leave **Report dropped frames during playback** checked on, as well as **Abort capture on dropped frames**. You may find that FCE is giving dropped frame warnings immediately when a capture begins. If this is happening, you might try switching this feature off and seeing if you can capture your material cleanly. Also, if it aborts 55 minutes into a one-hour capture, you've lost everything and have to start all over again. By far the most common causes of dropped frames can be traced to two things: one, capturing your material to the internal drive on which your operating systems resides; and two, that your media drive is not fast enough for digital video or is trying to do too many things at the same time.

The **Auto Render** settings are new to FCE2. These allow you to set a time for which the application will start rendering material based on your settings when your computer is idle. It's great to

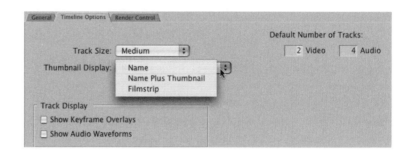

2.4   General Preferences Timeline
Options tab

find all of your rendering done when you come back from lunch
or after you leave your computer on overnight.

That's it for the first window of **Preferences**. Open the next tab,
Timeline Options (see Figure 2.4).

Timeline Options

Timeline Options is where you define your personal preferences
for your sequence timeline layout. You can set:

- The track size
- The default number of tracks a new **Timeline** opens with
- The style the tracks are displayed in: **Name, Name Plus
  Thumbnail,** or **Filmstrip** (Figures 2.5–2.7).

I leave the two checkboxes, **Show Keyframe Overlays** and **Show
Audio Waveforms,** off. They're more conveniently toggled on and
off in the **Timeline** as needed.

All these settings in **Timeline Options** affect only new sequences.
Existing sequences will not be affected. To change the **Timeline**

> **⏷ Note**
>
> **Filmstrip:** Although Filmstrip style
> may look like the best way to edit, it
> is very taxing on any computer.
> Using Filmstrip style on anything
> but the fastest computer will make
> the application work very slowly.

2.5   Name style

2.6   Name Plus Thumbnail style

2.7   Filmstrip style

Options of an existing sequence you'll have to open the sequence and use **Sequence>Settings** (**Command-0**) and change them there.

Render Control

Render Control is a new feature to FCE2 (see Figure 2.8). This panel allows you to change the render quality of your material from the default high-resolution to quite low-resolution rendering at low frame rates. The advantage of this is that low-resolution material will render out much more quickly than full DV resolution settings. Here you can also set to render Filters or just motion as well as adding in **Motion Blur** and **Frame Blending**. These last two, which produce better results, will slow down rendering considerably. **Render Control** for individual sequences, which is where you're more likely to need it, can also be accessed from **Sequence>Settings**. Be careful with changing these settings. See the lesson on outputting, Lesson 11 on page 263, for the problems this potentially creates.

System Settings

Systems Settings (**Shift-Q**) is a new set of panels to FCE2. Items that were previously in **User Preferences** have been moved here, and new items have been introduced.

Scratch Disks

The first panel in the tabbed window is **Scratch Disks** (see Figure 2.9). This is perhaps the most important of all the preferences panels.

Let's look at the bottom portion of the panel first. The locations of *Waveform Cache*, *Thumbnail Cache*, and *Autosave Vault* all default to the drive or partition that you set when you first launched the application.

Minimum Allowable Free Space On Scratch Disks defaults to 100MB. Most people feel that at this setting the hard drive will fragment heavily and slow down. Some go so far as to say that you should leave 25 percent of your drive free. For large drives, this seems a bit excessive. Experienced users recommend 10 percent or at least 1GB. If you have a large single partition larger than 60GB, I would suggest setting this number to 1GB, or 1000MB.

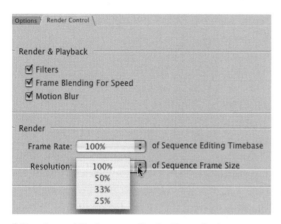

2.8 General Preferences Render Control tab

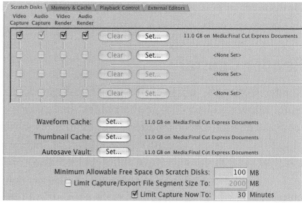

2.9 System Settings Scratch Disks tab

Unless you have a particular reason, you should leave **Limit capture/export segment size to** unchecked. This feature limits the size of segments FCE can capture or export. There isn't any particular reason to limit it.

The **Limit Capture Now To** box makes it easier to use **Capture Now** by improving the application's performance. Without it, FCE would check the available hard drive space before it started **Capture Now**. This could take a long time while the application rummaged through your assigned drives. This box allows you to limit the amount of space FCE will search for. It will stop searching either when it runs out of drive space or reaches the limit you designate. The default is 30 minutes, or about 6GB of file space at DV settings. FCE can search through this space quickly. If you're planning on capturing whole 60-minute tapes, you might want to uncheck this box.

2.10 Missing Disks warning

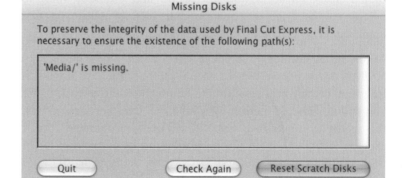

Let's get back to the main body of the **Scratch Disks** window. Here you assign scratch disks for your captured material and for your render files. Normally you set your project's video, audio, and render files in the same location.

By default, FCE assigns separate render folders for audio and video. When you click the **Set** button, a navigation window allows you to select the location for these files. Usually I go to the drive I want to use for a project and select the drive itself.

Selecting the drive will create some folders. There will be a folder called *Final Cut Express Documents*, inside of which will be folders called *Capture Scratch*, *Render Files*, and *Audio Render Files*. The next time you want to set a scratch disk, do not select the *Capture Scratch* folder; select the drive or partition. Selecting the folder rather than the drive will make another *Capture Scratch* folder inside the current one. As you capture your video material, it is stored in *Capture Scratch*.

If you have more than one hard drive or partition, you can set multiple locations in the **Scratch Disks Preferences** window. In FCE you can set up to 12 drives or partitions. The application automatically switches from one partition to another as they fill.

✎ *Note*

Scratch Disk Warning: A new feature in FCE2 is a scratch-disk warning if you start the application with the assigned scratch disk unmounted. The warning dialog in Figure 2.10 appears, giving you a chance to either **Quit**, mount drive and **Check Again, or Reset** the scratch disks to an available partition or disk. If the scratch disk with your media is missing, the items in your **Browser** as well as your render files will go offline. So it may be worth reconnecting that missing drive rather than reassigning the scratch disk to another location.

Memory & Cache

The next panel, **Memory & Cache**, is new to FCE2 (see Figure 2.11). It allows you to control the amount of memory used by the application. Normally the default values are fine. If you want to work in other applications—for instance, if you have an application such as Adobe After Effects that you would like to render in the background while you work in FCE—you can lower the application RAM to allow some for the other application to work with.

NTSC versus PAL

NTSC, which some wags say stands for Never Twice the Same Color, is actually the now-defunct National Television Standards Committee, which established the format used by television broadcasting in the United States. All of North America and Japan use this format as well. Europe and most of the rest of the world use PAL, for Phase Alternating Lines, which refers to the way color is handled. PAL uses a frame rate of 25fps. NTSC has a standard frame rate fixed at 29.97fps, not, as many think, a more manageable 30fps.

✎ *Note*

Remember: Using Filmstrip in your sequences will require considerably more system overhead and a larger **Thumbnail Cache** size.

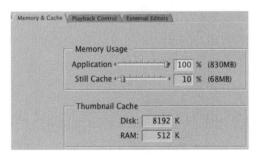

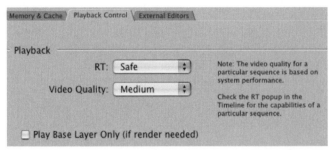

2.11 System Settings Memory & Cache tab   2.12 System Settings Playback Control tab

2.13 Timeline window RT pop-up menu

Also if you're working with a lot of large images in a sequence, you might want to set the **Still Cache** memory allocation higher. If you're working with a lot of stills, adding more physical RAM to your computer might also be a good idea.

Thumbnail Cache (Disk) and **(RAM)** values are relatively small. I'd keep them at the default values unless you like to work in the **Browser** with lots of bins in Icon view or like to keep thumbnails open in List view. If you do, you may want to raise these values from the default. Make sure you have extra RAM available. Some people make these numbers quite high, 30MB or more. I don't use icons much, so I leave it low.

Playback Control

Another new panel in FCE2, **Playback Control** (see Figure 2.12), is best left at its default settings. As with **Timeline Options**, these settings are best changed for individual sequences and can easily be done with the handy **RT** pop-up in the upper-left corner of the **Timeline** window (see Figure 2.13).

Here you can set **RT** (Real-Time Playback) to **Safe** or **Unlimited**. These two functions are available only when you are switched to real-time, not while you are feeding out through FireWire. Safe will give you ensured playback without dropped frames, your system and drives permitting. Unlimited allows you to play back more real-time capabilities but with the possibility of dropped frames.

Video Quality can be set to **High, Medium,** or **Low.** The lower the settings, the poorer the image quality but the greater the real-time playback capabilities. These settings effect only playback quality and do not change your render quality at all.

Scratch Disks	Memory & Cache	Playback Control	External Editors
Still Image Files	Clear	Set...	Macintosh HD:Applications:Adobe Photoshop 7:Adobe Photoshop 7.0
Video Files	Clear	Set...	Macintosh HD:Applications:QuickTime Player.app
Audio Files	Clear	Set...	<None Set>

2.14 System Settings External Editors tab

External Editors

The last panel is the **External Editors** tab. Here you can define which applications are used to work on different types of files outside of FCE (see Figure 2.14).

This allows you to launch an application to alter a clip in either the **Browser** or the **Timeline**. Select a clip and hold down the **Control** key for the shortcut menu choice **Open in Editor** (see Figure 2.15).

This will launch the application that you specify in this preferences panel. After you edit the clip—such as a still image in Photoshop—those changes will be reflected in FCE.

You can set **External Editors** for stills, video, and audio. Be aware, though, that if you set the QuickTime Player as your editor for video files and specify Peak or some other audio software as your editor for audio files, when you select **Open in Editor** for the audio portion of a sync sound clip, FCE will open the Quick-Time Player, not Peak. FCE thinks of the audio track as part of a single video clip and so uses the QT Player. Single audio files, even if the creator type is QuickTime, will still open with the different audio editor.

Easy Setup

From the **Final Cut Express** menu, select **Easy Setup**, or use the keyboard shortcut **Control-Q**. When you open Easy Setup, it brings up the panel in Figure 2.16.

The default setting is DV NTSC, based on standard DV with an audio sampling rate of 48kHz. If you check the **Show All** box in the upper-right corner from the pop-up you can select any of the 18 setups available, nine for NTSC and nine for PAL.

The trick to **Easy Setup** is to base it on the specifications used in your camera. If you're working with an audio sampling rate of 32kHz, choose one of those presets. If you work in anamorphic, sometimes called widescreen or 16:9, choose one of those set-

2.15 Open in Editor

✎ **Note**

Changes in Photoshop: Sometimes changes made to a file in Photoshop, particularly to the layer structure and opacity, will cause the file to appear to be offline. Select **Reconnect** and navigate to the Photoshop file on your hard drive. If the dialog does not come up and the file still appears to be offline, select it in the **Browser**, and from the shortcut menu choose **Reconnect Media**.

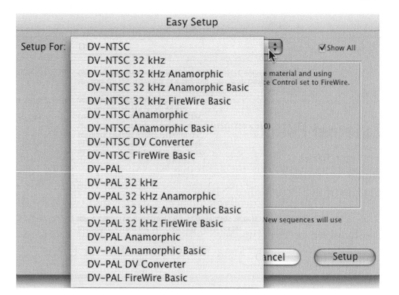

2.16 Easy Setup dialog box

What is anamorphic anyway?

Anamorphic is a 16:9 widescreen video. Though they have not caught on much yet in the United States, widescreen televisions are fairly common throughout Japan. Consequently, Japanese manufacturers have added this capability to many DV camcorders. The camera squeezes the pixels anamorphically (so that everything looks squashed, as though it's tall and narrow) to fit into a 4:3 frame and then unsqueezes them for playback on a widescreen TV.

The problem is that many people want to do 16:9 but don't have the equipment to do it properly. To monitor it, you need a widescreen monitor or one can switch between 4:3 and 16:9. FCE will output the correct 16:9 display if the presets are correct, but you won't see it correctly without the right monitor. You will not see a letterboxed version. Some fairly expensive decks will take a 16:9 image and output it as letterboxed 4:3. You can also place your 16:9 material in a 4:3 sequence and force it to render out the whole piece. You'll then have letterboxed 4:3.

Most DV camcorders will flag 16:9 material as such. They will read this regardless of whether you use the 16:9 setup. If you are shooting true 16:9 with an anamorphic lens, the correct setup will force FCE to treat it as widescreen material, even though it doesn't get the DV flag from the camera. So be careful. Don't select **Anamorphic** when your material is not 16:9, though this can be undone in the clip's **Item Properties** panel.

tings. If your camera or deck needs to use FireWire Basic instead of the standard FireWire, choose that. Check the Apple Final Cut Express web site's qualification page at http://www.apple.com/finalcutexpress/qualification.html.

All Canon cameras and many Panasonic and JVC cameras need FireWire Basic, but all Sony devices work with standard FireWire, also called iLink and IEEE1394. You should check with your camcorder manual to see its specifications. If you are using a DV converter box such as the Canopus ADVC100 to capture from analog material, choose one of the DV Converter options. This is for use with a noncontrollable device, a device that will not provide the machine with any timecode, which is what the application is looking for when it captures DV material.

The settings you choose here are for both your capturing and your sequences. The two need to match. Be careful that you don't use one setting to capture and then later change the settings for other material. Any sequences you create after changing the settings will reflect the new settings and will not work properly with material captured using the original settings.

Capture

So now you've set up your preferences, and you're ready to get your video material into your computer. To begin, go to **File>Capture (Command-8)**. This brings up the **Capture** window (see Figure 2.17).

The window is divided in two. On the left is a **Viewer** like the standard FCE **Viewer**, but this is a viewer for your tape deck or

➤**Tip**

Mixing Settings: Do not try to mix settings. If you shot your video in 32kHz, do not think that by capturing in 48kHz your material will become 48kHz. All that will happen will be that your audio is liable to drift out of sync.

2.17 Capture window

2.18 Time displays in the Capture window

2.19 Capture window controls

camera. The control buttons—**J**, **K**, **L**, **I**, and **O** keys and space-bar—work the same as in the FCE **Viewer** except that they control your deck or camera through the FireWire cable.

The **Timecode** in the upper-right of the **Viewer** portion of the **Capture** window is your current timecode on your tape, and the **Duration** on the upper left is the duration you set with your In and Out points as you mark the tape (see Figure 2.18). Notice the displays at the top of the window that tell you how much available drive space you have on the designated scratch disk and how many minutes of video you can store on it.

In addition to your keyboard shortcuts for **Mark In** and **Mark Out,** you also have buttons and timecode displays at the bottom of the viewer for these functions (see Figure 2.19).

The two inner buttons mark the In and Out points, **In** on the left, **Out** on the right. The timecode on the left is the In point, and the timecode on the right is the Out point. Of the buttons on the far outside, the left one will take the tape deck to the assigned In point, and the far right one to the assigned Out point, or you can use the keyboard shortcuts **Shift-I** to go to the In point and **Shift-O** to go to the Out point.

In the right half of the **Capture Viewer** window is the **Logging** window (see Figure 2.20).

At the top of the **Logging** window is the capture bin name. The button to the far right of the name will add a bin to the **Browser** and designate it the capture bin. Clicking the button again will add a new bin inside the previously designated bin. Using the button to the left, right next to the bin name, will take the capture bin up one level. If you click it enough times it will go right up to the **Browser** level. There is, however, no button to take you back down through the hierarchy. Creating a capture bin means that any material captured will be added directly to that designated bin. The bin appears in the **Browser** with a clapperboard icon on it when in Icon view or next to the bin's name when in List view.

➤*Tip*

Capture Size: The size of the Capture window is determined by the size of your **Canvas.** If you want a large display for the **Capture** window, set your window arrangement so that you have a large **Canvas.** If you want a smaller screen on your computer monitor, set the arrangement to the default **Standard** or even **Small Windows** before you launch the capture window.

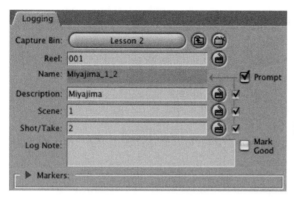

2.20 Logging window *(left)*

2.21 Set Capture Bin *(right)*

You can also select a capture bin directly in the **Browser** with a shortcut menu. **Control**-click on a bin, and from the shortcut menu choose **Set Capture Bin** (see Figure 2.21).

One critical piece of information in the **Logging** panel is the **Reel** name or number. These are really referencing the videotapes you shot, though it uses the film term *reel*. It is extremely important that reel or tape numbers be properly assigned. Each and every reel should have a separate number or name. The number should be written on the tape, and that number should be put in the **Logging** window. This number is actually attached to the QuickTime file when it's captured and is important for FCE being able to

Preferences Folder

If you have problems with FCE, one of the first remedies anyone will suggest is to trash your *Preferences* file. If there is a problem with your system, it's often your preferences that are corrupt. To delete them go into your user home folder, **Command-Option-H** from the **Finder**. Go to your *Library*, choose *Preferences*, and find the file *com.apple.finalcutexpress.plist*. This file should be deleted. In the same folder find the *Final Cut User Data folder* (see Figure 2.22).

Inside you can find four or five items, including two or three folders *(Custom Settings, Button Bars,* and *Plugins)*. The other items should be your *Final Cut Express* 2.0 *Prefs* and *Final Cut Express POA Cache*. If you do need to trash your preferences, the only files you should remove are 2.0 *Prefs* and *POA Cache*. You should do this with the application closed.

2.22 **Final Cut Express User Data folder**

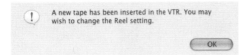

A new tape has been inserted in the VTR. You may wish to change the Reel setting.

OK

2.23 Reel Change warning *(left)* 2.24 Reel Number entry *(below)*

Reel: 001

recapture material should you ever need to. This is so important that when the application is in Capture mode, it will autodetect when the reel in your camera or deck has been ejected and a new reel inserted and will put up the warning message in Figure 2.23.

The reel number can be entered in the panel in Figure 2.24. The little clapperboard to the right can be clicked to increment the number.

In the **Logging** window you can enter information about your clips before you capture them. You can give them names based on **Description, Scene** and **Shot/Take** number, or other entry. You probably want to keep these as short as you can. They can be combined through the **Prompt** checkboxes, next to the tiny clapperboard icons, into creating a name for the clip. You can't enter a name for the clip in the **Name** area of the **Logging** window.

Below the **Naming** portion of the window is a box that you can twirl open with a disclosure triangle. This box allows you to add and name markers (see Figure 2.25). We'll look at markers more closely in later lessons, but here markers are a way of letting you add more information about a clip, keyed to a specific point somewhere inside the material. Once the clip has been captured, markers will appear attached to the clip, where they can be accessed from the **Browser**, as we'll see in the next lesson.

Strategies for Capturing

There are three strategies for capturing DV material, and you choose the one you want to use with the buttons at the bottom of the **Logging** window (see Figure 2.26). The options you have are:

- Now
- Clip
- Project

2.25 **Markers window** *(left)*

2.26 **Capture buttons** *(below)*

Capture Now

This is the simplest way to work, but it gives you least control. It also requires that your material be properly shot, preferably without timecode breaks. Breaks in the timecode can cause havoc with any capture, particularly if you use **Capture Now**. This version of FCE is capable of capturing across timecode breaks, but it should be avoided if at all possible, because it will still lose audio/video synchronization if it comes across a section of unstable video or a section of tape with no video at all, even if timecode is present.

FCE2 handles the capture across timecode breaks automatically. If there a break on the tape but the timecode continues getting higher, a new clip will start at the break, but the same reel number will be maintained. If the timecode resets to zero at the break, which is what most commonly happens on consumer cameras, the reel number will be changed and incremented as well as making a new clip. This will treat each portion of the tape where the timecode resets to zero as a separate tape. Avoid having breaks in your timecode if you can. It will make your life easier.

Capturing large chunks of video with **Now** is a common work strategy. To use **Now**, you put the deck in play and click the **Now** button. A capture screen comes up and begins recording as soon as it's checked your drives and found a video signal from your camera or deck.

If you are working with a noncontrollable device using the **DV Converter** preset, **Now** is the only capture choice available to you. I would recommend that, if possible, you dub your analog material to DV tape and then use the tape—properly reel-numbered, of course—as your master. Dubbing allows you to easily access the material again if you ever need to recapture.

FCE records the clip on your designated scratch disk until one of three events occur:

- It runs out of hard drive space.
- It hits your preference time limit.
- You hit the **Escape** key and stop the process.

If the capture stops because of the time limit, the deck also stops.

After your capture is complete, the video appears as a clip called *Untitled* inside the **Browser** or designated capture bin, unless you named the clip before capturing. Whenever a clip is captured, it is saved inside the *Capture Scratch* folder on the drive you selected

⬥ Note

Monitoring: When capturing, audio should be monitored through external speakers connected to the camcorder or deck you're playing back from. You will not be able to hear the sound through the computer's speaker during logging or capturing. See the sections "Monitors" and "Speakers" in the previous lesson on page 5.

in your **Preferences**. Inside *Capture Scratch* there will be a folder with the project's name, one folder for each project.

Inside that folder is where your captured material is stored. Your clip will be in that project's folder with the same name *Untitled* or the name you gave it. It's always a good idea to name the clip before you click the **Now** button so it will appear in the **Browser** and in your *Capture Scratch* folder with the name you assigned. If you capture a clip using **Now** and you decide you don't want to use it, you'll have to go into your *Capture Scratch* folder, dig it out, and throw it into the **Trash** to get it off your hard drive and retrieve that drive space.

Using **Capture Now**, you can bring all your video material into your computer for editing into smaller subclips rather than using your deck to select clips.

FCE has a wonderful tool for those working in DV with the **Capture Now** option. This is the ability to automatically mark up shot changes with **DV Start/Stop Shot Detect**. We'll look at this on page 58 in Lesson 3.

Clip

Another option in the **Capture** window is the **Clip** button. This requires that you enter In and Out points for where you want the capture to begin and where it should end. In the Clip method, you mark up the section of video you want to capture and then press the **Clip** button. This is a controlled form of **Capture Now**.

1. Mark an In point near the beginning of the reel and then an Out point near the end.

2. Click **Clip**.
   You will get a dialog box asking to confirm the name (see Figure 2.27). If you didn't name the clip in the **Logging** window, you'll have to enter one now. Notice the little clapperboard to the right of the name box. This lets you increment the name numerically.

3. Click the **OK** button and let the deck and the computer do its thing.

4. If you enter a clip name that already exists in the project's scratch folder, you'll get the dialog box in Figure 2.28 asking you to rename the clip, skip capture, or abort it.

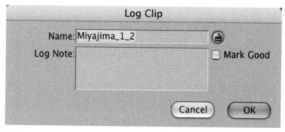

2.27   Log Clip window

2.28   Duplicate Item Filename dialog box *(right)*

✎ Note_____

Preroll and Postroll: Camcorders and decks cannot start and stop instantly. They require some time to get up to speed and to stop after they're playing. This is called preroll and postroll. This is a fixed preset in FCE of three seconds. So when you mark In and Out points to capture a clip, you need to make sure that your marked In point is no earlier than 03;00 from the beginning of the tape or from the last timecode break and that the Out point is no closer than three seconds to the end of the video material. In reality most cameras will need a bit more than three seconds of preroll, so I'd set 03;15 as the minimum. Most cameras don't need as much as three seconds of postroll and usually stop within one second. Still it's better to be safe if you can than lose a long capture because the camera ran out of timecode during postroll.

If the clip is not active in your project, or mistakenly got captured into the scratch folder, you'll also get an option to Overwrite the existing clip.

During capture you will get a large black window and, at the bottom, information about what's happening, such as in Figure 2.29, which shows that the deck is *cueing* source material, the clip that's being captured, the duration, and how much more to capture off that reel.

When capture begins, you'll see the image in the **Capture** window and the display in the bottom will change to the **Now Capturing** message in Figure 2.30, which gives the clip and duration.

Do not be dismayed that the quality of the video in the **Capture** window seems poor and stuttering. A computer monitor cannot display a full-screen interlaced image with full motion at full resolution during capture.

✎ Note_____
Renaming Clips: If you have to rename the clip because the name you've chosen is already used (as in Figure 2.28), the original incorrect name you assigned will appear in the **Browser**. This may mean that you have two clips in the **Browser** with the same name. The actual media file name will be correct, but the one in the **Browser** will not be. It's a good idea, if you do rename a clip in the warning dialog box, to immediately rename the clip in the **Browser** to match the media file name you gave the clip before capture.

Capture Project – CUEING SOURCE MATERIAL
Capturing File: Miyajima_1_2 (00:00:11:28) – Item 1 of 1
Remaining to capture on 001: 00:00:11:28

2.29   Cueing Source Material message

Capture Project – NOW CAPTURING (press 'ESC' to abort)
Capturing File: Miyajima_1_2 (00:00:11:28) – Item 1 of 1
Remaining to capture on 001: 00:00:11:28

2.30   Now Capturing message

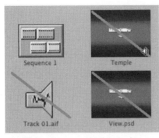

2.31   Browser with offline clips

2.32   Canvas with Media Offline

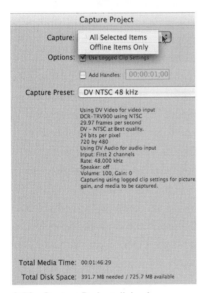

2.33   Capture Project dialog box

After you've captured your material, you are ready to edit. Close the **Capture** window before you start, however. You should not try to play video while **Capture** is open. So shut it down before you begin editing.

Once you've captured your material, you'll notice that it appears in the **Browser** in List view as a clip with a duration but with no In or Out points defined. Capturing only sets the media limit, and FCE assumes you will want to edit the material further, so no In or Out points are designated. The clip has the *de facto* In and Out points marked by the limits of the media; they're not displayed in the **Browser** in the **In** and **Out** columns.

Project Capture

Project capture is designed to let you recapture material for old projects to reconstruct them. To do this, reopen the project. If the material is not available, you will get the **Reconnect** dialog box we saw at the beginning of the previous lesson. Click the **OK** button and let the project open.

All the media will probably appear offline, with the **Browser** displaying clips with red slash marks through them (see Figure 2.31) and the words **Media Offline** across a glaringly red **Canvas** (see Figure 2.32).

You could at this point evoke the **Capture** window and press the **Project** button. This will bring up the dialog box in Figure 2.34.

Normally the pop-up at the top would display only **All Items**, but if some of the clips are available to you while others are offline, then you'll get the choice of either picking **All Items**, **Offline Items Only**, or **Selected Items**.

Notice the box that allows you to **Add Handles**. This will set the computer to capture a designated amount of material beyond the In and Out points defined in your clips. You can select any of the available **Capture Presets**, and the window will display what your selected settings are. At the bottom you get an indication of the hard drive requirements for **Total Media Time** and **Total Disk Space**. Check that you have enough drive space for the capture.

Also look closely at the media time to make sure it looks about right, that you're capturing all the media you need but not too much.

When you click **OK**, you'll get a window telling you what tapes will be required for the project capture and how much will be captured off each tape. Load the first reel and click **Continue**. FCE will prompt you whenever a reel change is required.

If you capture with handles, the clips will come into the **Browser** with your designated In and Out points marked already, not the usual **Not Set** indication, and if you open the clip into the **Viewer**, you'll see that there is the extra media beyond the marked In and Out points.

It's important to understand the way project capture works. It works best if you've captured your material using the Clip method—that is, selected the portions of the video you want to use and captured them as separate clips. But if you haven't, you can still use the **Project** button to trim down your material to just what you need, provided you had cut up your material into sub-clips, which we'll see how to do in the next lesson. If you have, this is how you do it:

1. Start by reopening your project file with the missing material that needs to be recaptured.

2. Delete everything except the sequence or clips you need to recapture. The clips inside the sequence need to be subclips. You'll probably get the warning message in Figure 2.35. Click **OK** and push on.

3. Select the sequences and from the **Modify** menu choose **Make Sequence Clips Independent**. This will separate the edited clips from the long masters you may have captured.

4. Start up the **Capture** window, and click the **Project** button.

The application will now recapture only those clips that it needs to reconstitute your sequence. It will not capture any of the clips that you didn't use and that you deleted from your project, nor all the rest of the material that is not part of your sequence. If you captured whole reels of tape or large chunks, FCE would want to recapture all the pieces that use even a very small portion of your clips. So if you originally captured a 60-minute reel and used only 10 seconds of it, the application would still want to capture the entire 60 minutes just to get that 10 seconds it needed to reconstitute your sequence. That's why you need to make the clips into subclips first and then use the **Make Sequence Clips Independent** function.

One or more of the clips you have selected are Master clips. By deleting them you will break their relationship to any clip or item affiliated with them. Do you want to continue?

Cancel   OK

2.34 Capture Project dialog box

Recapturing works only for the DV material for your project. When a project is complete, you should separately back up imported audio and graphics files. You should also be aware that tracks recorded using the **Voice Over** tool are not recapturable as they have no useful timecode. It's a good idea to build an **Import** bin that contains audio files, still images, graphics files, as well as your voice over tracks. The **Source** column will let you find the file path to where the media such as stills and voice overs are stored. These should be backed up separately if you want to re-create the project at a later time. It may be simplest to burn this data material onto a CD or DVD for storage.

2.36 Make Offline Dialog

> **➤Tip**
>
> **Secret Delete:** You can delete media from your hard drive directly from your **Browser** by using a secret keyboard shortcut. If you select a clip or clips and use **Shift-D** this will bring up the window in Figure 2.36. Here you can either delete the clip from the **Browser**, marking it as **Offline** (basically breaking the connection with the media on your hard drive); you can move the media to the trash; or you can delete it immediately and permanently from the hard drive. Be warned this last option will delete all the media for that file, and will affect all affiliate clips and well as all subclips made from the media. Use with caution.

Summary

With these two lessons, you have just about completed step one of the three steps of digital nonlinear editing. You have set up your system, moved your video material from the recording medium into the computer, imported some material—music or still images, perhaps—captured other material, and maybe consolidated your video. Having all the elements you need in your computer, you're now ready to begin the second part: editing, the fun part.

Timecode Breaks

Timecode breaks or control track breaks have been the bane of video editors since tape machines were invented. Many editors have cursed many a cameraperson for failing to keep good TC on the tapes. These days, most consumer and prosumer cameras are designed to generate frame-accurate time-code, and that's the way tape should be delivered. FireWire uses the TC recorded on tape when the video was shot to find your clips and control the deck during capture. This timecode information is passed to the application and remains with the clip throughout the editing process. It's important to understand what happens in the camera while you're shooting.

There are a number of ways to ensure that there are no breaks in your DV TC. The simplest way, which I recommend for beginners and students in particular, is to prestripe your tapes, that is, record black and timecode on your tape before you shoot. You can do this in any camera or VCR: put the device in VCR mode and press the **Record** button. With some cameras you might have to do it in camera mode; just put a lens cap on it or point it at a wall. Now whenever you shoot, your tape will have TC written on it. The camera will then read the TC and start writing from whatever it reads. No breaks.

If you don't want to prestripe the tape, you then just have to be careful when you shoot. After you shut off the camera to change batteries or play back your tape to review what you shot, for instance, not simply stop it after a shot, it's a good idea to back up the tape just a second to get back into the area of timecoded material. This is why it's always a good idea when shooting to let the camera run for a few moments after the action you're shooting is complete, before you stop the recording. That way you will have that moment or two of unnecessary material to back up into.

Any timecode break is liable to cause a sudden loss of AV sync when you capture across it. So if you do have a tape with TC breaks in it, one of the simplest ways to get around the problem is to dub the tape. By dubbing it from one deck or one camera to another, the video and audio portion of the tape is actually cloned exactly as it was on the original, while at the same time, the recording deck is creating new, unbroken timecode. Unfortunately this often means that you lose the ability to work with **DV Start/Stop Detect**.

Aside from shooting carefully, or prestriping the tape, another way around the problem is to use the Clip method to capture material between the timecode breaks.

Lesson 3

Cutting Up Those Shots

In this lesson we're going to look at some video and cut it up. After you capture your material, the first step in the editing process is to organize your material. FCE has a number of tools to help you do that and a number of different ways you can work with your video.

Loading the Lesson

1. Start by loading the DVD that came with this book into your DVD drive. Open the DVD.

This is a hybrid DVD and will probably start up your DVD Player application when you mount the disk. If your system is set to start up the DVD Player, you should quit that application. Double-click on the DVD icon on your desktop and you will find a folder called *Hybrid DVD-ROM Contents*. Inside that folder are a number of other folders.

2. To start, if you have not already done so, drag the folder called *Media 1* onto your media drive.

It contains the video material we'll need for this lesson, the same media that was used in Lesson 1.

3. When that's finished, drag the *Projects* folder on the DVD onto the system hard drive of your computer if you did not do so in Lesson 1. You should probably place it in your *Documents* folder.

4. Eject the DVD.

5. Open the *Projects* folder on your system hard drive and double-click the *Lesson 3* project to launch Final Cut Express 2.

The project is empty except for one sequence that is also blank.

Importing the Movie

1. Use **File>Import** (**Command-I**) to import the *Temple* file from the folder inside the *Media 1* folder on your hard drive. Or you can drag the clip directly from the *Media 1* folder into your **Browser**.

This is a *master clip*. Every time you import a clip or capture a clip or bring a new clip into the **Browser**, the first instance of that clip is always a master clip. This is a new term in Final Cut Express 2, and it refers to the new way the application handles media information. A master clip can be cut up into smaller clips called *affiliate clips*. Any copy or portion of a master clip has an affiliate relationship to the master. You can no longer cut up a master clip and rename all the pieces. Now all of the pieces, all the affiliates and the master clip, must have the same name. If you change one, they all change.

DV Start/Stop Detect

DV Start/Stop Detect is probably the best way to work with your material in FCE2. It uses the start/stop information from your camera to create markers on your video. This method works only if your camera has had its clock set. It doesn't have to be the right date or time, but it has to be set. No clock, no **DV Start/Stop Detect**. Once markers are set with **DV Start/Stop Detect**, they can be used to segment the master clip. Here's how it works.

1. Bring your long clip of DV material into FCE, either by importing it, capturing it with the Clip method or with **Now**.

2. Select the clip or clips. In this case select the *Temple* clip you imported into your **Browser**.

3. From the **Mark** menu, select **DV Start/Stop Detect**.

You will immediately see the **Scanning DV Movie(s)** progress bar (see Figure 3.1). It can scan multiple clips at once. It can handle even whole bins. It produces clips with markers at each camera start/stop.

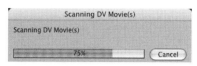

3.1 Scanning DV Movie(s) progress bar

After it's finished nothing seems to have changed, but it has. **DV Start/Stop Detect** will add markers at every shot change based on that date/time stamp. To see what's happened, double-click the clip *Temple* to open it into the **Viewer**. In Figure 3.2 notice that the playhead in the **Viewer** is sitting on the first marker, *Segment 1*; each of the other markers appears in the scrubber bar at the bottom of the **Viewer**.

3.2 Master clip with segments in the Viewer

> **Tip** _____

Marker Shortcuts: You can easily move between segments with keyboard shortcuts:

Shift-M (or Shift-Down arrow) takes you to the next marker.

Option-M (or Shift-Up arrow) takes you to the previous marker.

Command-` will delete a marker under the playhead as will the **Delete** button in the **Marker** dialog box. You can call this dialog box by pressing the **M** key while you're positioned on a marker.

A list of markers can be accessed by **Control**-clicking in the current time indicator window in the upper right of either the **Viewer** or **Canvas** (see Figure 3.3).

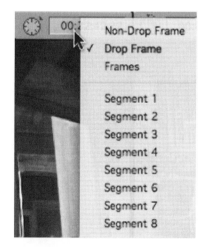

3.3 Markers in current time indicator window

Once the material has been segmented, it's easy enough to change the separate segments in shots.

1. Change the **Browser** into List view, either from the **View>Browser Items>as List,** or by using **Shift-H** to toggle through the **Browser** views.

2. You can twirl open the disclosure triangle in the **Browser** and marquee-drag through all the markers, as shown in Figure 3.4.

3. Then select from the menu **Modify>Make Subclip** or use the keyboard shortcut **Command-U.**

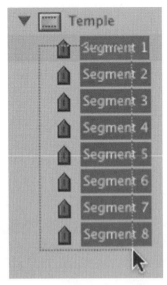

3.4 Marquee-dragging before making subclips

Before I do that, I often move the master clip into a bin appropriate for its content. To create a new bin, either use **File>New>Bin**, or **Control**-click in the **Browser** and from the shortcut menu choose **New Bin**, or use the keyboard shortcut **Command-B**. I do this so that when I make the subclips from *Temple*, they're already placed in the right bin.

✎ *Note*_____

Moving Shots Out of Bins: To move a shot out of the bin back to the top level of the **Browser**, drag the shot out of the bin and pull it onto the **Name** column header. That puts it at the top level of the project window.

_____

All subclips are master clips, and though you can rename your subclips anything you want, be aware that the underlying media that remains on your hard drive is unchanged in any way. Most importantly, its name is not changed. So if you ever need to reconnect the media or recapture it, FCE will want to do it under its original naming convention.

At this stage you're breaking down your material, organizing it, arranging it in bins, renaming clips, adding notes, and so on. This is critical if you're working on a project that's longer than 10 minutes or so, or a project with a lot of material, regardless of its finished length. This process of viewing, logging, and organizing should not be skimped, rushed, or dismissed as drudge work. It is crucial to the editing process.

Using Markers

If you're working with DV material without camera breaks, material captured from an analog to digital converter, or material that was dubbed to DV, you can still cut up your material using subclips. There are a few different ways to do this.

You can do this by adding markers to the clip similar to the way **DV Start/Stop Detect** worked. Open your long capture into the **Viewer**, and add markers as you play the clip—on the fly if you like—by tapping the **M** key or the ` (accent) key. You can create markers with more precision, of course, as well as set up extended markers to segment your material. Try this with *Temple*.

1. First, marquee-drag through any segment markers that may already be in the clip.

2. With the segment markers selected hit the **Delete** key to wipe them out.

3. Double-click *Temple* to open it into the **Viewer**.

4. Set a marker at the beginning of the clip. Do this by moving the playhead to the beginning of the clip with the **Home** key and pressing either the **M** key or the ` (accent) key.

If you wish, you can label the marker. Press the **M** (or `) key again while sitting over the marker. This brings up the dialog window in Figure 3.5. Change the name of the marker, and add comments if you wish.

This name will carry over into the name of the subclip. In this case, the subclip would be called *WS with memorials from "Temple" subclip*. The marker information and comments will displays in the **Viewer**. This stays with *Temple* and will appear whenever the playhead is over the marker, unless the marker is deleted, of course.

3.5   Edit Marker dialog box

5. Play through the clip either with the spacebar or by scrubbing in the scrubber bar until you find the shot change.

6. Use the **Left** and **Right** arrow keys to find the first frame of the next shot at 10;16.

7. Add another marker.

➤*Tip*_____

Scroll Wheel: FCE2 allows you do use the scroll wheel of a multibutton mouse to do a variety of tasks. It's quite a powerful tool. You can scroll the **Browser** window, of course. You can also use the scroll wheel to scrub the playhead in the **Viewer** window, in the **Timeline Ruler** of the **Timeline** window, as well as scrubbing the playhead when the cursor is over the **Canvas.** If the cursor is above one of FCE's sliders, it will move the slider, changing the values.

You can work your way through the clip, adding markers at each shot change. As with **DV Start/Stop Detect,** the markers can be turned quickly into subclips.

8. Marquee-drag to select the markers from *Temple* in List view and press **Command-U.**

➤*Tip*_____

Edit Marker: If you Shift-click the **Marker** button in either the **Canvas** or the **Viewer**, it not only sets a marker but also opens the **Edit Marker** dialog, where you can enter information. You can also use Command-Option-M to open the **Edit** window for the nearest marker before the current position of the playhead.

If you're working on narrative film or tightly scripted material, or material with lots of excess that you can discard, *extended markers* might be useful. When you capture large sections of material, there are often unnecessary pieces: clapperboards, director's instructions, setting the camera, bad takes. You can avoid adding these into your subclips by extending a marker.

1. Start by finding where you'd like the subclip to begin.

2. Add the marker with the **M** or ` key.

3. Play through the shot until the director shouts, "Cut!" or you find the end of the piece you want to make into a subclip.

4. Now extend the marker from the menus by going to **Mark>Markers>Extend**, or extend it even more simply by using the keyboard shortcut **Option-`** (accent mark).

The nice thing about this technique is that when you create your subclips by selecting them and pressing **Command-U** or using the **Modify** menu to **Modify>Make Subclip**, the subclips are only for the duration of the extended marker. By extending the markers you've defined the limits of the media available for each shot, basically defined rough In and Out points.

In the *Temple* clip, for instance, there are some camera bobbles, such as right at the end of the second shot, the glass-fronted hut. The start of the third shot also has a reframing zoom. By using extended markers, you can cut these areas out so that they don't appear unexpectedly during a transition. You might also not want to subclip a shot, for instance, the fourth shot in *Temple*. Extend the previous marker to the end of the third shot, and don't add a marker for the fourth shot. This is why there are only seven markers or extended markers in Figure 3.6.

Do not extend markers or define subclips too tightly. This should only be a rough cut covering the entire portion of usable media. FCE will treat the limits of the subclip as the limits of its media and will not allow you to extend the shot farther, so always make the ends of the subclips, the limits of the media, as far as you can without going into another shot or into some rough material, such as a swish pan or a quick zoom that you don't want to see on the screen.

3.6   Extended markers

Markers are an excellent tool for entering information about clips, even if you're not using the markers to edit your material. Here you can add comments, as well as create *chapter markers* and *compression markers* to use with iDVD or DVD Studio Pro and *scoring markers* to carry over to Apple's music-creation software Soundtrack. It's important to note that these specialized markers should always be added only to the **Timeline** itself. None of these markers, if added to clips, will carry over into other applications. Markers are also searchable within a sequence, as we shall see.

✎ Note

Removing Subclip Limits: Creating a subclip limits the available media to the length of the shot. If you ever need the rest of the captured material within the original shot, select the clip or clips in either the **Browser** or the Timeline and use Modify > Remove Subclip Limits. You'll then be able to open the shot in the **Viewer** and access the whole length of the clip, which is still on your hard drive.

Using In and Out Points

Another method of working with media without **DV Start/Stop Detect** is to open the original master clip into the **Viewer** and mark your shots with In and Out points.

1. If you have placed any markers in *Temple*, delete them as we did before so that you have only the long clip itself.

2. Next open *Temple* into the **Viewer** by double-clicking on it or dragging it into the **Viewer.**

3. Mark an In point at the beginning of the clip with the **I** key.

4. Play through the clip or scrub through it until you find the last frame of the first shot. Use the **Left** and **Right** arrow keys to find the frame at 10;15.

5. Mark an Out point with the **O** key.

Your **Viewer** will look like Figure 3.7. Notice the Out point mark in the upper-right corner of the picture, indicating that the playhead is at the Out point.

6. To make this shot a subclip, press **Command-U** or choose **Modify>Make Subclip.**

7. The clip will immediately appear in the **Browser** with its name highlighted, ready to be renamed.

8. Type in a name for the clip.

9. Switch back to **Viewer** (**Command-1**), and you're ready to mark new In and Out points to the master clip to make the next subclip.

3.7 Viewer with In and Out points marked

Although making a subclip does not create a separate QuickTime file, the subclip is treated as a separate piece of media, even though in reality it's not. The advantage to working in the subclip method is that it's easy to scrub the clip, running the mouse along the length of the media.

Slicing Your Clips

All of these methods described so far have been based on creating subclips. You can also work by making clips and turning them into master clips so that they can be renamed.

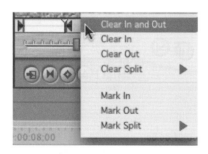

3.8 Clearing In and Out points in the Viewer

Slice 1

There are a few different ways to do this. Let's do this first in the **Viewer.**

1. Open *Temple* from the **Browser** into the **Viewer.**

It will probably have an In and Out point marked. We need to clear those.

2. **Control**-click on the scrubber bar at the bottom of the **Viewer** to evoke a shortcut menu, and select **Clear In and Out.** This will—surprise, surprise—clear the In and Out points (see Figure 3.8).

✎ *Note*

Clearing from the Browser: If you've opened a clip from the **Browser** and want to clear its In and Out points, you can use the keyboard shortcut **Option-X.** You can't, however, clear the In and Out from a clip that's been opened from the **Timeline**. A clip that's in a **Timeline** must by definition have an In and Out point, a start and end frame, even if it's the first and last frame of the clip.

3. Let's begin with the second shot in *Temple*. Find the shot change at 10;16.

4. Mark an In point by pressing the **I** key.

5. Press the spacebar to play *Temple*. Use the **Left** and **Right** arrow keys to find the end of the shot, the last frame of the thatched hut at 18;29.

6. Mark an Out point with the **O** key.

7. Create a new bin in the **Browser** (**Command-B**) and name it *Clips*.

8. Drag the marked clip of *Temple* from the **Viewer** and drop it into the **Clips** bin. Do not rename this clip; this would rename *Temple*. The new clip still has an affiliate clip relationship to the master clip.

9. Go back to the **Viewer** and repeat the process, marking In and Out points for each shot and dragging them into the **Clips** bin.

However, there is a feature that gets around this problem.

10. Select all the clips you've created in the **Clips** bin by marquee-dragging through them or by double-clicking on the bin and using **Command-A** to **Select All.**

11. With the clips selected from the **Modify** menu, go to **Modify>Make Master Clip.**

This will turn all of the clips into master clips, allowing you to rename them and organize your material.

Slice 2

The second Slice method is in the **Timeline**. This is where you really are slicing with a digital razor blade.

1. Open *Temple* from the **Browser** into the **Viewer.**

Edit Points

A note on the place where edit points occur. The shot change between edits takes place between the frames. That is, you see one frame, and the next frame you see is the first frame of a different shot. So when you're marking In and Out points, you should know where the shot change is taking place. If you mark the In point for a frame that you're looking at in the **Viewer**, that will be the first frame of the new clip. The edit will take place in the space before that frame. If you mark the frame you're looking at as an Out point, that will be the last frame in the clip, and the edit will take place after that frame.

It will probably have an In and Out point marked. We need to clear those.

2. **Control**-click on the scrubber bar at the bottom of the **Viewer** to select **Clear In and Out**, or use the shortcut **Option-X**.

3. If it's not already open, open the empty **Timeline** by double-clicking on *Sequence 1* in the **Browser**.

4. Drag *Temple* into it, dropping the clip on **V1**.

When you place a clip in the **Timeline**, the playhead automatically jumps to the end of the clip, ready for you to place another clip in position. In this case, we don't want it to do that.

5. Click in the **Timeline** window to make it active (or use **Command-3**), and press the **Home** key to take you back to the beginning of the **Timeline**.

6. Press the spacebar to play *Temple*. The video plays in the **Canvas**.

7. Use the spacebar to stop and the **Left** and **Right** arrow keys to find the start of the shot of the glass-fronted hut at 00:00:10;16.

8. Make sure **Snapping** is turned on. Check the indicator in the upper-right corner of the **Timeline** window. We saw this at the section on the **Timeline** in Lesson 1 on page 29. Toggle it on and off with the **N** key.

🐭 **Note**_____

Keyboard Shortcut: In addition to using the **Blade** tool, you can move the playhead to where you want to make the cut and press the keyboard shortcut **Control-V**. This will cut the clip right at the playhead.

_____

9. Select the **Blade** tool from the **Tools** palette and move it along the **Timeline** to the playhead line.

As you move along the clip in the **Timeline**, your cursor will show the **Blade** tool, rather than the **Selector** (see Figure 3.9). You'll see dark triangles at the top and bottom of the playhead line indicating that the cursor is at the playhead.

10. Click with the **Blade** tool to cut the clip at the playhead.

This will cut the video and audio on the clip as though you were cutting it with a knife or a razor blade, which is what used to be used to cut film and audiotape, and even videotape when it was first edited. What you are doing is the digital equivalent for the same process.

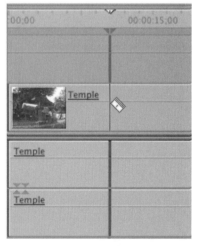

3.9 Blade tool in the Timeline

3.10 Cut clips in the Timeline

11. Go to the end of the shot, using the **Left** and **Right** arrow keys to find the first fame of the next shot.

12. Click the **Blade** tool again or use the keyboard shortcut **Control-V.**

13. Now that you've made one cut, find the next shot. Its first frame starts with the quick zoom at 00:00:19;00. Again use **Control-V or the Blade** tool to cut the shot.

14. Go through the **Timeline** and slice more clips by using **Control-V** to cut at the first frame of every new shot (see Figure 3.10).

15. After you've cut out the clips you want from the long shot in the **Timeline**, go to the **Browser** and select *Sequence 1.*

16. From the **Modify** menu, select **Modify>Make Sequence Clips Independent.**

17. Drag the clips into a bin in the **Browser.**

18. These clips are all master clips and can be renamed, reedited, and organized. They will have the same master/affiliate relationship as a captured clip, an imported clip, or a subclip.

Edit Points Redux

We talked about where the cut takes place when you're editing, that the In point cuts the space before the frame you're looking at, and the Out point cuts after the frame you're looking at. The **Blade** always cuts on the gap in front of the frame you're seeing in the **Canvas.** So to get the last frame of *Temple* when slicing in the **Timeline,** you have to be looking at the first frame of the shot after it. If you press **Control-V** on the last frame of the memorials shot, the thatched hut shot will have one frame of the memorials at its head.

➤*Tip*_____

Switching Cursors: The letter **B** will call up the **Blade** tool. The letter **A** is the shortcut that will return you to the Selection tool. (Think *A* for arrow.) Of course, with the cursor in **Blade** mode, you cannot select a clip. Trying to select a clip will cut it. So to do ripple deletes, you need to switch back and forth between the **Blade** and the Selector. You can do this quickly using **A** and **B.** Or you can leave your cursor in **Blade** mode, and instead of clicking to select a clip, hold down the **Control** key when the cursor is above the clip you want to remove. Holding down the **Control** key will change the cursor from the **Blade** to the shortcut menu. Clicking will open the menu, and from the menu you can select the function **Ripple Delete.** Neat, isn't it?

These *Temple* shots come into the **Browser** with an In and Out points marked, and if you open the clips you'll find that each contains all the video that's in the original master shot called *Temple.* The upside of this is obvious. Because a sliced clip is a copy of the

✎ Note

Browser and Timeline Clips: Now is a good time to explain the relationship between the clips in the Browser and the clips in the Timeline. Quite simply, there is no relationship—no direct, linked relationship, anyway. They are separate, distinct items. They may be copies of each other, but they are separate clips that share the same media. So in the first Slice method, when you mark up the master clip with In and Out points, you are marking one clip and making copies of it in the Clips bin. When you drag the master clip from the Browser and place it in a Timeline, you are placing a copy of the master clip. So when you razor blade and ripple delete the clip in the Timeline, you are not in any way affecting the master clip that remains untouched in your Browser.

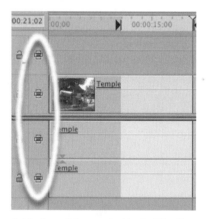

3.11 In and Out marked in the Timeline with Auto Select functions

master clip, you can now access any shot in the reel from inside any sliced clip.

That's the upside; the downside is scrubbing. The master clip is made up of a long length of material, perhaps even a whole reel of film or a roll of videotape, though I would advise against this. It's now difficult to scrub in the **Viewer** because even a tiny movement will move the playhead a long way up and down the scrubber bar.

Slice 3

With the Slice 2 method, you're cutting the pieces you want to keep and moving them into the **Browser**. Let's look at another method that works almost exclusively in the **Timeline**. Here we'll cut away the pieces we don't want to use and leave behind in the **Timeline** the shots that contain the good material.

1. Begin by deleting everything in *Sequence 1*. **Command-A** will **Select All**, and the **Delete** key will remove everything.

2. Make sure there aren't any In and Out points marked in the master clip *Temple*, and bring a fresh copy into the sequence by dragging it into the **Timeline**.

3. Press the **Home** key to return to the start of the sequence.

4. Play forward until you reach the beginning of the second shot at 00:00:10;16. We want to remove the second shot from the sequence, because we don't need it.

5. Mark an In point in the sequence by pressing the **I** key.

6. Play forward through the second shot and through the zoom at the beginning of the third shot, until about 00:00:21;02. We will cut out everything from the first frame of the second shot to and including the frame where the playhead is parked just as we mark In and Out points in the **Viewer**.

7. Press the **O** key to enter an Out point in the **Timeline**, which should look like Figure 3.11.

Notice the highlighted area in the tracks. This is the new **Auto Select** feature in FCE2. Tracks can have their selection toggled on and off with the buttons circled on the left in Figure 3.11. This allows you to select some tracks while not selecting others.

8. Now press **Shift-Delete** to execute a ripple delete, removing that section of the video.

Auto Select Shortcuts: There is a collection of keyboard shortcuts using the keypad of the extended keyboard to toggle off and on the **Auto Select** functions. **Command-1, 2, 3**, and so on will toggle tracks **V1, V2, V3**, and so on. **Option-1, 2, 3, 4**, and so on will toggle audio tracks **A1, A2, A3, A4**, and so on. **Option**-clicking on the **Auto Select** button for a video track will toggle soloing for just that one track. **Option**-clicking on the **Auto Select** for an audio track will do the same there.

This method, of cutting away the bad material in the **Timeline**, is a fast and efficient way to edit material. You end up with the shots you want to keep in the **Timeline**. If you do want to organize and rename your material again, choosing **Modify>Make Sequence Clips Independent** will separate the clips in the **Timeline** from their master/affiliate relationship. Now you can pull them into bins and rename them if you wish. I'd use this method for working on something like a news story, where fast turnaround and quick cutting is necessary, and you're not concerned with storage, organization, or logging your material carefully.

Slicing, whether in the **Viewer** or the **Timeline**, has the advantage of quickly and easily accessing all your material while still cutting it up into shots for editing. It has a couple of disadvantages:

- The problem of not being able to scrub easily in the **Viewer** when the shot is very long

- The problem of transitions, in which you might accidentally extend the transition into another shot, appearing as a flash on the screen. This cannot happen with properly made subclips.

Important: It is critical that you have nothing selected in the sequence when you use this technique. Anything that is selected—clip, audio, title, anything—will be ripple deleted instead of the marked In and Out section. The simplest way to avoid this is to press **Command-Shift-A** to Deselect All, the opposite of **Command-A, Select All**. This drops anything that's been selected. A good habit to get into before you execute this technique is to always make the **Timeline** the active window and press **Command-Shift-A**, or if you really like the menus, Edit > Deselect All.

Range Clipping

Another technique for slicing or making subclips is to use the **Range** tool in the **Timeline**. Some people prefer this method because it offers a visual display of the In and Out points as you work. Let's try this.

1. Again, make sure there are no In and Out points in the master clip *Temple* before dragging it into an empty *Sequence 1*.

2. Select the **Range** tool from the tools. It's under the second icon from the top. You can also call it up by pressing **GGG** (the letter **G** three times) (see Figure 3.12).

3. Position the playhead in the **Timeline** where you want the clip selection to begin.

3.12 **Range tool**

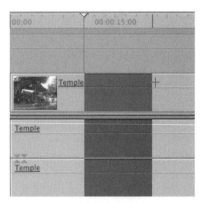

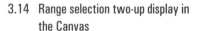

3.13 Range tool in the Timeline

4. With the **Range** tool, stroke one section of the clip (see Figure 3.13).

Unfortunately, the **Range** tool, unlike the **Blade**, does not respond as strongly to snapping, but the crosshairs let you position the **Range** selector very precisely. As you stroke the clip to make the selection, the **Canvas** will give you a two-up display that shows you the start and end frames as well as the timecode (see Figure 3.14).

Grab the selection from the **Timeline** and drag it to the **Browser**, where it can be changed into a master clip if you wish.

Organizing the Clips

Once you've got your material diced up, you should spend some time getting it put away so that you can find it again. There are no firm rules about this, and I find that each project tends to dictate its own organizational structure. Usually I begin with one bin that holds all the master shots. These are usually pretty big chunks of video: 10, 20, 30 minutes, usually not smaller. From the master shots, clips are separated out into bins. Keeping the master shots has the advantage that you can go back to the material in bulk to look through it again. As the project nears completion, I like to do this to see if I overlooked or discarded anything, which can be useful in light of the way the material gets cut together.

The separate bins can be organized in a variety of ways. Narrative projects tend to have material broken down in scene bins, with sub-bins for different types of shots or characters, depending on how complex the scene is. Documentary projects tend to break the material down into subject matter: a bin for all the forest shots, another for logging scenes, another for road work, another for weather, another for all the interviews, another for sound, another for narration tracks, another for music, another for

3.14 Range selection two-up display in the Canvas

graphics. As I said, there are no hard and fast rules on how material is organized.

The real trick is to break down your material into enough bins so that your material is organized, but not so many bins that it becomes difficult to find material. As you move clips into bins, add notes—lots of them. The more information you include on the clips, the easier it will be to find them.

Cutting up your shots and organizing them into bins is critical to working efficiently, particularly for long-form work, projects longer than 20 minutes or so. The longer the project, the more tapes you have, the more sequences, the more complex everything becomes. Having your material well-organized is crucial. Fortunately FCE provides ways to help you, such as the comments and logging information that we saw in the previous lesson. It's important to enter as much information as you can in the **Item Properties Logging Info** panel to take advantage of FCE's search capabilities.

5. Final Cut's search tool is called the **Finder**. To search for something in a project, use the same keyboard shortcut as the **Desktop Finder: Command-F**. This brings up the **Find** window (see Figure 3.15). The first pop-up menu lets you search:

    - The open project
    - All open projects
    - The *Effects* folder

It searches anything tabbed into the **Browser**.

The second pop-up menu selects **All Media** or a choice of **Used** or **Unused Media**, and the third pop-up menu lets you replace or add to existing results. The two pop-ups at the bottom define parameters. The left one sets where it's going to look. Unless you have a pretty good idea where the information is—for instance, if you're looking for a specific type of file—just leave it on the

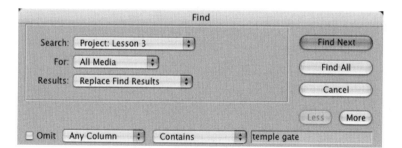

3.15 Find dialog box

default **Any Column**. The right pop-up menu lets you limit the search parameters to speed up the process by limiting the number of results.

➤**Tip**

Using Find to Keep Track: Because FCE doesn't keep track of shots that are taken from the **Browser** and put in a sequence, the **Find** window is one way to do this. By selecting the **Unused** pop-up menu, you can find the material. You can then use the check mark in the **Good** column to mark the unused clips. Unfortunately, **Find** searches only media, not subclips, so if any part of a piece of media is used, even one subclip, then all the sub-clips based on the same media are considered used.

3.16   Finder Results window

If you click the **Find All** button rather than the default **Find Next**, the requested clips appear in a new **Browser** window (see Figure 3.16).

Note the two buttons at the bottom, which let you:

- Show a selected item in the regular **Browser** bins
- Remove selected items from project

An important point to understand about this **Finder** is that all the items it locates are directly related to the items in the **Browser**. Unlike FCE's usual behavior where clips in sequences and bins can be copies of each other, here the found clips are directly linked to the clips in the **Browser**. Highlight a clip here, and it's highlighted in the **Browser**. Delete a clip here and it's deleted from the **Browser**.

➤**Tip**

Other Searches: The search engine isn't only for finding shots. You can search for anything in FCE. You might want to find a filter or a transition. You can search for those as well.

Look before You Cut

However you work your video into clips or subclips, what you're really doing is looking through your material. What you should watch for is relationships, shots that can easily be cut together. Getting familiar with the material is an important part of the editing process, learning what you have to work with and looking for cutting points.

While looking through the material in the **Timeline**, some editors even like to roughly cut up the shots into sequences as they sort through the pictures. As they come to groups of shots that work together, some editors put them together in sequences.

Look through the master shot *Temple*. It's quite short, but it shows a few shots that have obvious relationships. The same woman, in the white woolen hat, appears in four of them:

- In the third shot, as she bows before an incense bowl

- The shot from behind her that looks a little blue, in which she is walking up the stairs
- Another, in quick succession to the previous one, also from behind as she goes up the steps
- In medium shot from the side as she bows and prays

These shots can obviously be cut together to make a little sequence. You might want to put in a cutaway between the shot of her bowing at the bowl and her from behind walking up the steps or at the top of the steps already. From either of those two shots, a direct cut to her bowing would work without problem.

Searching for these relationships between shots is critical as you look through your material. Some editors like to immediately create small sequences and group them together, not finely honed, but roughly laid out, so that first important impression is preserved. You may not use it in your final project, but assembling related shots quickly into a sequence is an efficient way to make notes about your material. We'll look at assembling material into sequences in our next lesson.

You can have multiple sequences open at the same time. Timelines normally tab together into one **Timeline** window, but you can pull the timelines apart so that you have two sequences open on the screen at the same time. You can pull shots from one sequence into another. By doing this, you're copying the shot from one sequence into the new sequence.

Summary

In this lesson we've covered using **DV Start/Stop Detect** and working with markers, creating subclips, and slicing up our clips, as well as organizing our material so that we can work efficiently. In the next lesson. we'll look at more precise ways of editing sequences, moving your clips into the **Timeline**, and trimming them with some advanced editing tools.

Lesson 4

Editing Basics: Building Your Sequence

Now that you've got your material into Final Cut Express and cut it up, we're ready to begin putting it all together. There is no right way to edit a scene or a sequence or even a whole film or video; there are only bad ways, good ways, and better ways. Final Cut Express has a number of different ways, usually three or four, to do most of the editing functions. You can edit directly in the **Timeline** with the mouse, in the **Viewer** with buttons or shortcuts, and with various tools from the **Tools** palette.

Loading the Lesson

As in the previous lesson, start by loading the DVD into your DVD drive. When you begin any lesson that needs material from the DVD, you should first drag the needed media elements onto the media drive of your computer. The sound and video clips included there will play much better and more smoothly from your computer's high-speed media drive than from any DVD drive. For this lesson you'll also need the folders called *Media 2* as well as the *Projects* folder on the DVD.

1. Drag the *Projects* folder onto your internal system drive if you have not done so in previous lessons. Again, probably the best place for it is in your *Documents* folder.

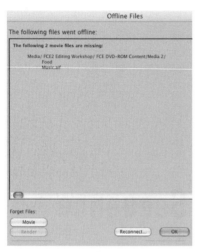

4.1   Offline Files dialog box

2. Copy the *Media 2* folder from inside the DVD's *Hybrid DVD-ROM Contents* folder onto your media hard drive.

3. Before opening anything, eject the DVD.

4. Open the *Projects* folder on your hard drive and double-click the project file, *Lesson 4*, to launch the application.

When the project finishes loading, you'll be greeted with the Reconnect dialog box we saw in Lesson 1.

5. Do *not* press **Return** or click **Movie** or **OK**. Instead click on the **Reconnect** button (see Figure 4.1).

The computer will now search through your hard drives looking for the QuickTime file called *Food*.

6. When the computer has found the correct file on your media drive, click the **Select** button.

Final Cut will reconnect all the material for the project. Then you're ready to go.

Setting Up the Project

Should the project ever get corrupted, you can always retrieve a fresh copy from your DVD, or from the *Autosave Vault* we saw in Lesson 2 on page 36.

Inside the **Browser** of your copy of *Lesson 4*, you'll see three sequences:

- *Sequence 1*
- *Food Sequence*
- *Slip & Slide*

Sequence 1 is empty. We'll look at *Food Sequence* in a moment and *Slip & Slide* later in the lesson. In the **Browser** there is also the master clip, *Food*, together with a bin called **Clips**. Open the **Clips** bin and you'll see that the shots from *Food* have been cut up into subclips.

Working with the Clips

Before we begin, take a quick look at *Food Sequence*. This is where we're going. To start, let's look at where we're coming from and the material we have to work with.

1. Open the empty *Sequence 1* and double-click on the master clip called *Food*, which will bring it into the **Viewer**.
    The material is one minute and 17 seconds long.

2. Play the shot, or scrub through it to see the material we'll be working with.

3. Open the **Clips** bin and double-click on the shot called *Food1*, which is 6;01 long, six seconds and one frame.

4. Play the shot. Let it pan from left to right across the trays of food, let the pan end, give it a beat, and then stop.

5. Enter an Out point by pressing the **O** key or the **Out** point button in the **Viewer**.

This will probably be around 4;12, about four and one-half seconds long.

Try it a few times until you get the pacing of the movement down. You might find that the more times you try it, the more you're shaving off the shot. Perhaps you'll feel that the front needs to be shortened as well. Instead of beginning right at the start of the shot, enter an In point just before the camera pans right. When you have it the way you want it, you're ready to move it into the **Timeline**.

There are three ways to get material from the **Viewer** to the **Timeline**:

- Drag it there. Grab the image from the **Viewer** and pull it directly into the **Timeline**, dropping it onto **V1** as shown in Figure 4.2.

- Drag the clip from the **Viewer** to the **Canvas**, and the visual dialog box, called the **Edit Overlay** (see Figure 4.3) immediately appears. Drop the clip on **Overwrite**.

- Use the **Overwrite** keyboard shortcut, **F10** (see the Note called "Exposé").

4.2   Dragging into the Timeline

> **Note**
>
> **Exposé:** When you're using OS X 10.3.x, called Panther, you have a great feature called **Exposé**, which allows you to reveal your **Desktop** as well as display all the open windows on your computer. Unfortunately for FCE users, the default shortcuts for **Exposé's** functions are F9, F10, and F11. These three keys are critical to working efficiently in FCE. What I would recommend is that you change the default **Exposé** keyboard shortcuts to **Option-F9**, **Option-F10**, and **Option-F11**. You can do this in your **System Preferences** in the **Exposé** panel as in Figure 4.4.

> **Tip**
>
> **Edit Buttons:** Although there are no buttons in the **Canvas**, you can make your own buttons for the primary edit functions that we'll be looking at in this chapter. I have created a button list for these functions for you that you can use. You'll find it in the *Extras* folder of the DVD. In addition to the edit functions, there are a couple of other buttons I find useful, which appear over the **Browser**.
>
> To load the buttons, **Control**-click in one of the coffee-bean button holders and choose **Load Main Button Bars** from the shortcut menu. Navigate to the *Extras* folder on the DVD and select **Editing Workshop Button Bar** to add the buttons to the windows.

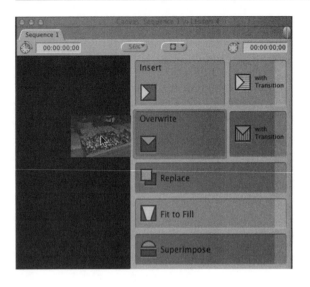

4.3   Edit Overlay

4.4   System Preferences > Exposé

4.5   Fit to Window

Which way you execute the edit is a question of personal preference. Many people prefer to drag to the **Timeline**. It can be easy when you're unpracticed to drop the clip into the wrong track or to do an Insert instead of an Overwrite when you drag to the **Timeline**. I prefer the accuracy and exactness of dragging to **Overwrite**. This seems to work well on a PowerBook, where there is no separate mouse and the **F** keys are awkward to use. On a full-sized keyboard, though, the speed of using shortcuts is hard to beat.

✎ Note

Dropped Frames: One of the most common causes of dropped frames, especially for new users of FCE, is that their viewing window is not fit to the video. If you look at your DV video in a small frame while the material is set to full size, you're expecting the computer to display only a portion of the video while playing it back. If this doesn't produce dropped frames on playback, it will at the very least show as stuttering video on your computer monitor. You can always tell if the image is too large for the viewing window when you see scroll bars on the sides, as in Figure 4.5. To correct this, select **Fit to Window** from the **Viewer Size** pop-up menu or the keyboard shortcut **Shift-Z**. **Shift-Z** is also used in the **Timeline** to fit the contents into the window.

Overwrite

Let's look at the **Edit Overlay** (see Figure 4.3). It offers seven different editing options. The most commonly used is the **Overwrite** command.

1.   Drag the clip from the **Viewer** until the box marked **Overwrite** highlights.

2.   Drop the clip.

It will overwrite whatever is in the timeline beginning at the point at which the playhead is parked. When you drag a clip onto the **Edit Overlay** or use a button or a keyboard shortcut to execute an edit, the clip is placed in the **Timeline** on the designated destination tracks, in this case **V1** and **A1/A2**. These are the default destination tracks set in the patch panel at the head of the **Timeline** (see Figure 4.6).

The number of tracks and the types available as destination tracks are controlled by what is loaded in the **Viewer.** For instance, if you have a still image in the **Viewer,** only one destination track for video will be available. Similarly, if you have a piece of stereo music loaded in the **Viewer,** only two tracks of audio will be available as destinations and no video tracks, as in Figure 4.7.

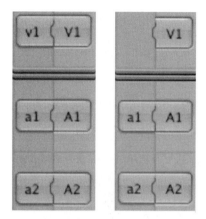

4.6   Patch panel *(left)*

4.7   Patch panel with stereo music only *(right)*

> **Note**_____
> **FCE2 Patch Panel:** The FCE2 patch panel has a number of distinct functions. One of them, Destination Track selection, controls how material gets placed into your sequence. The **Auto Select** is similar. It controls how edits—such as an Add edit—are executed, which items are copied, and even where items are pasted.
> If you copy a clip from the **Browser** and paste it into a sequence, this is still controlled by the patch panel as in the previous version of FCE. However, if you copy a clip from inside a sequence, either the one you're working in or another sequence, and paste the clip or clips into the **Timeline**, in FCE2 the application behavior has been changed. The patch panel and the **Destination Tracks** no longer determine where the pasted material goes. That is now set by the **Auto Select** function.

> **➤Tip**_____
> **Timeline In Point:** You can also define the In point in the **Timeline** to be a different point from the playhead. Go to the **Canvas** or the **Timeline** window and press the **I** key to mark an In point (see Figure 4.8). This will be the In point for the next edit, and when you drag the clip from the **Viewer** to the **Canvas** or press **F10**, the clip will drop at the marked In point and not at the playhead's current position.

4.8 In point mark in the Timeline

⚓ Note

Overwrite Constraint: Note that although you can drag a clip directly from the **Browser** to the **Edit Overlay**, **F10** does not overwrite directly from the **Browser**. **F10** works only when overwriting from the **Viewer**. If the **Viewer** is closed, **F10** will simply put in a slug, a long section of black with a stereo audio track.

So that we can look at the functionality offered in the **Edit Overlay**, let's quickly drag a few shots into the **Timeline** to see how they work.

1. If you haven't already done so, drag *Food1* from the **Viewer** and drop it on **Overwrite**.

2. Select clips *Food2* and *Food3* in the **Browser** and drag them directly to the **Overwrite** box in the **Edit Overlay**.

The clips will appear in the **Timeline** following *Food1* in their bin order. Every time you place a clip in the **Timeline**, the playhead automatically leaps to end of the clip, ready for the next edit event.

Insert

If **Overwrite** is the most commonly used of the **Edit Overlay** features, then the next most-used must be **Insert**. This is where a nonlinear editing system shows its power.

1. Move the playhead to the edit between *Food1* and *Food2*.

As you move the playhead onto the edit point, it should snap strongly to the join and display on the tracks the marks in Figure 4.9. If you don't see the snap marks, **Snapping** is turned off.

2. Press the **N** key. Try it several times, toggling the **Snapping** function on and off.

The **N** key may become one of your most often-used keys in Final Cut Express. You'll find that you'll be constantly changing from one mode to the other.

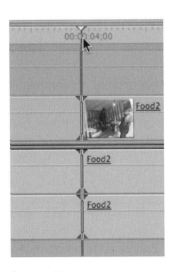

4.9 Snap markings

4.10 The Insert edit

Note

The Magic Frame: If the playhead moves to the end of the last clip in a sequence, the **Canvas** displays the last frame of the clip with a blue bar down the right side. This is the Magic Frame, because the playhead is actually sitting on the next frame of video—the blank, empty frame—but the display shows the previous frame.

Now with snapping on, you should have the playhead parked between the clips.

3. Grab *Food5* directly from the **Browser** and drag it to the **Canvas**, calling up the **Edit Overlay**.

4. Drop it on **Overwrite** to see what happens.

Food5 wipes out all of *Food2* and some of *Food3*.

5. Quickly undo that with **Command-Z**.

6. This time, instead of dragging *Food5* onto **Overwrite**, drag it onto **Insert**.

Immediately the **Timeline** rearranges itself. *Food5* drops into the **Timeline**, appears between *Food1* and *Food2*, and pushes everything farther down in the **Timeline**, as shown in Figure 4.10.

Insert will move everything down the track regardless of a clip's position. So if you insert into the middle of the clip, the clip will be cut, and everything on all the tracks will be pushed out of the way. This applies to all tracks, including music or narration, which you may not want to cut.

Track locks are useful in these circumstances. For instance, to prevent an insert from slicing into a music track, lock the track or tracks. All the other tracks will move, but the locked tracks will remain stationary.

Let's try this and see what happens.

> **Tip**
>
> **Select an Edit:** A useful keyboard shortcut is the V key, which selects the nearest edit point and moves the playhead to it.

1. Undo the insert edit that you did when moving *Food5* into the **Timeline**.

2. In the **Browser** is an audio track called *Music.aif*. Grab the icon and drag it directly into the **Timeline** and place it on tracks **A3/A4**. It's a stereo pair of music.

3. Move the playhead back between *Food1* and *Food2* again.

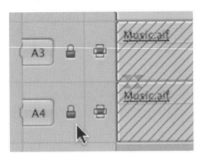

4. Execute the Insert edit with *Food5*. Immediately you'll notice that not only is the video being inserted into the sequence, but also the music track is being cut with the insert.

5. Undo that edit with **Command-Z**.

6. Click on the track locks (see Figure 4.11) at the head of each track. Remember that you need to lock or unlock both tracks of a stereo pair.

4.11 Track locks

7. Redo the Insert edit, and you'll see that although the video moves to accommodate the clip, the music track does not.

8. Before we go any further, let's undo the Insert edit and remove the audio on **A3/A4**, bringing the **Timeline** back to just three clips, *Food1*, *Food2*, and *Food3*.

You can also use **Control** key and the shortcut menu to do a ripple delete (see Figure 4.12), or ripple delete with **Shift-Delete**. You can also ripple delete using the **Forward Delete** key, sometimes marked as **Del**, on an extended keyboard.

4.12 Shortcut menu ripple delete

> ### 🐀 *Note*
> ***Keyboard Shortcuts:*** As usual in FCE, there are keyboard shortcuts for locking and unlocking tracks. To lock a video track, press **F4** and the track number. To lock an audio track, press **F5** and the track number. If you want to lock all the video tracks, press **Shift-F4**; for all the audio tracks, **Shift-F5**. These key commands are toggles: unlocked tracks will lock, and locked tracks will unlock.
>
> Sometimes it's handy to lock all the video or audio tracks except one. Use **Option**-click on the lock, and that track will remain unlocked while all the other tracks of that type, video or audio, will lock. Press **Option**-click on the track again to unlock everything.

Alternative Overwrite and Insert

Overwrite and **Insert** are the primary functions in the **Edit Overlay**, but let's look at another way to do them.

Drag *Food5* directly from the **Browser** to the **Timeline**. As you drag it onto the edit point between *Food1* and *Food2*, a little arrow appears, indicating how the edit will be performed. If the arrow is pointing downward as in Figure 4.13, the edit will over-write. If the little arrow is pointing to the right as in Figure 4.14, you will be doing an insert edit, which will ripple the sequence, pushing the other material in the **Timeline** out of the way. Notice as you do this how the two-up display in the **Canvas** changes. In Figure 4.15 the video is being overwritten, beginning at the end of *Food1* and wiping out all of *Food2* and most of *Food3*. In Figure 4.16 the shot is being inserted between *Food1* and *Food2*.

4.13 Overwrite arrow

You'll notice also as you work in the application that in addition to the arrow indicators, the clip colors change. In **Overwrite**, the track color changes to the highlighted brown color. In **Insert**, the track has an outline box.

The point at which the arrows switch from **Insert** to **Overwrite** is indicated by the faint line running horizontally through the clip about a third of the way from the top. If the clip is in the upper third, the edit will be an Insert. If it's in the lower two-thirds, the edit will be an Overwrite. It's the faint horizontal line you see running through the clips in Figures 4.13 and 4.14.

4.14 Insert arrow

Replace

We'll skip **Overwrite with Transition** and **Insert with Transition** for the next lesson and look at:

- **Replace**
- **Fit to Fill**
- **Superimpose**

Replace is remarkably sophisticated in the way it works. It will replace a clip in the **Timeline** with another clip either from the **Viewer** or dragged from the **Browser** to the **Canvas**. The trick to

4.15 Overwrite two-up canvas display

4.16 Insert two-up canvas display

understanding how **Replace** works is to understand that it works precisely from the point at which the playhead is positioned.

Let's do a Replace edit.

1. Start with your base three shots in the **Timeline:** *Food1*, *Food2*, and *Food3*.

2. Place the playhead at the edit point between *Food1* and *Food2* so that we're at the beginning of *Food2*.

3. Open *Food5* into the **Viewer** and make sure the playhead there is close to the beginning of the clip.

4. Drag it into **Replace** in the **Canvas,** or use the keyboard shortcut *F11*. *Food5* will immediately replace *Food2* in the **Timeline.**

The **Viewer** and the **Canvas** will show the same frame because Final Cut has taken the frame that was in the **Viewer** and placed it in exactly the same frame position as the shot it's replacing in the **Timeline.** It's extended the shot forward and backward from that point to exactly fill the duration of the shot it's replacing.

Take a look at the clips in Figure 4.17.

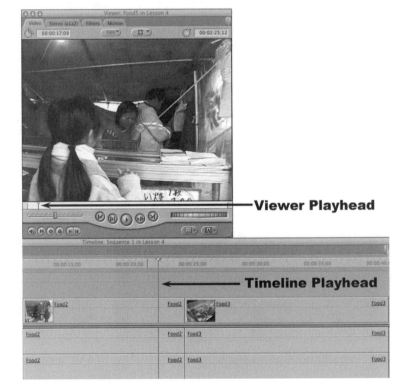

4.17 One clip trying to replace another

The clip in the **Timeline**, *Food2*, has the playhead parked toward the end of the shot. I want to replace it with the clip *Food5*. In the **Viewer,** *Food5* has the playhead parked near the beginning of the shot. The current position of the playhead in *Food5* is indicated. I won't be able to replace *Food2* with *Food5* even though the new clip is much longer than the clip it's replacing. Why? Because FCE calculates the Replace edit from the position of the playhead. There just aren't enough frames in front of the current position of the playhead in *Food5* in the **Viewer** to replace all the frames in front of the current position of the playhead in *Food2* in the sequence.

If you tried to do a Replace edit to *Food5* in place of *Food2* in the **Timeline** you'd get an **"Insufficient content for edit"** error message.

➤*Tip*

Alternative Replace: Another way to do a replace function is to use **Overwrite** after first defining the limits of the shot you want to replace. That's easy to do in FCE. With the playhead parked over the shot, press the **X** key. This sets In and Out points on the timeline that are exactly the length of the clip, as in Figure 4.18. If you now do an Overwrite edit, it will replace the shot in the **Timeline.** Remember that what gets selected and highlighted in the **Timeline** is controlled by the **Auto Select buttons** at the head of the tracks.

4.18 Ins and Outs in the timeline

Fit to Fill

Fit to Fill functions similarly to **Replace** except that it's never hampered by lack of media. **Fit to Fill** adjusts the speed of the clip to match the area it needs to occupy. This is a great tool for putting in still images or titles that you want to be a specific length. Because they aren't real video, Final Cut will produce the images very quickly and accurately. It's a little more problematic when using it with video where it can raise some serious problems.

1. To see how this functions, delete everything that you may already have in the **Timeline** and make sure the playhead is at the beginning of the **Timeline**.

2. Grab *Food4*, *Food5*, and *Food6* and drag them to **Overwrite** in the **Edit Overlay** to move them into the **Timeline**.

3. Move the playhead in the **Timeline** so that it's sitting over *Food5*, the middle of the three clips in the **Timeline**.

4. Open the clip *Food1* into the **Viewer**.

5. Press **Option-X** to clear any In and Out points that might be marked on the clip.

6. You can see by the duration in the upper left corner of the **Viewer** that *Food1* is quite a bit shorter than *Food5*. *Food1* is 6;01, while *Food5* is 17;09.

7. Drag the *Food1* clip from the **Viewer** to the **Edit Overlay** and drop it on the **Fit to Fill** box. Or use the keyboard shortcut **Shift-F11**.

The clip will immediately drop into the **Timeline**, and unless it is exactly the same size as the clip it's replacing, a colored render line will appear at the top of the **Timeline**, red if your system is not capable of playing back a speed change in real time and green if it is. The red or green render line indicates that the section of the **Timeline** needs to be rendered at some point before output. If the line is red, the clip will have to be rendered immediately to be viewed; if it's green you will have real-time preview. This section needs to be rendered because of the speed change to *Food1*, which is now in slow motion to accommodate the **Fit to Fill** edit. The clip in the sequence shows the speed change, in this case, 35 percent of real speed (see Figure 4.19). You will also see a green colored line at top of the audio portion of the clip, indicating that it too, because is the sound is also slowed down, will need to be rendered before outputting.

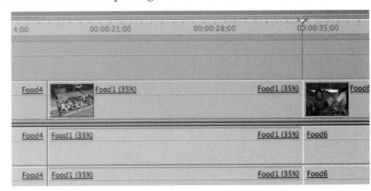

4.19 Slow-motion clip in the Timeline

Changing to Slow Motion

When a speed change is done in a sequence, a Ripple edit is performed, that is, the contents of the Timeline shift, based on the new length of the clip. This is usually good, but sometimes you just don't want that to happen. If you're speeding up the material, the easiest way is to go to the head of the clip and use the **F** key to match back to the clip in the **Browser**. Mark an In point and press **Command-J** to call up the **Speed Change** dialog. Change the speed to, say, 200 percent and then **Overwrite** back into the **Timeline**, cutting away what's left of the clip that you don't need.

If you're slowing down the material, it's slightly different. Here with the playhead in the **Timeline** at the start of the clip, use the **F** key to match back to a new copy of the clip, and then mark an In point. Execute the speed change, say, to 50 percent, and drag the clip to **Replace**. The slomo will be the duration of the clip it's replacing without rippling the sequence.

But the 35 percent shown in the **Timeline** is not quite true. Let's check the speed.

8. Select the clip *Food1* in the **Timeline** and press **Command-J**, which calls up the **Speed** dialog box (see Figure 4.20).

In this case the speed is 34.68 percent. The real problem with speed changes is that it is difficult to create smooth motion, particularly at odd speeds such as 34.68 percent. At full-size, interlaced DV, you can get some nasty stuttering effects, particularly if the clips are speeded up. It's better if you want to do slow or fast motion to use simple multiples: 50, 150, 25, or 200 percent. These are much easier to calculate and generally produce better results. **Fit to Fill** calculates an absolute number and, as you can see, usually a bizarre one.

4.20 Speed dialog box

Modify>Speed (**Command-J**) is where all clip speed changes are made. It is unfortunately not possible to ramp speed up or down so that it accelerates and decelerates.

Frame blending can help, but it will slow down render time. The default is to have **Frame Blending** turned on. With **Frame Blending** off, FCE merely duplicates or drops frames as necessary to make up the right speed. For slow motion you usually want to have **Frame Blending** turned on, but for clips being speeded up, it works better to have it switched off.

⚛ Note

Superimpose: There is often some misunderstanding about the term *superimpose*. In FCE it is used to mean placing a clip on the track above the current destination track. It does not mean what many people expect, that the superimposed image will appear partially transparent and that the underlying image will still be visible beneath it.

Superimpose

Superimpose is used primarily to place titles on the track above the video. It again works a bit like **Replace**. The clip you're superimposing takes its duration from the clip you're placing it above. Drag the clip on **Superimpose**, and it will be placed above the clip that the playhead is sitting on.

Let's ripple delete the **Fit to Fill** shot, the middle of the three in the **Timeline** so that we're left with only *Food4* and *Food6*.

1. Place the playhead somewhere over the middle of the *Food6*.

2. Drag *Food5* from the **Browser** to the **Canvas** and drop it on the **Superimpose** box, or use the keyboard shortcut **F12**.

The clip appears in the **Timeline** above the clip on the destination track, above *Food6* in this case, as in Figure 4.21. Notice where the audio track has gone onto **A3** and **A4**, the tracks below the destination tracks.

⚛ Note

Different In Point: If you want to superimpose at some point other than right over a clip you can do this by entering an In point in the **Timeline**. Go to the **Canvas** or the **Timeline** window and press the **I** key to mark an In point. This will be the In point for the next edit, and when you drag the clip from **Viewer** to **Canvas** to **Superimpose**, the clip will drop at the marked In point and not at the playhead's current position.

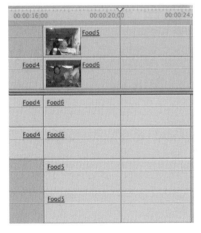

4.21 Superimposed clip

Making a Sequence

Now that we've gone through the principal means of going from **Viewer** to **Canvas**, let's edit in the **Timeline** itself, trimming and adjusting the clips. We'll edit together a quickly paced sequence of shots.

I like to begin by looking at the material I'm going to use for the sequence. Open the master clip *Food* in the **Viewer** and look through the material the way it was shot.

Rather than working on the clips in the **Timeline**, let's start afresh with the first clip.

1. Again, select all and delete everything in the **Timeline**.

2. Double-click on *Food1* in the **Browser** to open it into the **Viewer**.

3. Scrub through to the point where the camera starts moving from left to right.

4. Find the beginning of the movement and mark the In point.

5. Now find the end of the movement and mark the Out point. We can leave the shots a little loose at this stage.

6. After you've marked the In and Out points, drag the clip to **Overwrite** or press **F10**.

I'm not sure which part of the second shot, *Food2*, I'll use at this stage. I'll probably use something, so I'll cut a long piece.

7. Open *Food2* into the **Viewer** and take the shot from just before the zoom starts and let it run almost to the end, including the part with the hands turning the skewers.

8. Again **Overwrite** to the **Timeline**.

Food3 is a little more complex. I want to use more than one part of the shot.

9. Start by marking the In point at the beginning of the shot.

10. Mark the Out point just before the short zoom out.

11. Overwrite the clip.

Ins and Outs

By putting the shot in the **Timeline,** I made a copy of the shot that's currently loaded in the **Viewer.** So now I can set new In and Out points for the clip that's still in the **Viewer** without affecting what I've already done to the shot in the sequence.

1. Set a new In point in the **Viewer** just before the pan left begins.

2. Let the shot carry over to the steaming kettle, until about the 8;18 mark.

Marking Edit Points

Many editors like to mark their Out points on the fly. This has the advantage of allowing you to judge the pace of the shot and of the sequence, to do it almost tactilely, to feel the rhythm of the shot. After a few tries you'll probably find you're hitting the Out point consistently on the same frame. If you're not, perhaps it isn't the right shot to be using, or perhaps you should look again at the pace the sequence is imposing on you. It's possible the shot doesn't work where it is.

Marking the In point is a little different because often you want to mark the edit point before an action begins, but judging how far in front of the action to begin on the fly is difficult. Some editors like to mark the In point while the video is playing backwards. By playing it backwards, you see where the action begins, and you get to judge the pace of how far before the action you want the edit to occur.

3. Add an Out point and add that to the **Timeline**.

4. Take a third section from that clip, from just before the camera tilts up until shortly before the shot ends and add that to the **Timeline**.

Food4 might fit nicely before the close-up of the steaming tray.

5. Position the **Timeline** playhead between *Food2* and *Food3* in sequence.

6. Mark an In point at the beginning of *Food4* and an Out point just before the pan to the right, around 2;28.

7. Drag the clip to **Insert** or use the shortcut **F9**.

We might be able to get another piece out of *Food4*.

8. Mark an In point around 5;15, just at the beginning of the static portion of the shot of the man hunched over his soup.

9. Mark an Out point just before the camera pans left around 9;09.

10. Move the playhead in the **Timeline** in front of the first portion of *Food4*, to the edit point that separates *Food2* and *Food4*.

11. Execute an Insert edit to move the shot from the **Viewer** into the **Timeline**.

Bookends

Let's look at *Food5*. It's the most human part of the material, the little girl at the food stall. My thought is to use it as bookends: the little girl at the beginning of the sequence and at the end.

1. Make the first part of the shot one clip, basically until after she hands the vendor her money. Mark an In point near the beginning of the shot and an Out point around 6;12.

2. Make sure the playhead is at the start of the **Timeline**, then drag to **Insert**.

3. Make the second part of *Food5* begin shortly before the vendor reaches for the biscuit, around 7;27. Mark an In point there and let it go until just before the end.

4. Move the playhead to the end of the **Timeline** with the **End** key.

5. Drag the second half of *Food5* from the **Viewer** to **Overwrite**, or press **F10**.

We want *Food6* to go just before the last shot.

4.22 Timeline after first cuts

6. Open *Food6* in the **Viewer** and play it.

7. Set the In point near the beginning.

8. Set the Out point before the move with the biscuits, around 3;16.

9. In the **Timeline**, the playhead is probably at the end of the material. Use the **Up** arrow to move backwards one edit.

10. Now drag the clip from **Viewer** to **Insert**, or use **F9**.

The duration of this little sequence should be about 45 seconds, depending on how tightly you cut the shots. Looking through it, it's obvious it needs to be tightened up as well as have the order rearranged. Your **Timeline** should look like Figure 4.22.

Swap Edit

There are three pieces of *Food3* in the sequence. Let's begin by moving *Food1*, which is now the second shot in sequence, between the first two pieces of *Food3* in the **Timeline**. This is called a *Swap edit*.

1. Grab the shot and start to pull it along the timeline.

2. After you've started the movement, hold down the **Option** key.

> **Tip** _____
>
> **Timecode Location:** To go to a specific timecode point in either the **Canvas**, the **Viewer**, or the **Timeline**, tap out the number on your keypad. (In the case of working with *Food6*, type in *24513*.) and press **Return**. The playhead will immediately move to that point.

Jump Cuts

The sequence as we've laid it out so far has the most obvious form of jump cut, which is any abrupt edit that jars the viewer. This is generally considered bad editing. The most common cause is placing side-by-side shots, such as the two halves of F*ood5*, that are very similar but not the same. You get this disconcerting little jump, as if you blacked out for a fraction of a second. It suddenly pulls the viewers out from the content of the video as they say to themselves, or perhaps even out loud, "What was that?" You can also get a jump cut if you put together two very different shots, such as the shot of a long street with the small figure of a person in the distance, cutting to a tight close-up. It's disorienting because the viewer has no reference that the close-up belongs to the person seen in the far distance in the previous shot. These are jump cuts. The general rule is to avoid them if you can. Or use them so often that it becomes your style. Then it's art.

4.23 Swap Edit arrow

Don't press the **Option** key until after you've started to move the clip, while you're already in mouse-down mode. As you move, a downward hooked arrow appears on the clip (see Figure 4.23). You'll also see a number displayed. This tells you how far in the sequence you have moved the clip.

3. When you get to the edit point between the first and second portions of *Food3* in the sequence, drop the clip.

If you look at the **Timeline**, you'll see that you've done an insert edit as well as a ripple delete. You've removed the clip from one point on the timeline, placed it somewhere else in the timeline, and pushed everything out of the way to make room for it. Figure 4.24 shows the sequence after the Swap edit. This is a great hidden tool that I often use.

4.24 After using Swap Edit

Note

Swap Edit Limit: The Swap Edit function that lets you move clips will work on only one clip at a time. Unfortunately, you can't grab a couple of clips or a small section of clips and do the same thing. It also works best if you have **Snapping** turned on to avoid slicing off a little bit of a shot by accident.

Tip

Gaps and Syncing: FCE defines a gap as a space in the **Timeline** that extends across all tracks. So if you have a music track on **A3** and **A4**, for instance, FCE will not see the space between the shots on the video tracks as a gap. This is where the ability to lock tracks really helps. If you lock those music tracks, you can then close the gap. Or use **Option**-lock to lock all other tracks, and again you can close the gap. There are a number of ways to close a gap:

• **Control**-click in the gap and from the shortcut menu choose **Close Gap**.

• With the playhead over the gap, press **Control-G**.

• Click on the gap to select it and then press the **Delete** key.

Ripple Cut and Paste Insert

Although you can move only one shot at a time when you do a Swap, there is a handy way to move groups of clips. Look at the two pieces of *Food4* followed by the first part of *Food3*. These three shots should be moved together right after *Food5* at the head of the **Timeline**. This would make them the second, third, and fourth shots in the sequence. I could just move *Food2* after them, but let me show you a way to move groups of clips.

1. Start by selecting the clips. It's simplest to marquee-drag through them, or select the first clip and **Shift**-select the third clip.

2. Next, cut them out, but not with the usual **Command-X**, but with **Shift-X**.

Using **Command-X** would create what's called a Lift edit but leave a gap in the sequence. Sometimes you do want to do this, but in this instance we use **Shift-X**, which performs a **Ripple Cut** instead of the simple Lift. This not only cuts the clips out of the timeline but also closes the gap the missing clips leave behind.

3. Now move the playhead to the edit is at the end of *Food5*, between *Food5* and *Food2*. This is where you want to place the clips. Press **Shift-V**, which will paste the clips as a Paste Insert edit. **Command-V** would also paste but as an Overwrite edit.

Your timeline should be laid out something like Figure 4.25.

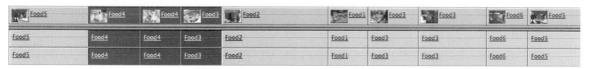

4.25 Timeline after Paste Insert

Let's look through the sequence again. It's getting better, but there are still a few edits I don't like and quite a few shots that need trimming. We'll get to trimming in a moment, but let's rearrange a few more shots.

Add Edits

In the first shot, I like the way the camera moves around the girl at the beginning, and I like the way she hands over her money with her fingers splayed out. I'd like to lengthen the effect of this scene by basically making it take more time than it actually did. What I'd like to do is move *Food2* right into the middle of that first shot. I know *Food2* is too long; we'll get to trimming it shortly.

✎ **Note**
Moving the Playhead: Shift-Left
or **Right**-arrow will move the playhead forward or backward in one-
second increments.

1. Scrub or play through the beginning of the **Timeline** to find the point just after the camera moves around the girl and the vendor picks up the bag, around 2;15 into the sequence.

2. Make sure nothing is selected in the sequence and use **Control-V** to slice the clip in the sequence.

3. Play or scrub forward in the **Timeline** to find the point just before the vendor reaches his hand out for the money, around 2;21.

4. Press **Control-V** again. You have now isolated a short section to cut out.

5. Ripple delete it either by **Control**-clicking to call up the short-cut menu or by selecting it and pressing **Shift-Delete**.

Instead of using the **Add Edit** function with **Control-V**, you could also have done this, by marking an In and Out point in the **Timeline** as we did in the previous lesson and ripple-deleting the short section.

Range Clipping

A third way to do this would be to use the **Range** tool (**GGG**), which we saw in the previous lesson. You can use this feature to select a portion of the clip to ripple delete. This functionality is new to FCE2 (see Figure 4.26). You may have to switch off **Snapping** to make such a short edit. While you're dragging with the **Range** tool, you'll see a two-up display in the **Canvas** showing you the start and end points of the edit (see Figure 4.27). The timecode display in the **Canvas** is that of the clip, beginning from the clip's start time of 00:00:00;00.

Rearranging Clips

Obviously the sequence now has a jump cut. So let's take *Food2*, which we moved earlier and should now be the sixth shot in the

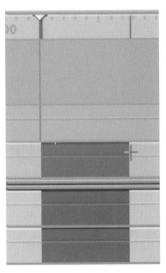

4.26 Range tool selection in the Timeline

4.27 Two-up Canvas display

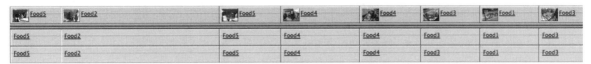

4.28 Food sequence beginning

sequence, and do a Swap edit. Drag with **Option** to drop *Food2* between the two halves of *Food5* at the beginning of the sequence. The beginning of the **Timeline** should look like Figure 4.28.

As you go through the sequence, you'll see another jump cut between two parts of *Food3*. The camera pans right from the cooking tray to the steaming kettle and then in a separate shot tilts up from the kettle to the cook. I would remove the first of these shots, taking out the pan. I've seen that cooking tray already, but the kettle and the chef are new.

The arrangement is almost right, but there is a problem with the very last shot that I don't care for. Just after the vendor puts the biscuit in the bag, the camera jiggles. I'd like to remove this. So let's do this in the **Timeline**.

1. Scrub or play through *Food5*, the last shot in the sequence, to the frame when the biscuit just disappears into the bag behind the counter.

2. Use **I** to mark the In point in the **Timeline**.

Right after this the camera is jostled.

3. Move further down to where the vendor is about to reach forward with the bag, just before his hands separate.

4. Mark the Out point with the **O** key and ripple delete the middle portion.

Now we have the same problem we had in the first shot.

This time we're going to move *Food3* from its earlier position. This is the shot of the tilt from kettle to cook.

5. Drag and then add the **Option** key before you drop it between the two halves of *Food5* that you just split.

If you look through the sequence, you'll see that the shots are in the order we want, but we still need to tighten it up, trimming the shots to make them faster-paced.

➤**Tip**

Timeline Scaling: You can change the scale of the **Timeline** to zoom in and out with the tabbed slider at the bottom of the window. Pulling either end of the tab will change the scale of the **Timeline** window. At the bottom left is a little slider that will adjust the scale (see Figure 4.29).

4.29 Scaling slider and tabbed slider

My favorite is to use the keyboard shortcuts **Option-** = (think **Option-** +) to zoom in and **Option--** (that's **Option-**minus) to zoom out. What's nice about using the keyboard shortcuts is that it leaves the playhead centered in the **Timeline** as you zoom in and out. Just be careful a clip isn't selected in the **Timeline**, because the scaling will take place around that rather than around the playhead. You can use **Command-** + and **Command--** to scale in other windows, but **Option-** + and – will always scale the **Timeline** even if the **Viewer** or the **Canvas** is the active window.

Storyboarding

Another way to lay out your sequences is by building storyboards in bins. Some editors like to do this. In Large or Medium Icon mode, you can:

- Trim and set the clips
- Set the Poster frame
- Arrange the layout order of the shots in the **Browser**

To set the Poster frame of a clip when you're in Icon view, either:

- Open the clip into the **Viewer**, find the frame, and use **Mark>Set Poster Frame** (**Control-P**), or
- Press **Control-Shift** while you click on the icon in the bin. This will let you scrub the clip. Hold down the two modifier keys and release the mouse over the clip where you want to set the Poster frame.

Storyboarding is a fast, easy way to move the shot order around, to try different arrangements and sequences. Although you can't play the clips back as a sequence, you can make a quick arrangement of shots in your bin. Then marquee through the shots and drag them into the **Timeline** (see Figure 4.30).

The shots will appear in the sequence in the order they are in the bin. Notice that the shots in the **Timeline** in Figure 4.30 follow the bin order as they are laid out, left to right, top to bottom. Be careful with the row heights: clips that are placed higher up in the bin will appear earlier.

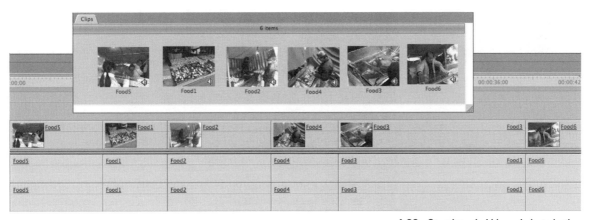

4.30 Storyboarded bin and shots in the Timeline

The Trim Tools

The trim tools—**Roll** and **Ripple**, **Slip** and **Slide**—are among the tools shown in Figure 4.31. The trim tools are clustered in the fourth and fifth buttons.

The first two trim tools, **Ripple** and **Roll**, change the duration of clips, and the second two, **Slip** and **Slide**, leave the clip duration intact.

A *Ripple* edit moves an edit point up and down the timeline by pushing or pulling all the material on the track, shortening or lengthening the whole sequence. In a Ripple edit, only one clip changes duration, getting longer or shorter. Everything else that comes after it in the track adjusts to accommodate it. In Figure 4.32 the edit is rippled to the left, and everything after moves left to accompany it, just as in a ripple delete.

A *Roll* edit moves an edit point up and down the timeline between two adjacent shots. Only those two shots have their durations changed. One gets longer, and the adjacent shot gets shorter to accommodate it. The overall length of the track remains unchanged. In Figure 4.33 the edit point itself can be moved either left or right.

A *Slip* edit changes the In and Out points of a single clip. The duration of the clip remains the same, and all the clips around it remain the same. Only the In and Out of the slipped clip change. If more frames are added on the front, the same amount are cut off the end, and vice versa, if some are added to the end, an equal amount are taken off the beginning.

4.31 The tools *(left)*

4.32 Ripple edit left *(below)*

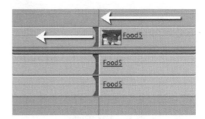

4.33 Roll edit directions

4.34 Slip edit direction

4.35 Slide edit directions

4.36 The Ripple tool

4.37 Ripple tool right (Left)

4.38 Ripple tool left (Right)

In Figure 4.34 the contents of the shot change by changing In and Out points, but neither its position in the **Timeline** nor either of the adjacent shots are affected.

A *Slide* edit moves a clip forward or backward along the timeline. The clip itself, its duration, and its In and Out points remain unchanged. Only its position on the timeline, earlier or later, shortens and lengthens the adjacent shots as it slides up and down the track. In Figure 4.35 the shot *Food6* can slide up and down the timeline. The shot itself doesn't change, only the two adjacent shots.

The Ripple Tool

We're first going to work with the **Ripple** tool. Press the fourth button and extend the popout to select the tool as in Figure 4.38. You can also call it up by pressing **RR**; that's the **R** key twice.

Let's use it on some of the shots we want to work on. Start with the edit between shots *Food4* and *Food3*. Take the tool and place it near the edit. Notice that it changes direction as you move it across the edit as in Figures 4.34 and 4.35.

When the tool is on the right side it will ripple the second shot; when it's on the left side, it will ripple the first shot.

In this case, we want to ripple the second shot. The edit almost works, but it can perhaps be a little improved by tightening up. The little pause at the beginning of *Food3* before the ladle moves makes the edit look awkward. You can ripple right in the timeline. As you grab the clip, you will get a small two-up display in the **Canvas**.

A word of caution about rippling: if you're working with material that's cut to narration or music, rippling will easily upset the timing of the sequence, because it's pulling and pushing the entire track and its sync sound. So what's working for you at this moment in the edit may be ruining something else further down the timeline. In these cases, the **Roll** tool may work better for you.

The Roll Tool

The **Roll** tool is also under the fourth button in the **Tools**, shown in Figure 4.39. It can be evoked with the **R** key. It works similarly to **Ripple** and can be used in the **Timeline** as in Figure 4.40.

The **Roll** tool acts on both shots, extending one shot while shortening the other. Although the **Ripple** tool changes the overall length of the sequence by moving everything up and down the line, the **Roll** tool only affects the two adjacent shots.

Using **Roll** and **Ripple**, tighten up some of the shots in the sequence. I rippled the zoom into the skewers in *Food2* until all you see are the hands turning over the sticks on the grill.

4.39   The Roll tool

> ➤ *Tip*
> _____
> **Ripple and Roll Shortcuts:** You can also use the Ripple and Roll tools incrementally with keyboard shortcuts in the **Timeline**. Select the edit point by moving the playhead over it and pressing the **V** key. Now, by using the **U** key, you can toggle through **Ripple Right**, **Ripple Left**, and **Roll**. Whichever edit you have selected, you can now move incremental with the less-than bracket < and the greater-than bracket >. (Actually, it's the comma and period, but I always think of it as < and >.) Each tap will move the edit one frame left or right in the direction the bracket is pointed. **Shift-<** and **Shift->** will move the edit whatever duration you have set for **Multi-Frame Trimming** in your **User Preferences**. This also works if you select a clip in the **Timeline** and choose either the **Slip** or **Slide** tools.

4.40   The Roll tool in the Timeline

Extend Edit

Final Cut's **Extend Edit** is another nice way to perform a Roll edit. It's a simple way to move an edit point, even one with a transition.

1. Select an edit by clicking on it or by using the **V** key.

2. Move the playhead in the **Timeline** to where you want to move the edit. Press **E** or select **Sequence>Extend Edit**.

If the selection is dimmed in the menu or you hear a system warning, it's because you don't have enough media to perform the Extend edit.

3. Undo that edit when you're done.

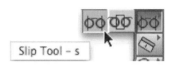

4.41 The Slip tool

The Slip Tool

Let's look at **Slip** and **Slide** next. Slip works in the **Timeline** and the **Viewer**, while **Slide** works in the **Timeline** only. They do pretty much what their names imply. **Slip** is one of my favorite tools, though I'm not very keen on the display in Final Cut Express. You can select the **Slip** tool from the fifth button in the **Tools**, as shown in Figure 4.41, or call it with the **S** key.

I've created the *Slip & Slide Sequence* to help explain these two tools. Open the sequence by double-clicking it in the **Browser**. Use the **Slip** tool to grab the middle clip in the sequence. Move the clip from side to side, and you'll see the display in Figure 4.42. What you're doing is slipping the media for the clip up and down its length. The overall duration of the clip remains unchanged, but the section of media for that duration is adjusted.

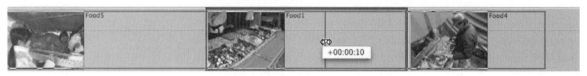

4.42 The Slip tool in the Timeline

The **Canvas** again shows you a two-up display. This is showing you the first and the last frames of the video. The shot in the sequence begins at 3;00 and ends at 4;29, a two-second shot. By slipping the clip 10 frames as we see in the figure, the shot will now start at 2;20, 10 frames earlier, and end at 4;19, keeping the same duration. It starts earlier so it will end earlier. If the shot slipped in the other direction it would start later in time but also end later.

The two-up display will help you from slipping the clip too far into some unwanted material. If you're working without subclipping your material as we discussed in the last lesson, you can see if you're slipping into the next shot.

It is also possible to slip in the **Viewer**, which can be especially beneficial when you're adjusting a clip before you bring it into the **Timeline**.

1. To slip in the **Viewer**, double-click the clip to load it into the **Viewer**.

2. Hold down the **Shift** key as you grab either the In point or the Out point and drag. This way you will drag both points together and maintain a constant duration.

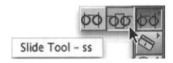

4.43 Slipping in the Viewer with the Canvas display

This is *slipping,* and what you see in the display (see Figure 4.43) is the start frame in the **Viewer** and the end frame in the **Canvas**. It doesn't matter which end you grab to pull; the display is always the same: start in the **Viewer**, end in the **Canvas**.

The Slide Tool

Let's look at the last trimming tool, the **Slide** tool, also in the fifth **Tools** button (see Figure 4.44). The **Slide** tool can be brought out with **SS** (S twice).

4.44 The Slide tool in the Timeline

Like the **Slip** tool, it also works in the **Timeline**, though not in the **Viewer**. The **Slide** tool doesn't change anything in the clip you're working on; it grabs the clip and pulls it forward or backward along the timeline, wiping out material on one side and extending the material on the other side, as shown in Figure 4.45.

4.45 The Slide tool in the Timeline

Notice that you're not only moving the clip but also affecting the two adjacent clips, which is why they're highlighted with boxes.

The **Canvas** display (see Figure 4.46) is unlike other two-up displays. You don't see the clip you're moving at all. What's displayed are the two adjacent shots:

- On the left, the end of the shot in front of the one you're moving
- On the right, the beginning of the shot after the one you're moving

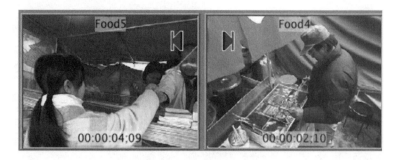

4.46 The Slide tool Canvas display

In these figures, by moving *Clip2* earlier in time, the first shot *Clip1* is being shortened by 20 frames, and the last shot *Clip3* is being lengthened by 20 frames.

You are limited in how far you can slide a clip by the amount of media available in the adjacent shots. If you move to the end of the available media, the film sprocket overlay will appear in the two-up display.

Look at your finished sequence. It should look something like the sequence called *Food* in the **Browser**. I still wouldn't be very happy with the piece, principally because the audio is so abrupt and choppy, marking each cut. Work would need to be done to smooth out the sound, perhaps extend sound from a single clip, or add some constant underlying sound from somewhere else. But that's for another lesson.

How Long Is Long Enough?

A static shot, either close-up or medium shot, needs to be on the screen a much shorter time than a long shot in which the audience is following a movement. A shot that has been seen before, a repeat, can be on the screen quite briefly for the audience to get the information. Though there is no hard and fast rule, generally shots without dialog remain on the screen no more than six to eight seconds on television with its small screen. In feature films shots can be held for quite a bit longer because the viewer's eye has a lot more traveling to do to take in the full scope of the image. This is probably why movies seem much slower on the television screen than they do in the theater. While a close-up can be on the screen quite briefly, a long shot will often contain a great deal of information and needs to be held longer so that your viewer has time for his or her eye to rove around it. You can often hold a moving shot such as a pan longer because the audience is basically looking at two shots, one at the beginning and the other at the end. If the movement is well shown—a fairly brisk move, no more than about five seconds—you can also cut it quite tightly. All you need to show is a brief glimpse of the static shot, the movement, and then cut out as soon as the camera settles at the end of the move.

Summary

In this lesson you've learned how to use the **Canvas** editing tools:

- Overwrite
- Insert
- Fit to Fill
- Replace
- Superimpose

You've learned how to use the various sequence-editing tools:

- **Roll** and **Ripple**
- **Slip** and **Slide**

When you want to smooth out cuts or to change between scenes, you might want to use transitions. That's what we're going to look at in the next lesson: lots and lots of transitions, how they work, and how to use them.

Lesson 5

Adding Transitions

Transitions can add life to a sequence, ease a difficult edit into something smoother, or give you a way to mark a change of time or place. The traditional grammar of film that audiences still accept is that dissolves denote small changes, and a fade to black followed by a fade from black mark a greater passage of time. With the introduction of digital effects, every imaginable movement or contortion of the image to replace one with another quickly became possible—and were quickly applied everywhere, seemingly randomly, to every possible edit. They can be hideously inappropriate, garish, and ugly. But to each his own taste. Transitions can be used effectively, or they can look terribly hackneyed. Final Cut Express gives you the option to do either or anything in between. Let's look at the transitions FCE has to offer. There are quite a few of them, 60 to be exact, although there is quite a bit of redundancy in the transitions. Some people seem to think that just because Apple put all those transitions in there you have to use them all. Remember that most movies use only cuts and the occasional dissolve. Most television programs are cuts only, with a fade in at the beginning and a fade out at the commercial breaks.

Loading the Lesson

Let's begin by loading the material you need on the hard drive of your computer, if you have not done so already.

1. Open the hybrid DVD. From the folder called *Hybrid DVD-ROM Contents*, drag the *Media 3* folder from the DVD to your media drive. This contains the media needed for this project.

2. You may also want to drag the folder called *Transitions* from the DVD onto your media drive. This contains samples of each of the 60 transitions available in Final Cut Express 2.

3. Also make sure your have the *Projects* folder on your system hard drive.

4. Eject the DVD and launch the *Lesson 5* project from the *Projects* folder on your hard drive.

5. Once again, you may have to go through the reconnect process as in the previous "Loading the Lesson" on page 106 in Lesson 4. You will first get the **Offline Files** window. Click the **Reconnect** button.

Inside your copy of the project *Lesson 5* you'll find in the **Browser**:

- An empty sequence called *Sequence 1*
- The master clip *Village*
- A still image called *Gradient.pct*, which we'll use later
- The bin called **Clips**

To see the basic settings for each of the 60 FCE transitions, use **File>Import>Folder** to bring into the application the *Transitions* folder you copied onto your hard drive. The folder contains bins with all the transitions grouped in the same fashion they are in the application.

5.1   Effects window

Applying Transitions

In the **Browser**, usually behind the **Lesson 5** project window, is a tab called **Effects**. If you open it, you see a window with a group of folders—sorry, bins—as in Figure 5.1. You'll notice more than transitions in this window. For the moment, we're going to concentrate on the **Video Transitions** bin.

One of the bins in the **Effects** window is **Favorites**. We'll look at **Favorites** a bit later in the lesson. Here is where you can park your special transitions and effects. It's probably empty now.

Double-click on **Video Transitions** to open the bin. It should look like Figure 5.2 The **Video Transitions** window shows yet more bins, and these bins contain the available transitions grouped into categories. I'd be very surprised if any one has ever used them all in earnest on real projects, not just playing with them to try them out. The **Transitions** bin you imported contains previews of each of the transitions available in FCE. We're going to try some of them out in this lesson.

The default transition in Final Cut Express is the **Cross Dissolve** with a default duration of one second. In the bins in the **Effects** window and in the menus, you may see some transitions highlighted in bold. These are real-time capable transitions, if your system is fast enough to support them. If you system isn't fast enough, very few will be in bold.

There are a number of different ways to apply a transition in Final Cut Express:

- Drag the transition you want from the **Effects** panel of the **Browser,** and drop it on an edit point.
- Select the edit point. (Remember, **V** will select the nearest edit point.) Then use the **Effects>Video Transitions** menu and choose one.
- Select the edit point, and apply the default transition with the keyboard shortcut **Command-T.**
- Select the edit point, and by **Control**-clicking on the edit point, call up the default transition from the shortcut menu.

There are a couple of other ways that we skipped in the last lesson, using the two items in the **Edit Overlay:**

- **Insert with Transition**
- **Overwrite with Transition**

The default transition will appear in your sequence when you select **Insert with Transition (Shift-F9)** or **Overwrite with Transition (Shift-F10.)**

5.2   Video Transitions window

Checking the Media

1. Let's begin by opening *Sequence 1*.
2. Select the three clips in the **Clips** bin and drag them directly to the sequence.

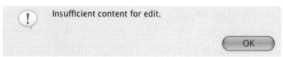

5.3 Transition error

5.4 Insufficient Content error

3. It might be helpful to use **Shift-Z** (**Fit to Window**) if the clips appear too small in the **Timeline**.

Remember that these are all subclips, and so each shot you just placed in the timeline contains the full extent of the media for that clip on the hard drive. Or at least so Final Cut Express thinks.

Let's try putting a transition onto the sequence we've laid out.

4. Grab the **Cross Dissolve** transition from the **Dissolve** bin and drag it onto the edit point between *Village1* and *Village2*.

You see that this isn't possible because you get the transition drag icon with a small **X**, as shown in Figure 5.3. If you try to perform the edit by using the keyboard shortcut **Command-T**, you'll get the error message in Figure 5.4. Why is this happening? The answer is simple. There isn't enough media in either clip beyond the edit point to perform the transition. The shots must overlap; frames from both shots must appear on the screen simultaneously. For a one-second transition, both shots have to have one second of media that overlaps with the other shot. These frames come partly from inside the clip, and partly from media beyond the edit point. The extra video frames, those beyond the edit point separating the two shots, are called *handles*.

5.5 Film sprocket overlay in the Viewer

1. Double-click *Village 1* in the **Timeline** to open it into the **Viewer**.

2. Go to the end of the shot. Use **Shift-O** to take you to the Out point.

If **Overlays** are switched on in the **View** pop-up as they normally are, you'll see the telltale film sprocket hole indicator on the right edge of the frame (see Figure 5.5).

This overlay tells you that you're right at the end of the available media for that shot. There needs to be extra media available to create the overlap for the transition, as shown in Figure 5.6.

The pale shot on the left has to overlap the dark shot on the right by half the length of the transition, and vice versa. If that media does not exist, you can't do the transition. FCE usually assumes

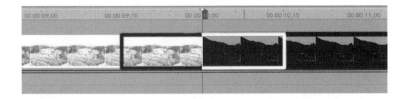

5.6 Overlapping video

as a default that the transition takes place centered around the marked edit point, not that it ends at the edit point. Therefore, to execute the default one-second transition, you need at least half a second, 15 frames, of available media after the Out point on the outgoing shot and 15 frames in front of the In point of the incoming shot. In this case there is nothing, hence the error messages when you try to execute the transition. Unless you think of it ahead of time—and many times you don't—you'll have to deal with it when you're fine-tuning your edit. Often you'd rather not deal with transitions while you're laying out your sequence, leaving them until you've laid out the shot order.

If you know you have extra media in the original clip, you can always go back to extend the media. If this option is available, it's easy to do in FCE. Select **Remove Subclip Limits** from the **Modify** menu.

However, in this case, extending the media will push it into another shot, producing a flash frame during the transition, something to be avoided. This is one of the benefits of subclipping. It prevents you from going beyond the shot when you're laying in a transition.

To be able to put in transitions, we'll have to trim the Out point of *Village1* and the In point of *Village2*. We could do this by dragging the ends of the shots to make them shorter, but that would leave a hole in the **Timeline**. Instead, we'll use the **Ripple** tool to shorten the shots.

1. Select the **Ripple** tool from the **Tools** palette, or use the keyboard shortcut **RR**.
2. With the **Ripple** tool, click just to the left of the edit point between *Village1* and *Village2*, as in Figure 5.7.
3. With **Ripple** active, type in *–15* for 15 frames. Notice the display that appears in the middle of the **Timeline** window (see Figure 5.8). Press the **Return** key.

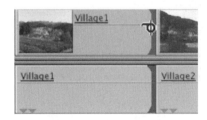

5.7 Ripple tool in the Timeline

5.8 Ripple value in the Timeline

We know this is the navigation shortcut for going backward half a second. Because we're in the **Ripple** tool, we're rippling it backwards one-half second.

4. Click on the right side of the edit point at the start of *Village2*. Remember that you can use the U key to toggle from rippling one side, to roll edit, and to ripple the other side of an edit point.

5. This time type **+15** and press **Return** to ripple the edit point half a second.

We've now rippled *Village2's* In point by half a second, half a second off the end of the first shot, half a second off the beginning of the second. So we have removed a half second of material from both clips, leaving this as handles, so that there is enough room for the transition.

Over these three shots laid in the **Timeline**, if I ripple the Ins and Outs on both edits in the **Timeline**, taking 15 frames off the end and the beginning of each shot, I reduce the overall duration by two seconds. This will substantially change the timing of my sequence. If you plan to use transitions between shots, it's best to allow for the extra material within the shot before you lay it in the **Timeline**.

6. Once you've rippled the edits, go the edit point in the sequence between *Village1* and *Village2* and apply the transition.

If you drag a transition from the **Transitions** bin to an edit point, it does not need to be dragged only to the center line. It can also be dragged to the out clip so that the transition ends at the edit point (the A side) or to the in clip so the transition begins at the start of the clip (the B side). This can be done, of course, only if there is sufficient material for this type of transition. If you only have video available for the transition overlap on one side of the edit, you should not try to execute the transition from the menu or with **Command-T**. These methods will usually execute the default Center on Edit transition. If one of the shots does not have enough material to do the transition, you'll get a one-frame transition. Just be careful, because it may seem that a transition has been entered into your sequence when there isn't anything there of value.

After you've applied a transition, if you double-click on the transition itself in the **Timeline**, it will open into the **Viewer**. This is

5.9   Clips overlapping in the Transition Editor

the **Transition Editor,** which we'll look at in detail in a moment. Here you can see how the video overlaps and why extra material—handles—are needed on either end of the transition to create the effect (see Figure 5.9).

Once it's in the **Timeline,** the transition displays in one of three ways, depending on how it was placed. Figure 5.10 shows the center position; the other two appear as in Figures 5.11 and 5.12.

5.10   Center on Edit transition   5.11   End on Edit transition   5.12   Start on Edit transition

Making the transition to start or end on edit is useful if you have media available on only one side of the edit point, if you have a title or other clip on a track without any material adjacent to it, and of course at the beginning or end of your program.

Notice the sloping line indicators showing the type of alignment only in each case. The last two transitions can be only half-second dissolves. When we rippled the sequence by 15 frames on each side of the edit point, only enough media was made available for a half-second Start or End on Edit transition. If the transition is to end on the edit point, the incoming shot has to be extended a whole second underneath the outgoing shot to accommodate it. Similarly, if you wanted to start the transition on the edit point, the outgoing shot has to extend one second into the incoming shot, one second beyond the start of the edit point. If we made these changes, then we could also easily change the type of transition alignment with the shortcut menu on the transition in the **Timeline** (see Figure 5.13).

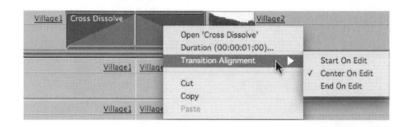

5.13 Transition Alignment shortcut menu

Using the Edit Overlay

Let's back up a bit to see another way to do this.

1. Delete everything in the **Timeline**.

2. Open *Village1* from the **Browser** into the **Viewer**.

Because this will be the first shot in the timeline, I won't need to shorten the front of the clip.

3. Press the **End** key to take you to the end of the shot.

4. Type *–1.* (minus one period) and **Return**. This will move the playhead back one second.

5. Press **O** to enter the Out point and drag to the **Edit Overlay Overwrite** box, or press **F10** to overwrite it into the **Timeline**.

6. Open *Village2* in the **Viewer** from the **Browser**.

This clip we should shorten on both ends.

7. Go to the beginning of the clip. Type *+1.* and **Return**. Enter an In point.

8. Then go to the end of the clip and enter an Out point one second before the end (type *–1.*, press **Return**, and then press **O**).

9. Drag *Village2* from the **Viewer** to **Overwrite with Transition**—not to **Overwrite**. Or use the keyboard shortcut **Shift-F10**.

The clip immediately drops into the **Timeline** after the first clip. The default transition has been added at the beginning of the clip, as well as a default audio crossfade. Adding the audio crossfade is a bonus that enhances the edit and helps to smooth the transition (see Figure 5.14). If you use the shortcut menu to create a transition in the **Timeline**, this also will add the audio crossfade.

5.14 Transition with audio crossfade

Rendering

In adding your transition to your sequence, you may have encountered the need for rendering for the first time. After you've entered a transition, you'll see that the narrow bar at the top of the **Timeline** has changed color from the normal mid-gray. It will have changed to red, green, yellow, or orange, depending on the type of transition you applied, your system capabilities, and your **RT** settings. If you are working with a system with no real-time capabilities, then a bright red line will appear over the transition, indicating that a portion of the sequence needs to be rendered, the bar inside the circled area in Figure 5.15.

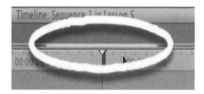

5.15 Render indicator

Rendering means that the application has to create media for which none exists. Most of the two shots are on your hard drive, but not for the 30 frames that make up this one-second cross dissolve, during which one shot is changing into the other. The material of one shot mixed together with another is not on your hard drive. All you've done is give the computer instructions to create that media. If you try to play across that part of the timeline with a non–real-time system, the **Canvas** will momentarily display the message in Figure 5.16.

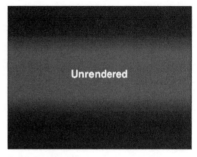

5.16 Unrendered warning

If you have real-time capabilities, Final Cut can play through the timeline without prior rendering. It processes the transition on the fly in real time as it plays. If you have your **RT** settings, which we saw in Lesson 2 on page 42, on **Unlimited RT**, you may get a yellow or an orange bar. The yellow bar indicates that playback is a

---

Real-Time Preview

FCE's real time can be seen only in the **Canvas** and only when the external viewing is switched off. It will not send a real-time DV signal out the FireWire cable. So you have a choice: either monitor through FireWire but not in real time, or monitor on your desktop screen.

So if you think you have real-time capabilities and you're still seeing a red line in your sequence, it's probably because you have **External Viewing** turned on. You can switch it off from the **View** menu by going right down at the bottom to the **Video** submenu. Here you can select either **Real-Time** or FireWire. Fortunately there is a keyboard shortcut that will quickly toggle this on and off: **Command-F12**.

Remember, this is real-time preview only. As soon as you revert to viewing your video externally or you want to output your material to tape, all those items that were in real time on your desktop a moment ago now have to be rendered out.

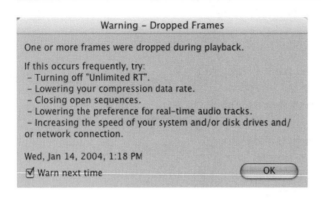

5.17 Unlimited RT dropped frame warning

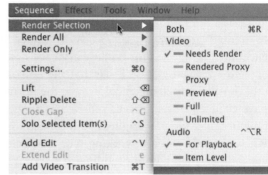

5.18 Sequence > Render Selection

proxy only; that is, if you've created a complex setting for your transition, only the default will be visible in real time. Orange indicates that you will likely get dropped frames when playing through this area. If you do play through you may get the dropped frame warning message in Figure 5.17. If you switch this warning off in the lower-left corner, you can then work in **Unlimited RT** without hindrance but with the occasional frame drop. To turn on the dropped frame warning, you'll have to go back to your **User Preferences** and switch it back on in the first tab.

Render Commands

FCE2 has made rendering extremely flexible, if perhaps a bit confusing. What gets rendered is controlled by a complex combination of settings in the **Sequence** menu under **Render Selection, Render All,** and **Render Only.**

The **Render Selection** menu (see Figure 5.18) controls rendering of a selection, either a clip, clips, or a segment of the **Timeline** marked with In and Out points. Normally only the red **Needs Render** bar is checked for both video and audio. If you want to force a render on any of the other available items, select it. It will remain checked in the menu. Whenever you give the **Render Selection** command (see Table 5.1), those checked items would be included in the render.

Table 5.1   Render commands

Command	Shortcut
Render All	Option-R
Render Selection	Command-R
Render Audio Selection	Control-Option-R
Render Proxy	Command-Option-P
Render Preview	Control-R
Mixdown Audio	Command-Option-R

➤*Tip*

Playing the Red: By using Option-P, you can still play through a red transition without leaving the sequence, not in real time but in slow motion. This is a good way to see if the transition will play smoothly, if there are any unforeseen flash frames or other unpleasant hiccups in the effect. The faster your system, the faster it will play through the transition. More complex effects that we will see later will only play slowly, even on the fastest computers, without hardware assistance. What's good is that FCE caches the playback so that the first time you play back using Option-P, it might take quite a while, but the next time the playback will be considerably faster. This applies only to using Option-P. Regular play with the spacebar will still produce the unrendered message. You can also scrub through a transition by switching **Snapping** off and mousing down in the **Timeline Ruler**, slowly moving the playhead through the transition area.

In FCE2's render options is the new ability to render audio at **Item Level**. This allows you to render a piece of sound, such as an MP3 file or a piece of 441kHz CD music, into the correct sampling rate as a separate item. Wherever you place that audio in your **Timeline,** it will be fully rendered to the correct settings. It will have a blue indictor bar on it to tell you it's been rendered as an item and will not need to be re-rendered. To render an audio selection, use the keyboard shortcut **Control-Option-R**.

The **Render All** menu (see Figure 5.19) gives you the same list except that many more items are checked by default. The **Render Only** menu (see Figure 5.20) is similar. It allows you to render selected items without changing the settings in **Render** and **Render All**. Note the inclusion in the **Render Only** menu of **Mixdown** for audio. This allows you to render out a mixed audio file of all your tracks, allowing easier playback. This is particularly important when outputting to tape.

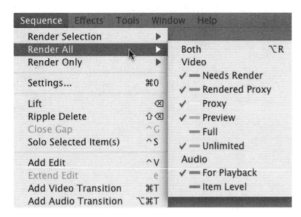

5.19 Sequence > Render All

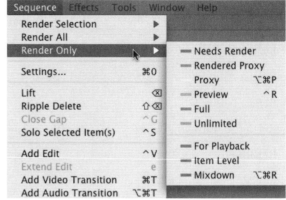

5.20 Sequence > Render Only

Render Control

Rendering settings are a new feature FCE2. Normally FCE will render to full resolution, but it's possible now to adjust your render settings.

Render settings are now set in the **Render Control** tab (see Figure 5.21) in **Sequence Settings**, which can be called up from the **Sequence** menu or with the keyboard shortcut **Command-0**. Here you can set what you want to render, as well as control your render quality with the **Frame Rate** and **Resolution** pop-up menus. Setting these two pop-up menus to lower numbers will greatly speed up your rendering process.

In FCE2 you can switch between render settings at any time, which means that you can have material in various render resolutions throughout your sequence simultaneously. This can be a useful feature, because it allows you to render complex material at lower resolution to speed up your workflow and to switch to full resolution for easier material. The feature does create one substantial problem, which we shall look at in the lesson on Outputting, Lesson 11 on page 263.

Render Management

Render files are stored in the *Audio Render Files* folder and the *Render Files* folder of your designated scratch disk. The renders are stored in separate folders based on the project name, one folder for each project. FCE keeps track of the renders required

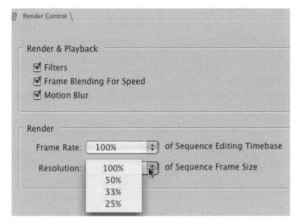

Name	Date Modified
Sequence 5-FIN-0000000b	Today, 7:41 AM
Sequence 5-FIN-0000000a	Today, 7:41 AM
Sequence 5-FIN-00000007	Today, 7:40 AM
Sequence 5-FIN-00000006	Today, 6:55 AM
Sequence 5-FIN-00000001	Today, 5:16 AM
Sequence 5-FIN-00000005	Today, 5:06 AM
Sequence 5-FIN-00000004	Today, 4:53 AM
Sequence 5-FIN-00000003	Today, 4:02 AM
Sequence 5-FIN-00000002	Today, 3:46 AM
Sequence 3-FIN-00000008	Yesterday, 9:49 PM
Sequence 3-FIN-00000007	Yesterday, 7:16 PM
Sequence 3-FIN-00000006	Yesterday, 7:16 PM
Sequence 1-FIN-00000015	Yesterday, 7:15 PM
Sequence 1-FIN-00000014	Yesterday, 7:15 PM
Sequence 1-FIN-00000011	Yesterday, 5:38 PM
Sequence 1-FIN-00000010	Yesterday, 5:38 PM
Sequence 1-FIN-0000000f	Yesterday, 3:51 PM
Sequence 1-FIN-00000008	Yesterday, 2:43 PM

5.21   Render Control tab *(above)*

5.22   Render files in List View *(right)*

for the output of each sequence. It keeps all the renders it generates for each session so that you can step back through those 32 levels of undo and not lose your renders. As you keep rendering and changing and re-rendering, FCE holds onto all those renders it creates while the application is open. When you quit the application, it dumps any render files it no longer needs to play back any of the sequences in the project. It will hold onto any renders it needs for playback. All these render files will start to pile up after a while. If you delete a project, its render files won't go with it. They'll just sit on your hard drive taking up space in the folder with the project's name.

It's a good idea to weed out the old files in your render folders, video more than audio because the files are much larger. Sometimes it might be as simple as discarding an old project folder, throwing out all the renders associated with it. Sometimes, for long-form projects that go on for a long time, managing your render files requires you to go in and dig out these old files. The simplest way to do this is to open up the *Render Files* folder for that project and switch the window to List view as in Figure 5.22. List view will show you not only the file names, which are pretty meaningless, but also the date modified. By clicking on the **Date Modified** column, you can sort the renders by when they where created, giving you a clue about which ones are worth keeping and which aren't. If you're uncertain, select the render file and switch to Column view, where you can use the preview window to look at the little QuickTime file that the render generates (see

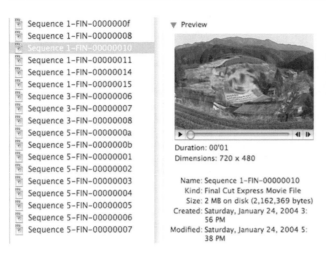

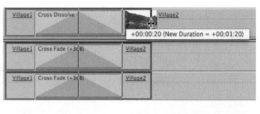

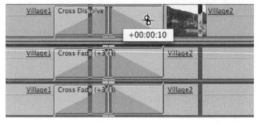

5.23   Render files and Preview window

5.24   Lengthening a transition in the Timeline *(top)*

5.25   Rolling the transition edit point *(bottom)*

Figure 5.23). Move the files you think don't need into the trash and run the project. If the project needs some of the render files, you'll get the **Reconnect** dialog box. That will give you a chance to move the missing items back into the *Render Files* folder.

Controlling Transitions

Once you've played back your transition with **Option-P** a couple of times or rendered it and looked at it, you may discover that it isn't quite the way you'd want it to be. You may want to shorten or lengthen it or shift the actual edit point. Assuming you have material available for this, it is easiest to do in the **Timeline** itself. To change the duration of the transition, grab one end of it and pull, as in Figure 5.24. It's a good idea to switch **Snapping** off (toggle with the **N** key) before you do this, because it's easy to snap the transition down to nothing. As you pull the transition, a little window displays the amount of change as well as the new duration of the transition. If you have an audio crossfade as well as a transition, that will also change with your action. While you're dragging the transition end, you'll get the two-up display in the **Canvas** that shows you the frames at the edit point.

You can also reposition the edit point in the center of the transition. Move the **Selector** to the center of the edit, and it will change to the **Roll** tool, allowing you to move the edit point, together with the transition along the **Timeline**, left and right as desired (see Figure 5.25). You can also ripple either shot, but to do that you have to call up the **Ripple** tool (**RR**) and pull either shot left or right, shortening or lengthening the sequence while not affecting the transition (see Figure 5.26). Again, the two-up display in the **Canvas** will show you the frames you're working on.

Transition Editor

Final Cut gives you another way to fine tune the transition. This is done in the **Transition Editor** (see Figure 5.27), which we briefly saw earlier.

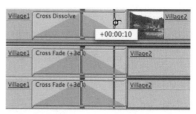

Double-click on the transition in the **Timeline** window to evoke the **Transition Editor**. It opens in the **Viewer**. The **Viewer** displays the transition as a separate track between the two video tracks on which the clips sit.

5.26 Rippling the transition edit point

The **Transition Editor** allows you to control the transition. Some of them, such as **Swing** in Figure 5.27, have quite a few controls. At the top in the center is a small group of buttons that lets you position where the transition will occur. The transition will be placed in the default centered position between the two clips, shown by the middle button. Using the left button moves the transition so that it begins at the edit point. The right button moves the transition so that it ends at the edit point.

The primary purpose of the **Transition Editor** is to access the controls some transitions offer you. Here you can also fine-tune the

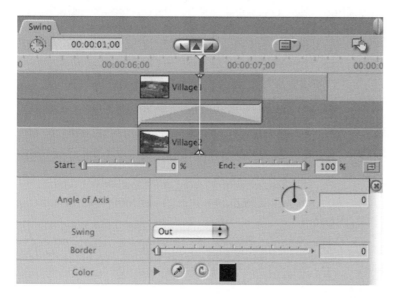

5.27 Swing Transition Editor

effect, to shorten or lengthen it as needed. As in the **Timeline,** you can do this by dragging either end of the transition. The **Canvas** displays the end and start frames for the two shots.

➤**Tip**

Navigating the Transition Editor: The grab handle in the upper-right corner lets you pull a transition from the **Transition Editor** onto an edit point in the **Timeline.** This is useful if you've opened the editor directly from the **Transitions** bin. This is the only way you can grab the transition. There is also a pop-up menu for recent clips in the **Transition Editor.**

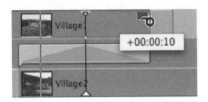

5.28 Rippling a clip in Transition Editor

By grabbing the center of the transition, you evoke the **Roll** tool, which allows you to drag the transition forward and backward along the clips, provided that there is available media.

You can also Ripple edit the end of either outgoing or incoming clip by pulling it (see Figure 5.28). You don't have to call up the **Ripple** tool. By moving the cursor into position, it will change to the appropriate tool. As with all Ripple edits, you are changing the duration of the tracks involved and may be pulling the alignment of clips on different tracks out of kilter.

Notice the two sliders in the **Transition Editor,** one for **Start** and the other for **End,** each with percentage boxes adjacent. The transition starts at 0 percent completed and ends at 100 percent completed. You can adjust these sliders so that the **Cross Dissolve** will pop in at more than zero to start or suddenly finish before the transition reaches completion. In **Cross Dissolve** this produces a rather ugly effect. There is also a small arrow button to the right of the **End** slider. This will swap the effect for you, usually reversing the direction. Below that is a small circle with a red cross in it. This is the **Parameters Reset** button. This is useful for more complex transitions. Also note that the **Reset** button does not reset the **Start** and **End** sliders, nor the arrow, only the other parameters.

Using Transitions

Now that we know how to add and trim transitions, let's look at the transitions themselves. To change the transition:

- Drag the new transition from the transitions folder in the **Effects** window and drop it on the existing transition in the timeline or

- Select the transition in the **Timeline** by clicking on it and then select a new choice from the **Effects>Video Transitions** menu.

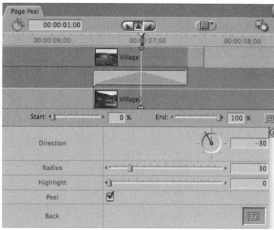

5.29 Page Peel

5.30 Page Peel controls

I'm not going to go through each of the transitions, although I would like to highlight a couple because they will show you how the controls work in some of the other changeable transitions. To see all the transitions, look at the individual QuickTime movies in the *Transitions* folder on the DVD. Many of the transitions have lots of variables, such as colored borders and the direction in which a motion transition such as Swing occurs.

Page Peel

Page Peel (see Figure 5.29) is often overused, but sometimes it really is the right effect, especially for wedding videos. This is also the first introduction to FCE's **Well**.

Apply the transition and double-click on it to open it into the **Transition Editor** (see Figure 5.30).The **Direction** dial changes the angle at which the page peels back. The default is –30 and pulls the lower-right corner toward the upper center of the image.

The **Radius** slider sets the tightness of the peel. A small number will make it peel very tightly, and a high number will make the turn of the page quite loose.

The **Highlight** slider puts a gleam of light on the back of the turning page. The farther to the left you move the **Highlight** slider, the more muted the shine becomes. There is no control of the width of the highlight area.

If you uncheck the **Peel** checkbox, the image will not only peel back but also curl in on itself. With a tight **Radius** you'll get the image rolling up like it's a scroll.

✎ Note

Static Well: Unfortunately, the Well won't track an image or change if a video clip is used. The Well uses the In point of the video clip as its map. In the case of **Page Peel**, there is no movement on the backside of the page. Sorry.

5.31 Generators button

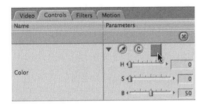

5.32 Color Matte Controls tab

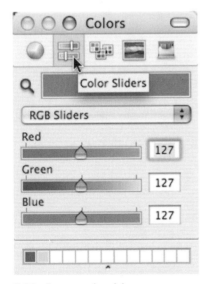

5.33 System color picker

One of **Page Peel**'s interesting features is the **Well**, which lets you use another image as part of an effect. The **Well**, the indented filmstrip icon that controls the **Back** function, lets you map another image onto the back of the page peel. The default is to place the same image, flopped, on the back of the page, but you can use any image in your project.

The tiny **Arrow** checkbox at the top right of the controls toggles between peeling the page off, the default, and peeling the page on, an unusual variation.

To put a color on the back, as in Figure 5.29, use the **Video Generator** in the **Viewer** to create a color matte.

1. Open any clip into the **Viewer**. The **A** with the **Filmstrip** icon in the lower-left corner evokes the **Generators** (Figure 5.31).

2. Select **Matte>Color**.

3. Set the color in the **Controls** tab (Figure 5.32). Click on the swatch to access the system color picker (Figure 5.33).

Note the swatch tray at the bottom, which lets you move color selections from application to application, not just within FCE.

4. Switch back to the **Video** tab and drag the Color Matte from the **Viewer** into the **Browser**.

5. Reopen the **Page Peel** transition from the **Timeline**, and pull the **Color Matte** from the **Browser**. Drop it into the **Well**, making it part of the transition.

➤Tip

Selecting Color: Whenever you need to select a color from anywhere on your desktop, click on the color swatch to open the color picker. If you click on the magnifying glass next to the color swatch, you can move around anywhere on the computer desktop.

Push Slide

The **Push Slide** transition is often used when making still slide shows where one image pushes the other out of the frame and replaces it. The controls (Figure 5.34) are pretty straightforward: an **Angle** dial and controls for adding a border.

Angle defaults to straight up, but you can set to any angle you want. At −90 the incoming image will slide in from the right and push the outgoing image off the left side of the screen.

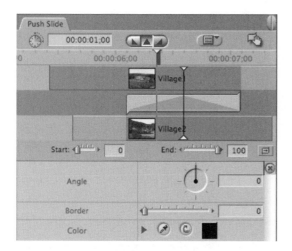

5.34 Push Slide controls

5.35 Gradient Wipe controls

The **Border** control can be quite useful. It not only helps in separating the images more clearly but also covers the black band that appears on the edge of some digitized images. This is normally in the blanking area under the television mask and not seen by the viewer. However, if the image is moved, as it is here and in other digital video effects, the black edge becomes visible. The **Border** will help to disguise that or at least make it a feature.

Gradient Wipe

The **Gradient Wipe** transition is a deceptively simple-looking filter with very few controls. Its real power lies in the **Gradient Well** (Figure 5.35). In its default condition, it's nothing more than a simple wipe from left to right.

In the **Browser** is an image called *Gradient.pct*. If you open it in the **Viewer**, you'll see that it's a complex, grayscale checkerboard pattern. This is the basis of patterning in a gradient wipe. The image will be wiped on or off, based on the grayscale values of pattern image. The darkest parts of the pattern image will be where the incoming image will appear first, and the lightest parts will be where the image will appear last. In the gradient pattern we have, some of the outside boxes will appear first, as in Figure 5.36. The lower left to upper right diagonal of the image will still be from the outgoing shot. There is no end to the variety of patterns you can get to manipulate this control. If you don't like a pattern, replace it with another. To really see the power of transition effects, you should look at what Michael Feerer has

5.36   Gradient Wipe pattern *(left)*

5.37   Favorites bin *(below)*

▼ 🗀 Favorites	Bin	
🎞 **8Frames**	Video Transition	00:00:00;08
🎞 Checkerboard Gradient Wipe	Video Transition	00:00:01;00
🎞 Logo Page Peel	Video Transition	00:00:02;00

created with his Video Spices. Check them out at http://www.pixelan.com. They add an important tool to Final Cut's transitions. His patterns can be used not only inside his own transitions but also inside **Gradient Wipe** as well.

I like the **Gradient Wipe** because it is so infinitely variable and you can always find some way to make it look just a little different and just right for the effect you want. A trick I've used in the past is to use a grayscale frame of either the outgoing shot or the incoming shot as the image for the **Well**. It makes the transition like a slightly sharp-edged dissolve because the elements of the shot itself are affecting how the transition happens.

Favorites

Once you've started to make a few transitions that you like, maybe a special Page Peel with your logo on the back, or a Gradient Wipe with a particular pattern, you might want to save these in your **Favorites** bin in the **Effects** tab behind your **Browser**.

To see how to do this: open the *Dissolves* folder, which holds seven different types of dissolves.

1. Grab the **Cross Dissolve**, and drag and drop the transition over to the **Favorites** bin. You can also drag a transition directly from the **Timeline** into *Favorites*, or from the **Transition Editor** with the grab handle.

2. Open **Favorites** and switch it to List view as in Figure 5.37. Remember that **Shift-H** will toggle through the views.

3. In List view you can change the duration of the transition to your favorite length. Other transitions that have different parameters such as borders and adjustable shapes can also be saved here in favorite configurations.

You may notice that the transition in the **Favorites** bin is a duplicate. The usual behavior when moving items from one bin to another is that the item is relocated. But when moving an element to **Favorites**, a copy is created. You can put any transitions, video or audio, any effect; or even a generator into **Favorites**. You can rename the transition or effect to anything you want.

Note that although *8Frames* appears underlined, it is not the default transition. Only the standard **Cross Dissolve** with the standard one-second duration can be the default.

Conclusion

That's it for transitions. Everybody has his or her favorites. Mine are fairly simple: mostly **Cross Dissolves** and **Gradient Wipes** occasionally, or a **Push Slide**. Many I've never used. Many should probably never be used, and most you'll probably never see.

Next we go on to advanced editing techniques and working with audio.

✎ Note

Saving Favorites: It's important to note that **Favorites** are saved as part of your FCE preferences. If you trash your *Preferences* file, as you may need to from time to time, your **Favorites** go with it. There is a simple solution to this. Drag the **Favorites** bin from the **Effects** panel and place it in your **Browser**. This is a copy of the **Favorites** bin in **Effects** and will remain with the project, even if the prefs are trashed. I keep a **Favorites** project and in it a bin with my favorite effects and filters, sometimes in stacks in separate folders. Whenever I want to access these effects, I open the **Favorites** project and drag the folder into the new project. I add new effects to it and occasionally I burn the project onto a CD as a backup.

Lesson 6

Advanced Editing: Using Sound

Film and video are primarily visual media. Oddly enough, though, the moment an edit occurs is often driven as much by the sound as by the picture. So let's take a look at sound editing in Final Cut Express. How sound is used, where it comes in, and how long it lasts are key to good editing. With few exceptions, sound almost never cuts with the picture. Sometimes the sound comes first and then the picture; sometimes the picture leads the sound. The principal reason video and audio are so often cut separately is that we see and hear quite differently. We see in cuts. I look from one person to another, from one object to another, from the keyboard to the monitor. Though my head turns or my eyes travel across the room, I really only see the objects I'm interested in looking at. We hear, on the other hand, in fades. I walk into a room, the door closes behind me, and the sound of the other room fades away. As a car approaches, the sound gets louder. Screams, gunshots, and doors slamming being exceptions, our aural perception is based on smooth transitions from one to another. Sounds, especially background sounds such as the ambient noise in a room, generally need to overlap to smooth out the jarring abruptness of a hard cut.

127

Setting Up the Project

This is going to sound familiar, but it's worth repeating. Begin by loading the material you need on the media hard drive of your computer

1. Drag the *Media 4* folder from the *Hybrid DVD-ROM Contents* folder from the book's DVD to your media drive.

2. Make sure the *Projects* folder from the DVD has been installed on your system drive.

3. Eject the DVD and launch the *Lesson 6* project.

4. Once again, choose the **Reconnect** option to relink the media files when the **Offline Files** dialog appears.

You'll find in the project's **Browser** an empty sequence called *Sequence 1* and a number of other sequences that we'll look at during this lesson. There is also the master clip *Backstage* and the folder called *Clips*, which contains the subclips pulled from the master

In this lesson we're going to look at backstage preparations for a kabuki performance. Before beginning the lesson, it might be a good idea to look through the material, which is about three and one-half minutes long. You can start by double-clicking the shot *Backstage* to open it in the **Viewer** and then playing through the material.

The Trim Edit Window

Before we get into editing this material, we should take a look at FCE's **Trim Edit** window, which is a powerful tool for precisely editing your material and looking at edit points.

1. You open the **Trim Edit** window by double-clicking on an edit point or by moving the playhead to an edit point and using the menu **Sequence>Trim Edit** or the keyboard shortcut **Command-7**.

2. Let's bring a couple of shots into the **Timeline**. Select *Backstage01* and *Backstage02* in the **Clips** bin and drag them directly to **Overwrite** in the **Canvas**.

3. Double-click on the edit point between the shots in the **Timeline**. This will call up the window in Figure 6.1.

Notice the sprocket hole indicators on the inner edges of the frames. This overlay indicates that the clips are at the limits of

6.1   Trim Edit window

their media, but we can still ripple this edit just as we did in the previous lesson when we had to ripple the two shots to create room for a transition.

The green bars over the frames in the **Trim Edit** window indicate what mode you're in. When a green bar appears over both sides, as in Figure 6.2, you're in Roll edit mode. By clicking on one side or the other, you can either ripple the outgoing shot (as in Figure 6.3) or the incoming shot (as in Figure 6.4). To get back to Roll edit, click on the space between the two frames.

6.2   Roll Edit indicator in Trim Edit

6.3   Ripple Left indicator in Trim Edit

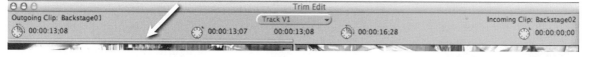

6.4   Ripple Right indicator in Trim Edit

You can toggle between the **Ripple** and **Roll** tools in the **Trim Edit** window with the U key. The ways the U key cycles between **Ripple Left, Ripple Right,** and the **Roll** tool is also reflected in the way the edit point is selected in the **Timeline** (Figures 6.5–6.7).

You can ripple and roll the edit points by dragging them in either window. When you're in Ripple mode, the cursor will change to the **Ripple** tool, and when you're in Roll mode, the cursor automatically becomes the **Roll** tool.

You can also use the little plus and minus buttons at the bottom of the window to make incremental edits on either side of the **Trim Edit** window. FCE allows you to move the edit point by one or five frames at a time. The five-frame value can be changed anywhere from two to 99 in the preferences in **User Preferences** in **Multi-Frame Trim Size,** although 5–10 are probably the most practical settings.

There's a lot of useful timecode information at the top of the **Trim Edit** window, information about the where the A side ends and the B begins and the durations of the shot and their place in the **Timeline.**

6.5   Roll Edit indicator in the Timeline *(upper left)*

6.6   Ripple Left indicator in the Timeline *(upper right)*

6.7   Ripple Right indicator in the Timeline

- The number to the far left is the duration of the outgoing shot, *Backstage01* in this case (*A* in Figure 6.8).
- The next timecode number is the Out point of the outgoing shot (*B* in Figure 6.8).
- The center number under the track indicator is the current time in the sequence (*C* in Figure 6.8).
- The next number displayed is the duration of the incoming shot (*D* in Figure 6.8).
- On the far right of the window, the number is the current In point of the incoming shot, *Backstage02* (*E* in Figure 6.8).

You can play either side of the **Trim Edit** window with the **J, K,** and **L** keys. The green bars at the top determine which side plays. If you're rippling the left side, that side will play; if you're rippling the right side, the incoming shot will play.

6.8   Timecode display at the top of the Trim Edit window

Outgoing Clip: Backstage01   Track V1   Incoming Clip: Backstage02
00:00:13;08   00:00:13;07   00:00:13;08   00:00:16;28   00:00:00;00

A   **B** **C** **D**   **E**

When you're in Roll mode, the green bar above both displays and the side that plays is determined by the position of the cursor. If the cursor is over the left or outgoing side, that side will play. If the cursor is over the right or incoming side, that side will play.

The spacebar serves an interesting function in the **Trim Edit** window. It acts in looped Play-around mode. It will play around the edit point again and again so that you can view it repeatedly. The amount of Play-around, how much before the edit and how far after the edit, is controlled in **User Preferences** under **Preview Pre-Roll** and **Preview Post-Roll**. The default is five seconds before the edit and two seconds after. I usually set it down to two or three seconds before and two after.

New to Final Cut Express 2 is the ability to do *dynamic trimming* in the **Trim Edit** window. You'll see a little checkbox at the bottom of the window that activates this function, which can also be turned on in **User Preferences**. Dynamic trimming effects the control of the **J**, **K**, and **L** keys. Whenever you press the **K** key to pause, the edit will automatically execute. This will work in any edit mode: Roll, Ripple Left, or Ripple Right. As soon as you press the key to pause, the edit will be executed. Try it. It's pretty slick.

To trim an edit, you modify the In or Out point with the **I** and **O** keys. Your change will be reflected in the edit, either as a ripple or as a roll, in the **Timeline**.

The Split Edit

A common method of editing is to first lay down the shots in scene order entirely as straight cuts. Take a look at the sequence called *Rough Cut*. This is the edited material cut as straight edits. What's most striking as you play it is how abruptly the audio changes at each shot. But audio and video seldom cut in parallel in a finished video, so you will have to offset them. Take a look at the sequence called *Final*. The three and one-half minutes that is *Backstage* have been cut down to one minute and 23 seconds for the *Final* sequence. This is where we're going. Notice how the audio overlaps and the way it fades in and out.

➤*Tip*

Moving Slowly in the Trim Window: You can move forward slowly by holding down the K and L keys together. To move backwards slowly, hold down the K and J keys together. To go forward one frame, hold down the K key and tap L. Backwards one frame, tap J.

➤*Tip*

Trim Edit Shortcut: In the Trim Edit window, in addition to the trim buttons, you can use the keyboard shortcuts [and] to trim plus or minus one frame and Shift-[and Shift-] to trim plus or minus the multiframe trim size. As with the buttons, these will work on the fly while you're in looped Play-around mode.

6.9   Split Edit

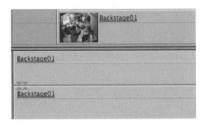

6.10   J-cut

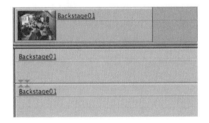

6.11   L-cut

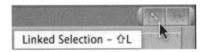

6.12   Linked Selection button

When audio and video have separate In and Out points that aren't at the same time, the edit is called a split edit (see Figure 6.9), J-cut (see Figure 6.10), or L-cut (see Figure 6.11). Whatever you call it, the effect is the same. There are many ways to create these edits, which I lump together as split edits.

In the Timeline

Many instructors tell you to perform these edits in the **Viewer**, but I think the **Viewer** is the least flexible place to create them. Let's set up a split edit inside the **Timeline**. It's a much more logical place to perform this type of work and very effective.

In making split edits, particularly in the **Timeline**, you will be frequently linking and unlinking clips, switching off the link between synced video and audio. You can do this with the little switch in the upper-right corner of the **Timeline** window that toggles **Linked Selection** off and on (see Figure 6.12). When **Linked Selection** is turned on, the button is green; when it's off, the icon is black.

You might want to switch **Linked Selection** off if you want to move a lot of synced sound clips, splitting the audio and the video. But I don't think that's ever a good idea. I think **Linked Selection** should be maintained at all times and toggled on and off only as needed for individual clips. You might get away with leaving it off most of the time, but one day it will leap up and bite you hard. So for these lessons, let's leave **Linked Selection** turned on.

Before we begin working on the sequence, it is probably be a good idea to duplicate the *Rough Cut* sequence. Select it and use **Edit>Duplicate** or the keyboard shortcut **Option-D**. This way you can also refer back to the original *Rough Cut* should you ever need to.

1. Start by double-clicking the copy of *Rough Cut* and take a look at the **Timeline**.

➤*Tip*

Disappearing Buttons: Should your Linked Selection button or your Snapping button disappear from the Timeline window, Control-click on the button holder and from the shortcut menu choose **Restore Default**. Or choose **Load Main Buttons Bars** and pick your favorite configuration.

The trick to smoothing out the audio for this type of sequence—or any sequence with abrupt sound changes at the edit points—is to overlap sounds and create sound beds that carry

The Cutaway

Any editor will tell you that cutaways are the most useful shots. You can never have too many, and you never seem to have enough. No editor will ever complain that you have shot too many cutaways. A cutaway shot shows a subsidiary action or reaction that you can use to bridge an edit, like the shot of the interviewer nodding in response to an answer. The cutaway allows you to bridge a portion of the interviewee's answer where the person has stumbled over the words or has digressed into something pointless. A wide shot that shows the whole scene can often be used as a cutaway. Make note of these useful shots as you're watching your material.

through other shots. Ideally, a wild track was shot on location, sometimes called room tone when it's the ambient sound indoors. This is a long section of continuous sound from the scene, a couple of minutes or more, which can be used as a bed to which the sync sound is added as needed. Here there was no wild track as such, but some of the shots are lengthy enough to have a similar effect.

Before we get started, we want to change the type of audio that's used in the sequence. Double-click on the first shot, *Backstage01*, to bring it into the **Viewer**. Notice at the top of the **Viewer** that there are two tabs for the two audio tracks **Mono (a1)** and **Mono (a2)**. This is the default capture setting for FCE material. Unfortunately it's more difficult to work with audio such as this because you have to adjust the two tracks separately. The best thing to do is to change your audio in the **Timeline** to a *stereo pair*. This is very simple to do.

1. Select everything in the **Timeline, Command-A**.

2. From the **Modify** menu use **Stereo Pair** or the keyboard shortcut **Option-L**.

As soon as you do this, the clip that was in the **Viewer** will disappear. If you reopen it into the **Viewer**, you'll see that there is only one audio tab marked **Stereo (a1a2)** and each of the clips in the **Timeline** has little inward pointing pairs of green triangles on each of the tracks. This indicates that these are grouped as stereo pairs. It's much easier to work with your audio when the tracks are stereo pairs, because both channels will move in unison.

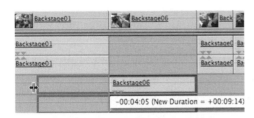

6.13 Dragging audio to create a split edit

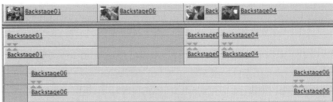

6.14 Timeline after making split edits

Making Split Edits

1. Play through the first three or four shots in the *Rough Cut* copy sequence. The change between the first and second shot is quite noticeable, even more so between the second and third.

2. Hold down the **Option** key and select the audio portion of the second shot, *Backstage06*.

3. With the **Option** key still pressed, tap the **Down** Arrow key twice. This will move the stereo pair of audio down two tracks. This can be done with any tracks, video or audio, as long as there is nothing in the way, such as another clip.

4. Again holding down the **Option** key, drag the head of the audio edit point toward the beginning of the **Timeline** (see Figure 6.13). While you drag it, a small box will appear. It gives you a time duration change for the edit you are making. It may be helpful to toggle **Snapping** off with the **N** key.

5. Repeat the process on the other side of the audio. Holding down the **Option** key, drag out the audio so that your sequence looks like Figure 6.14.

You have now created two split edits for the clip *Backstage06*.

Adding Audio Transitions

We want the sound of the first shot, *Background01*, to fade out before it ends. The simplest way to do this is to apply an audio crossfade.

1. Select the edit point by clicking on it.

2. To add the audio transition, either use the menu **Effects>Audio Transitions>Cross Fade (+3dB)**, or use the keyboard shortcut **Command-Option-T**.

Note_____

Linear or Logarithmic: FCE has two crossfades, the default + 3dB as well as a 0dB transition. The + 3dB crossfade that FCE calls an equal power crossfade is generally preferred because it gives a logarithmic roll of sound, which is the way sound works. The 0dB crossfade is a linear fade. It will often produce an apparent dip in the audio level at the midpoint of the crossover from one track to the other.

Because the audio is not butted against anything, the application will by default create an End on Edit transition, as shown in Figure 6.15.

In the Viewer

You can also create a split edit in the **Viewer**. Let's first set up a.new sequence.

6.15 Cross Fade Transition applied

1.   Begin by again duplicating the *Rough Cut* sequence.

2.   Open the new duplicate sequence and delete everything but the first shot.

Let's make a split edit with a clip from the **Browser**.

3.   Find the clip *Backstage06* in the **Clips** bin in the **Browser**.

4.   Double-click on it to open it into the **Viewer**. Because we want to use all the audio, begin by marking a split audio In point at the beginning of the clip. With the playhead at the very start of the shot, either **Control**-click and from the shortcut menu choose **Mark Split>Audio In** (see Figure 6.16), or use the keyboard shortcut **Command-Option-I**.

6.16 Marking Split Audio In

5.   Play through the clip until you find the In point for the edit at 4;10.

6.   Instead of pressing **I** to enter the In point, press **Control-I**.

Next we'll make the split edit for the Out point.

7.   Play forward till you get to the Out point at 9;18.

8.   Instead of pressing **O** to enter the Out point, press **Control-O**.

Note the markings in the **Viewer** scrubber bar and on screen in Figure 6.17 that indicate the split edit.

6.17 Split edit in the Viewer

Viewer to Timeline

The simplest way to work with the split edit in the **Viewer** is to drag and drop to the **Timeline**.

6.18 Setting destination tracks in the patch panel

9. Reset the destination tracks in your **Timeline** by pulling the **a2** button down to **A4** and the **a1** button down to **A3** in the patch panel at the head of the tracks as in Figure 6.18.

10. With the playhead at the end of the shot in the **Timeline**, drag the clip from the **Viewer** to the **Timeline**, as in Figure 6.19.

What will happen is that the edit will be performed as in Figure 6.20. This seems to be a bug in the software that has not been fixed as of this writing (version 2.0.3). Should that happen, grab the clip and slide it to butt up against the first shot, as shown in Figure 6.21.

Controlling Levels

Next we need to look at how to control the audio levels. This can be done either in the **Timeline** or in the **Viewer**. It's easier and quicker in the **Timeline**, but the **Viewer** controls afford a great deal more precision.

In the Timeline

To work in the **Timeline**, let's return to the first *Rough Cut* duplicated sequence that still contains all the clips. To adjust the audio levels in the **Timeline**, you first need to turn on the **Clip Overlays**

6.19 Dragging a split edit to the Timeline

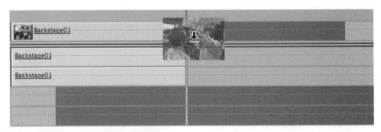

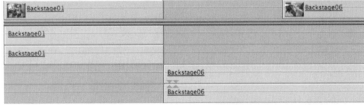

6.20 Displaced split edit in the Timeline

6.21 Correctly placed split edit

Slipping Out of Sync

Sometimes when you move an unlinked audio track it may accidentally slip out of sync with the video material. If that happens, you'll see time indicators in the **Timeline tracks** (see Figure 6.22) showing you how far out of sync the clips have slipped. The time slippage shows in a red box. The minus number means that the audio is three frames ahead of the picture. A plus number indicates that the audio is behind the video.

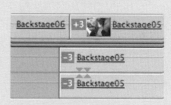

6.22 Out-of-sync audio

If the audio does slip out of sync, the easiest way to get it back in sync is to **Control**-click on the red box and choose from the options available in the shortcut menu (see Figure 6.23).

You could also nudge the clip back into sync. **Option**-click on the audio to select the audio portion of the clip. If you just click on the audio, you'll select both video and audio even though they are out of sync. With only the audio selected, use the < or > keys to slide the clip forward or backwards.

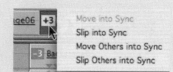

6.23 Out-of-sync shortcut menu

As it moves, the time displays will update and finally disappear when the clip is back in sync. Every press of the < or > keys nudges the clip one frame. Holding down the **Shift** key will nudge the clip the trim amount you selected in **Multi-Frame Trim Size** in **User Preferences**.

You can also select the audio portion of the clip (or whichever portion has free track space around it) and type plus or minus the value in the **Move** box as in Figure 6.24. Then press the **Return** key to move the clip.

6.24 Typing in a numeric value to move audio

button in the lower-left corner of the **Timeline** window (see Figure 6.25), or use the keyboard shortcut **Option-W**. It's a good idea to leave the **Clip Overlays** turned off when you're not using them, because it's easy to accidentally shift the level line while just trying to grab a clip to move it.

When the **Clip Overlays** are turned on, a thin pink line appears through the middle of the audio portion of the clips. This is the audio level control for the clips. Notice also the thin black line that appears at the top of the video. This controls the opacity for the video portion.

6.25 Clip Overlay button

6.26 Dragging the level line

6.27 Pen tools

6.28 Adding a keyframe

6.29 Lowering the keyframe level

6.30 Fade-out in the Timeline

Play the audio for the third shot in the sequence, *Backstage05*. It's pretty low and adds nothing to the soundtrack except to muddy it a bit. To eliminate the audio, you could select the audio portion of the clip with the **Option** key and delete it. However, if you ever decide you want that audio or if you move the clip to a place where the audio is needed, it's a bit of a nuisance to get it back.

A simpler way is to reduce the audio level to zero. With **Clip Overlays** turned on, move the cursor over the line. It will change to the **Resizing** tool. Grab the line and pull it down to the bottom of the clip as shown in Figure 6.26.

Fading Levels in the Timeline

You usually don't want to reduce the overall levels. More often you'll want to reduce the levels of portions of the sound, raise other portions, or fade in or out. For a simple fade, you could use the crossfade transition that we saw earlier, or you can do it by fading the level line. To do this you use the **Pen** tool. There are a number of them available at the bottom of the **Tools** palette (see Figure 6.27). You can also call up the **Pen** tool with the **P** key.

Let's create a fade-in at the beginning of the second shot, *Backstage06*, which is on **A3/A4**.

1. Move the **Pen** over the pink level line in the clip. The cursor will change to a pen nib, allowing you to click on the line to create a point(see Figure 6.28). This adds a tiny diamond to the levels line called a *keyframe*.

2. Put a keyframe about one second from the beginning of the shot by clicking with the **Pen** tool on the level line.

3. As you move the cursor to the newly created keyframe it will change into a crosshairs cursor. This lets you grab the keyframe and move it up or down. Pull the keyframe down to about −7dB as in Figure 6.29. Notice that because there are no other keyframes on the level line, the volume for the entire clip is reduced.

4. Take the **Pen** tool and grab the very left end of the level line. Pull it down to create a curved fade-up ramp (see Figure 6.30).

✎ Note

What Is a Keyframe?: We'll be talking more and more about keyframes as we get further into the book. A keyframe is a way of defining the values for a clip at a specific moment in time, a specific frame of video. Here we're dealing with audio levels. We're saying at this frame we want the sound to be at a particular level. By then going to a different point in the clip and altering the levels we will have created another keyframe, defining the sound level at that particular frame. The computer will figure out how quickly it needs to change the levels to get from one setting to the other. The closer together the keyframes are, the more quickly the levels will change; the farther apart they are, the more gradually the change will take place.

➤Tip

No Switching Necessary: If you don't want to switch to the **Pen** tool from the standard **Selector** tool, as you move the cursor to the level line and it changes to the **Resizing** tool, hold down the **Option** key and the cursor will automatically change to the **Pen** tool. If you are working with the **Pen** tool and you want to switch to the straight-level line-moving **Resizing** tool, hold down the **Command** key.

We haven't finished with *Backstage06* yet. We still need to bring the sound up to full level as the shot is introduced and fade it out at the end.

5. To bring the level back up, add a keyframe at about the point where the crossfade begins on **A1/A2**.

6. Next, add another keyframe at about the point where the crossfade ends. Push the level line back up to 0dB (see Figure 6.31). Because this is the last keyframe on the level line, everything after that point will come back up to full volume.

7. Finally, to finish *Backstage06*, we want to fade out the audio at the end. With the **Pen** tool, add a keyframe to the level line about two seconds before the end of the clip. Go to the end of the clip, and pull the end of the line all the way down to create a slow fade-out as in Figure 6.32.

8. On **A1/A2** it would be a good idea to add a crossfade transition between the silent *Backstage05* and the next shot, *Backstage04*.

Controlling Track Levels

There may be occasions when you want to change the audio level for an entire track—say, of music—to give it a lower base level, especially CD music, which is often recorded and compressed at maximum audio levels, often too high for use with most digital video systems. You can do this by selecting the track you want with the **Track** tool, which is the first button the third group in the **Tools** palette (see Figure 6.33).

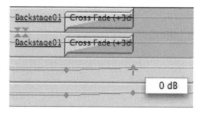

6.31 Ramping up the audio

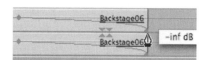

6.32 Slow fade-out

6.33 Track tools

Waveform in the Timeline

When you're working in the **Timeline**, it may be beneficial to turn on the waveform display in Timeline window(see Figure 6.34).

6.34 Waveform in the Timeline

Do this by going to the **Timeline Options** pop-up menu by clicking the tiny triangle in the bottom left of the **Timeline** window (see Figure 6.35), and select **Show Audio Waveforms**, or use the keyboard shortcut **Command-Option-W**.

Because displaying the audio waveform in the **Timeline** takes a good deal of processing power (pre-reading the audio and then displaying it), the redraw ability and video playback capabilities of the computer are markedly slowed down. So it's a good idea to toggle the waveform display on and off as needed with that handy keyboard shortcut.

6.35 Timeline Options pop-up menu

You can select a single track, multiple tracks forward and backward, a single track forward and backward, or a whole track of audio and adjust its level globally.

Select the items or the track with the **Track** tool (**T**). Once you have your track or clips selected, go to **Modify>Levels**, or use the keyboard shortcut **Command-Option-L**.

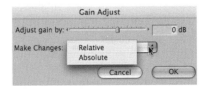

6.36 Level controls

This command calls up a dialog box that allows you to adjust the audio levels of the clips (see Figure 6.36). The slider or the value box will change the gain setting for all the clips selected. The **Relative** and **Absolute** pop-up menu sets how the gain is affected. **Absolute** will make the level you set affect all the clips, eliminating any fades. Using the **Relative** setting will change the value of the levels relative to any current settings or fades. This global levels control work not only on audio but also on opacity on a title or on the video portion of a clip.

Another way to change the audio level of more than one clip is to change its attributes. You can copy an audio clip by selecting it and pressing **Command-C**. Select the clips you want by marquee-ing or **Command**-clicking, and choose **Paste Attributes** from the **Edit** menu or press **Option-V**. Then check the attributes you want to paste to the other clips' **Levels** or **Pan** values (see Figure 6.37).

Notice the **Scale Attributes Over Time** checkbox at the top. It defaults to the on position. If you have keyframed the levels in the copied clips, that keyframing will be distributed proportionately onto the pasted clip, based on the relative durations of the clips. If the copied clip is longer, the keyframing will be tighten up; if it is shorter, the keyframing will be spread out. If you want to paste the keyframes in the same duration as in the copied clip, uncheck **Scale Attributes Over Time**.

Paste Attributes	
Attributes from Backstage06:	
☑ Scale Attribute Times	
Video Attributes:	Audio Attributes:
☐ Content	☐ Content
☐ Basic Motion	☐ Levels
☐ Crop	☐ Pan
☐ Distort	☐ Filters

6.37   Pasting audio attributes

➤**Tip**_____

Changing a Range of Keyframes: You can also change the relative or absolute levels of a group of audio key-frames. Use the **Range** tool (**GGG**) to select the area that includes the audio keyframe (see Figure 6.38)

6.38   Range selection of audio keyframes

If you then apply the **Levels** function, it will raise or lower the relative or absolute values of the keyframes in the selected area.

More Fades

Before we look at how to control audio levels in the **Viewer,** let's do some more work on the *Rough Cut copy* sequence.

Take a look at the fifth shot in the sequence *Backstage11.* We need to overlap its audio underneath the adjacent clips.

1. With the **Option** key pressed, select the audio portion of the clip. Still holding down the **Option** key, tap the **Down** arrow key twice to move the stereo pair onto **A3/A4**.

2. Holding down the **Option** key again, drag out the front and end of the audio portion of *Backstage11* so that it overlaps the adjacent clips as in Figure 6.39.

3. The next step is to add a fade out at the end of *Backstage04* on **A1/A2**. Select the edit point and use the keyboard shortcut **Command-Option-T** to put in the default audio transition.

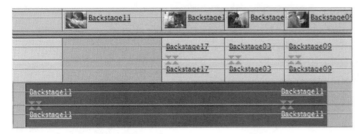

6.39   Backstage11 overlapping clips

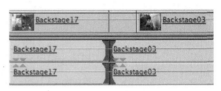

6.40   Roll or Extend audio edit

Backstage17, which immediately follows *Backstage11*, is quite loud and has a pronounced music track. As you did with *Backstage05* earlier in the sequence, suppress its sound completely by dragging the level line right down to the bottom.

For the next shot, *Backstage03*, I want to fade up the sound, but as so often when working with video, I want the fade to come up before the shot begins.

1. Use a Roll edit or Extend edit to move the audio portion of the shot earlier in the sequence.

2. To do this, again hold down the **Option** key and click on the edit point in the audio portion of the clip.

3. Now either use the **Roll** tool to move that audio edit about a second earlier, or do an Extend edit, moving the playhead about one second earlier and pressing the E key to create a split edit that looks like Figure 6.40.

4. To complete the fade, with the edit still selected, press **Command-Option-T** to add the crossfade.

I would like to fade in the overlapping *Backstage11* a little earlier. To do this I need to ripple the sequence to move the overlapping on A3/A4 so that they butt up against each other. We'll do this with the **Ripple** tool.

1. With the **Ripple** tool, select the left side of the edit between *Backstage04* and *Backstage11*.

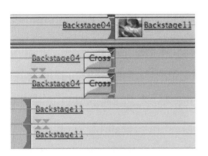

6.41   Multitrack Ripple edit

2. Hold down the **Command** key and click just to the left of the audio portion of *Backstage11*, in the empty space between it and the previous shot (see Figure 6.41). You can now ripple the empty space together with *Backstage04*.

3. Pull the edit until the audio tracks collide on **A3/A4**.

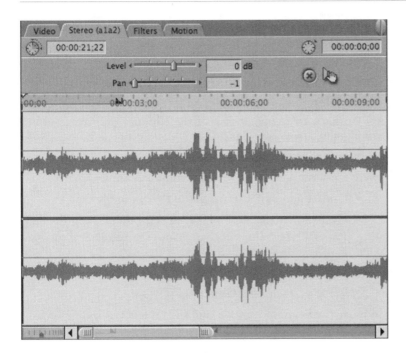

6.42 Stereo (a1a2) Viewer

In the Viewer

Let's add the fade at the beginning of *Background11* in the **Viewer**.

1. Double-click on the audio portion of the clip. This opens the clip to the **Viewer** but with the **Stereo (a1a2)** tab in front (see Figure 6.42). Here you can see the clip's audio waveform.

Notice the pink line in the center of the audio track. As you move the cursor over the line, it changes to the **Resizing** tool we saw earlier, which allows you to raise and lower the audio level.

At the top of Figure 6.42 you'll notice the **Level** slider and the **Decibel Indicator** box. It's currently at 0, which is the level at which the audio was digitized or captured.

As you move the line up or down with the cursor, both the **Level** slider and the **Decibel Indicator** box at the top move. A small window appears in the waveform as well that shows the amount in decibels that you're changing the audio level (see Figure 6.43). Notice also that, because this is a stereo pair, you are seeing two waveforms in this window and that they move together when you raise and lower the level of one track.

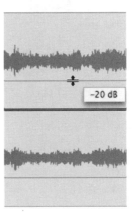

6.43 Decibel level change indicators

6.44 Audio fade-in

6.45 Pen Delete tool

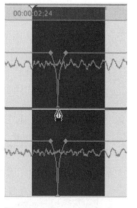

6.46 Zoom tool in the waveform with audio slice

2. To add a keyframe, either use the **Pen** tool or hold down the **Option** key as the cursor approaches the level line. The cursor changes into the **Pen** tool.

3. Go about one second into the shot in the **Viewer** and add a keyframe.

4. Go back to the beginning of the clip and pull the level line down so that the audio fades up from the beginning of the shot (see Figure 6.44).

There are several ways to delete an audio keyframe:

- Grab it and pull it down out of the audio timeline.
- Hold down the **Option** key when you're over the keyframe. The cursor will change into the **Pen Delete** tool (see Figure 6.45).
- Use the shortcut menu by **Control**-clicking on the keyframe and selecting **Clear**.

To move the keyframe, grab it and slide it left and right along the line.

One of the great features for editing sound in the **Viewer** is that you can do it with great precision, down to 1/100th of a second. To do this you have to zoom into the waveform, either with the scaling tab at the bottom of the **Viewer** window or with the **Zoom** tool (see Figure 6.46), which you can call up with the **Z** key. To zoom out, hold down the **Option** key while you click in the waveform. You can also use **Command-+** to zoom in and **Command-** to zoom out. The black band in Figure 6.46 represents one frame of video, and you can zoom in farther still. Notice the tiny slice of audio that has been cut out of the track, less than one video frame in length.

A new feature in FCE2 is the ability to automatically record slider movements while playing back a clip in the **Viewer**. This is switched on in the **User Preferences** by checking the box for **Record Audio Keyframes**, or you can make a button for it and park it in a button holder.

Because the **Viewer** is a pretty cramped space, a nice trick is to pull your **Stereo (a1a2)** tab out of the **Viewer** and dock it into your **Timeline** as in Figure 6.47. Then as you play back your audio you can monitor it on the meters and ride the levels up and down as you like. When you stop playback, the keyframes necessary to reproduce your level control will be added to the clip.

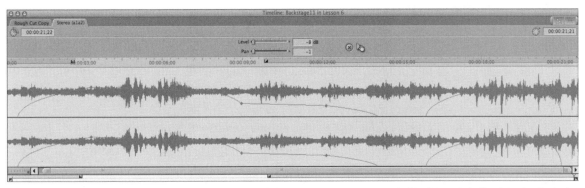

6.47 Stereo (a1a2) tab in the docked Timeline

Middle of the Sequence

Let's finish off the *Rough Cut copy* sequence. There are only a few more levels to tweak. Further along in the **Timeline** is another portion of *Backstage05*. This time we do want to use the sound.

1. Again with the **Option** key, select the audio portion of the clip and move the stereo pair down to **A3/A4**.

2. Extend the front of the sound until it butts up against *Backstage11*, also on **A3/A4**.

3. Extend the end of the sound as far as it will go, which isn't that far.

Between *Backstage03* and *05* are two shots, *Backstage09* and *10*. Both of these shots are quite loud.

➤ *Tip*

Zoom a Marquee: You can also use the **Zoom** tool to drag a marquee along a section of the waveform to zoom into just that portion of the display. This technique will work in the **Viewer**, the **Canvas**, as well as the **Timeline**.

Fixing Soft Audio

Sometimes audio is too low to be as forceful as you'd like, even after you crank it up with FCE's level controls. A neat little trick is to double up the audio tracks. Put another copy of the same sound on the track below. A simple way to do that is to hold the **Option** key to select just the audio. Hold the **Option** key and drag down to see the right-pointing **Insert** arrow. Add the **Shift** key to constrain the direction, and change the arrow to the downward-pointing **Overwrite** arrow. Drop the audio on the tracks below. You will have created a duplicate. Now push that audio level up as well. Double your pleasure.

A neat new feature of FCE2 is the ability to merge up to 24 tracks of audio with a single track of video. This is normally done in the **Browser**, but you can still do it in the **Timeline** to your audio-doubled clip. Select the clip, then **Command**-click the duplicate audio tracks to select them as well, and use **Modify > Link** or **Command-L** to link them all together as a single clip with four or more audio tracks.

Pan Values

In addition to the pink levels line in the **Viewer**, there is a purple pan line. In a stereo pair such as this material, the pan lines are defaulted to –1. This indicates that the left channel is going to the left speaker and the right channel to the right speaker. By moving the lines up toward zero as in Figure 6.48, the two tracks are centered between the speakers. Going to 1 will make the channels cross over and swap sides. You can also type in a value in the **Pan** slider box.

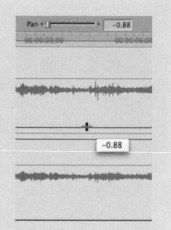

When you have a multitrack recording with separate **Mono (a1)** and **Mono (a2)** sound, the **Viewer** appears with separate tabs, one for each channel. **Level** and **Pan** values can then be set separately for each channel, one set to –1 and the other to 1. This allows you to move the audio from one side of the stereo speakers to the other.

6.48 Changing spread value

When you're working with separate channels using the pan line, you can shift the sound to come from either the left side or the right side. Moving the **Pan** slider to the left to –1 will move all the sound to the left speaker, and moving the **Pan** slider all the way to the right to 1 will move the sound to the right speaker. As with **Level**, **Pan** values can be keyframed. The classic example is the racing car that approaches from the left with all sound coming from the left speaker, roars by, and disappears to the right while the sounds sweeps past to the right speaker.

A little trick to quickly get the channels centered between the speakers is to select the clips in the **Timeline** and use the keyboard shortcut **Control-period** to center the tracks to the zero value.

4. Marquee-drag or **Command**-click to select the pair of them, and use **Modify>Levels** or **Command-Option-L** to reduce their levels to –9dB.

5. To smooth the transition between *Backstage09* and *Backstage10*, add a crossfade transition between the pair (**Command-Option-T**).

6. Extend the end of the audio on *Backstage10* so that it's underneath the following shot *Backstage05*.

7. With the **Pen** tool, make a slow fade-down on the audio of *Backstage10* that you extended under *Backstage05*. Or you could a crossfade transition on the end and lengthen it.

8. Add a crossfade transition to the beginning of *Backstage13*, which follows *Backstage05*.

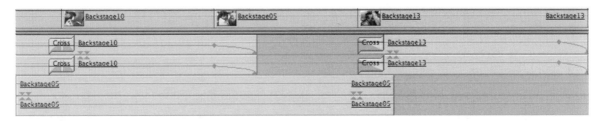

6.49 Middle portion of the completed sequence

9. With the **Pen** tool, add a slow fade-out to the end of *Backstage13*. The middle portion of the sequence should now look like Figure 6.49.

End of the Sequence

There is an interesting little problem in the ending portion of the sequence that will again require a Ripple edit of empty space.

1. Pull the audio tracks for *Backstage02* down onto **A3/A4** and extend them front and end as far as you can.

2. There is one more stereo pair to pull down onto **A3/A4**, the last shot, *Background14*. Bring the audio down to **A3/A4** and extend the front until it meets *Backstage02* on **A3/A4**.

I want to put a crossfade transition between the two shots on **A3/A4**, but I can't because there isn't enough media available on the end of *Backstage02*. I need to ripple that shot back by 15 frames to create enough space for the overlap.

3. With the **Ripple** tool, select the edit at the end of *Backstage02*. Holding down the **Command** key, click just to the left of the beginning of *Backstage16* tracks on **A1/A2**, as shown in Figure 6.50.

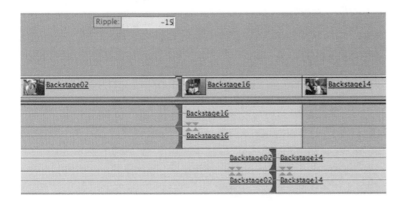

6.50 Selecting the Ripple edits and numerically editing

Metering

Key tools for working with sound in Final Cut are its audio meters (see Figure 6.51). The standard audio level for digital audio is –12dB. Unlike analog audio, which has quite a bit of headroom and allows you to record sound above 0dB, in digital recording 0dB is an absolute. Sound cannot be recorded at a higher level. It gets clipped off. Very often on playback of very loud levels, the recording will seem to drop out completely and become inaudible as the levels are crushed beyond the range of digital audio's capabilities.

For normal speech it's probably best to keep the recording around –12dB, perhaps a little higher for louder passages, a bit lower for softer ones. Many audio CDs are very heavily compressed, right up to the limits of digital audio. If you see your audio meters hitting the top of the scale, lighting up the two little orange indicators at the top, bring down your audio levels a few dB. You'll probably find you have to do this for most audio CD material.

Monitor not only single tracks but also your mixed track. Often a single track will not exceed peak level, but a mix of all your tracks may send your meters well into the red.

6.51 Audio meters

4. Pull the edit point to the left so that it moves 15 frames, or edit it numerically (Type *–15* and press the **Return** key). As you type, a little box will appear at the top of the **Timeline** window telling you that you're rippling the edit as in Figure 6.50.

5. Add the crossfade between the two audio clips on **A3/A4**.

6. Finally, for *Backstage16* just add a crossfade at the edit point. You have to add the crossfade after you do the Ripple edit, because for some reason you can't select the empty space in front of a transition.

Voice Over

Final Cut Express has a feature called **Voice Over,** which allows you to record narration or other audio tracks directly to your hard drive while playing back your **Timeline. Voice Over** is most valuable for making *scratch tracks,* test narrations used to try out pacing and content with picture. It could be used for final recording, although you'd probably want to isolate the computer and other extraneous sounds from the recording artist. Many people prefer to record narrations before beginning final editing so that the picture and sound can be controlled more tightly. Others feel that recording to the picture allows for a more spontaneous delivery from the narrator. However you use it, **Voice Over** is an important tool in the application.

Voice Over is found under the **Tools** menu. This brings up the window in Figure 6.52. Or better still, call it up from the menus under **Window>Arrange>Voice Over Recording**, which brings a three-up display, **Viewer** on the left, **Voice Over** in the center, **Canvas** on the right, **Browser** and **Timeline** below.

🐾 *Note*_____

More RAM for VO: Because Voice Over works in RAM, storing the sound before recording it to disk, you may need to put more RAM into your computer than the minimum requirements asked for by FCE because the audio is buffered in RAM as it's recorded. 48kHz audio consumes 6MB per minute. So a half-hour track would take 180MB. Once they are recorded, all of these recordings are stored in your *Capture Scratch* folder with the project name.

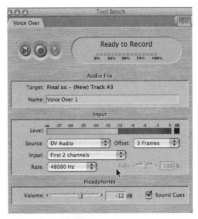

6.52 Voice Over tool

The first steps you'll have to take are to configure your recording setup for your **Source, Input,** and **Sampling Rate.**

Source defines where the sound is coming from: the computer mic input, a USB device, a camcorder, or an installed digitizing card.

Input controls the type of signal being received, whether it's line level, balanced audio in, digital audio, or whatever your source device is capable of handling.

---

iMovie Sound Effects

It is possible to bring iMovie4 sound effects into Final Cut Express, such as those great Skywalker sound effects. The trick is to know where they are and to copy them to somewhere else. Do this very carefully.

1. **Control**-click on the iMovie application inside your *Applications* folder.

2. From the shortcut menu select **Show Package Contents.**

3. Go inside the *Contents* folder to the *Resources* folder and find inside that the *Sound Effects* folder.

Most of the iMovie sound effects are AIFF files. Copy what you need from that folder. Do not move them. The Skywalker sounds are MP3s and should be converted to AIFF using iTunes or the QuickTime Pro Player, if you have that.

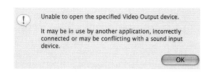

6.53   DV device error message

6.54   Discard warning dialog

Offset adjusts for the delay taken by the analog to digital conversion. USB devices typically take one frame. DV cameras can be three frames or more.

Let's look at some of the controls in this panel. The large red button, the middle of the three in the top portion of the window, is the **Record** button. It will also stop the recording, as will the **Escape** key. The button to its left is the **Preview/Review** button and will play the selected area of your sequence. The button to the right is the **Discard** button. Immediately after a recording or after aborting a recording, pressing the **Discard** button will bring up the warning dialog in Figure 6.54.

The **Gain** slider, next to the **Input** pop-up, allows you to control the recording level based on the horizontal LCD display meter. This is fine for scratch tracks, but for finished work it is probably better to have a hardware mixer before the input for good mic level control.

The **Headphones** volume does just what it says. If there is nothing jacked into the headphone output of your computer, the sound will come out of the computer speaker itself. To avoid recording it or the sound cues, uncheck the **Sound Cues** box.

FCE gives the recording artist elaborate sound cues, which are turned on with the little checkbox. Together with the aural sound cues in the headphones, there is visual cuing as well, which appears in the window to the right of the **Record** button. As the recording starts, a countdown begins, with cue tones as the display changes. It starts pale yellow and becomes darker and more orange until recording begins. Then the display changes to red. There is a cue tone at 15 seconds from the end of the recording as well as beeps counting down the last five seconds to the end of the recording. Recording begins during countdown and continues two seconds after the end of the recording during **Finishing**. Although this doesn't appear in the **Timeline** after the recording, you can drag out the front and end of the clip if the voice started early or overran the end.

I think the best way to work with **Voice Over** in the **Timeline** is to define an In and Out point. If no points are defined, recording will begin at the point at which the playhead is parked and go until the end of the sequence or until you run out of available memory, whichever comes first. You can also simply define an In point and go from there, or define an Out and go from the playhead until the Out is reached. Because the **Timeline** doesn't scroll as the sequence plays, it might be helpful to reduce the sequence to fit the **Timeline** window. **Shift-Z** will do this with a keystroke.

Sometimes during recording you don't want to hear certain tracks, or you just want to hear a single pair of tracks. FCE2 has a new feature to make it simple to do this with the new **Mute/Solo** buttons. You open them by clicking on the tiny speaker button in the far lower-left corner of the **Timeline** window, which pops open the array of **Mute/Solo** buttons (see Figure 6.55). Clicking on the headphones will turn them red and Solo that track, muting the others. You can turn on or off any combination of **Mute** and **Solo** buttons that you need. Notice the green **Visibility** (audibility) buttons at the head of the **Timeline**. The difference between these and the **Mute/Solo** buttons is that when audibility is switched off, that track will not play out to tape. If a track is muted, it will still output even though it can't be heard during playback in the **Timeline**.

6.55 Mute/Solo buttons

Recording is always done to a destination track that has free space. **Voice Over** always records a mono track. It does not make a stereo recording and take up two tracks. If there is no free space within the defined area of the recording, **Voice Over** will create a new track. So if you record multiple takes, they will record onto the next lower track or onto a new track. The **Audio File** window will give you the track information (see Figure 6.56). You can name the recording in the **Audio File** window, and each take will be numbered incrementally.

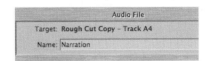

6.56 Audio File window

After recording, the new voice-over clip appears selected. You can play it back for review, but if you want to record further takes, use **Control-B** to switch off the clip audio so you don't hear it during playback of the next take.

After a discarded take, **Voice Over** will record to the previously assigned track with the previously assigned name. After a few takes, you may want to discard a previous take and reassign the targeted track so that **Voice Over** will work with the empty tracks you vacated.

Also, you should be careful to switch off previous takes as you go so that the talent doesn't hear the previous recording in the headphones while recording.

After a recording session with **Voice Over**, it would not be a bad idea to go into your hard drive and root out old tracks that aren't needed and may be filling up your drive. Those takes you recorded that you no longer want can be deleted from your sequence, but they aren't automatically deleted from your hard drive. Also remember, the recordings are only a part of your sequence and will not appear in your **Browser** at all, unless you put them there.

Summary

In this lesson we looked at working with sound in Final Cut Express. We covered performing split edits, overlapping sound, cutting with sound, overlapping and crossfading tracks, transitions, meters, and FCE's **Voice Over** tool. Sound is often overlooked, seeming insignificant or of minor importance, but it is crucial to making a sequence appear professionally edited.

In the next lesson we'll look at some of the titling options available in Final Cut Express.

Lesson 7

Adding Titles

Every program is enhanced with graphics, whether they are a simple opening title and closing credits or elaborate motion-graphics sequences illuminating some obscure point that can best be expressed in animation. This could be simply a map with a path snaking across it or a full-scale 3D animation explaining the details of how an airplane is built. Obviously, the latter is beyond the scope of both this book and of Final Cut Express alone. But many simpler graphics can be easily created within FCE.

In this lesson, we will look at typical titling problems and how to deal with them. As always, we begin by loading the project.

Loading the Lesson

This should be familiar to you by now. Let's begin by loading the material you need onto your media drive.

1. Drag the *Media 5* folder from the DVD's *Hybrid DVD-ROM Contents* folder.

2. Make sure the *Projects* folder from the DVD is installed on your system drive and eject the DVD.

3. Double-click on the project file *Lesson 7* to launch the application.

4. Reconnect the media file as we have done before.

Setting Up the Project

Inside the project in the **Browser** you'll find some sequences, which we shall look at in the course of this lesson. One of the sequences, *Sequence 1*, is empty, ready for you to use. There is also the master clip, *Kabuki*, and the **Clips** bin.

1. Begin by opening *Sequence 1*.

2. We'll be working only with the picture here, so deselect the **a1/a2** destination tracks in the patch panel by clicking on them.

3. Drag a clip—let's say *Kabuki1*—from the **Clips** bin and drop it onto **Overwrite** in the **Edit Overlay**.

Text Generator

Now let's look at FCE's **Text Generator**.

1. To get to it, click the small **A** in the lower right corner of the **Viewer**.

2. Go into the pop-up menu, drop down to **Text**, slide across, and pick **Text** again, as in Figure 7.1.

In addition to **Text,** there is also **Lower 3rd, Outline Text,** and the basic animations **Scrolling Text, Crawl,** and **Typewriter,** as well as the Boris title tools **Title 3D** and **Title Crawl.** We'll look at the Boris tools a bit later in the lesson, but let's start by looking at the way FCE's basic **Text** tool works.

7.1 Text Generator

Note

Scrolling Text, Crawl, and Outline Text: Neither FCE's **Scrolling Text** nor **Crawl** should be used as a first choice. To create text animations for scrolling or rolling titles (vertical movement) or crawling titles (horizontal movement) you should use **Title Crawl,** which can be set to do either movement. This should always be the preferred tool. Nor should **Outline Text** be used. The primary text tools should always be **Title 3D** and **Title Crawl.**

Text

This is for very basic text graphics indeed, simple on-screen words. The **Text** generator should be used only for very simple, quick text blocks. Your normal titler of choice should be **Title 3D,** which we'll look at a bit later. But let's just have a look at the **Text** generator because it has many of the typical text controls you can work with in Final Cut Express. Select **Text** from the **Generator** pop-up menu, which immediately loads a generic text generator into the **Viewer** (see Figure 7.2).

Notice that this generator has:

- A default duration of 10 seconds
- A default length of two minutes

➢ *Tip*_____

Launching Text Generator: The default, basic text generator can be opened into the **Viewer** with the keyboard shortcut **Control-X**. It's handy if you need to create a lot of basic titles quickly.

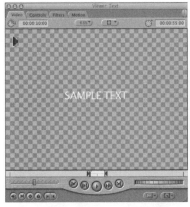

7.2 Generic sample text in the Viewer

You can designate any duration for a text file up to four hours. However, once the text file has been placed in a sequence, its duration can no longer be extended beyond the designated duration. So if I accept the default length and I place the text file in a sequence, I can no longer make the duration go beyond two minutes. If you know you're going to need to make a very long text file, change the duration before you place it in the sequence. You can always make it shorter, but not longer. It's a good way to create a video bug, that little graphic that's always in the bottom right of your TV screen—or your warning that a tape is only a sample copy and not for distribution.

The first point to realize about this text generator is that at the moment it exists only in the **Viewer**. Usually the next step I take is to put it somewhere useful, either into the **Browser** or the **Timeline**. If you park the playhead anywhere over the shot that's in the Timeline and drag the generic text generator from the **Viewer** to the **Edit Overlay** to **Superimpose**, the text will appear above the shot, with the same duration as the shot (see Figure 7.3). Notice that the application ignores the marked Out point and takes its duration from the length of the shot on **V1**.

7.3 Supered text in the Timeline

➢*Tip*_____

Background: I always leave the playhead in the **Timeline** parked over the middle of the clip with the text supered on it. That way whatever I do in the **Text** controls appears a moment later supered on the clip in the **Canvas**. If you place a clip in the **Timeline** over nothing, the blackness you see in the **Canvas** behind the clip is the emptiness of space. You can make it a variety of colors, including checkerboard under the View > Background menu, but this is only for viewing purposes. If you want an actual color layer, use the **Generators** to make a color matte. Make it any color you want and place it on the layer below all other material.

You can also drag and drop the generator into the **Timeline** onto an empty track or the space above the tracks. Whether you drag the generic text generator to the **Timeline** or the **Browser**, you are creating a copy of that generator. Be careful not to do anything to the generator in the **Viewer**. I've seen countless people do this. They lay the generator in the **Timeline**, work in the **Viewer**, and then wonder why the text in the sequence still says "Sample Text."

First, you should open the new generator you created in the **Timeline**. Open it by double-clicking on the **Text Generator** in the **Timeline** window. The **Viewer** screen will look the same, of course, except now you'll be working on the generator in the **Timeline**, which is what you want. The label area at the top of the **Viewer** will tell you where the text came from. Figure 7.4 shows the label for text generated in the **Viewer**. Figure 7.5 shows the label for text that's been opened from a sequence.

The other telltale sign that indicates whether a title or a clip has been opened from the **Browser** (or generated in the **Viewer**) or has been opened from a sequence is in the scrubber bar at the bottom of the **Viewer**. In Figure 7.6 the clip has been opened from the **Browser**. The scrubber bar is plain. In Figure 7.7 the clip has been opened from the **Timeline**. The scrubber bar shows a double row of dots, like film sprocket holes.

Now we're ready to start making that graphic.

1. After you've opened the generator from the **Timeline** into the **Viewer**, click on the **Controls** tab at the top. You might also want to stretch down the **Viewer** to see all the controls (see Figure 7.8).

These are the default settings. At the top is the text input window in which you type whatever you want to appear on the screen.

2. Click on **SAMPLE TEXT** and type in *Kabuki*, press **Return**, and type *Performance*.

Click out of the window or tab to the **Size** box. The default is 36 point, which is quite small for video display.

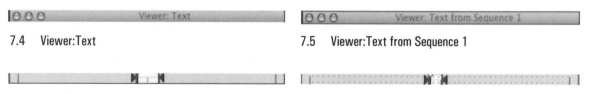

7.4 Viewer:Text

7.5 Viewer:Text from Sequence 1

7.6 Plain scrubber bar on clip opened from the Browser

7.7 Dotted scrubber bar on clip opened from the Timeline

3. Type in a size of *72* and press **Return**, which loads the size setting.

Note

Computer Display: Because much of FCE2 is real time, text will not require rendering on many computers. This means that as soon as the text is put into the **Timeline** it is at render quality. The title is rendered into interlaced DV material ready for display on a television set. That's what it is designed to do. It is not designed for display on a computer screen, which is why the text on your computer screen, and in these graphics, looks somewhat jagged and poorly rendered. You *must* judge your graphics output on a television set or video monitor. You cannot assess them properly on your computer monitor.

Above the **Size** slider is the **Font** pop-up menu, in which you can pick whatever TrueType fonts you have loaded in your system. It defaults to Lucida Grande, which is a pretty good font to use with video. If you have fonts on your computer that are not showing up here, then they are probably PostScript fonts. Unfortunately, FCE's titling tools tool do not work with PostScript, only with TrueType fonts.

An important point to note: the **Font** pop-up menu and all the settings in the text block will change all the letters for everything in the text block. You cannot control individual letters, or words, or lines of text. This applies to all of Final Cut Express's text generators except for Boris. Both **Title 3D** and **Title Crawl** have full text control, as we shall see.

The **Style** pop-up menu lets you set text styles such as bold and italic. Below **Style** is the **Alignment** pop-up menu, what's usually called *justification*.

A word of caution: though the default setting is **Center,** the words in the text window are left-justified. Ignore that. The choice in the pop-up menu rules; the text window just doesn't display intelligently.

The left and right alignments are not to the screen but to the Origin point, the way it works in Illustrator and Photoshop. So if you want left-justified text on the left side of the screen, you have to move the origin point about –300 or a little less to keep it in the **Safe Title Area,** if you also set the **Alignment** to **Left.** This applies only in the **Text** tool. Other tools such as **Scrolling Text** align to

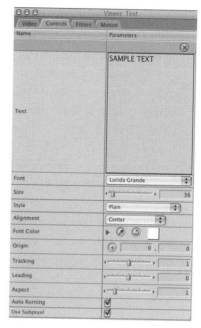

7.8   **Text Control window**

Note

No Word Wrapping: FCE's titler is limited in many ways, and word wrapping is one of them. You have to put in the line breaks where appropriate, or your text is liable to run off the screen.

Safe Areas

Televisions have a mask on the edge that cuts off some of the displayed picture area. What you see in the **Viewer** and the **Canvas** is not what you get—far from WYSI-WYG—and can vary substantially from television to television. That is why the **Canvas** and **Viewer** are thoughtfully marked with a **Safe Action Area** and a smaller area that is defined as the **Safe Title Area**, the marked boxes seen in Figure 7.9. These are turned on with the **View** pop-up menu at the top of the **Viewer** and **Canvas**. Make sure that both **Overlay** and **Title Safe** are checked to see the **Safe Action** and **Safe Title** areas. What's within the **SAA** will appear on every television set. Because television tubes used to be curved, and some still are, a smaller area was defined as the **Safe Title Area** in which text could appear without distortion if

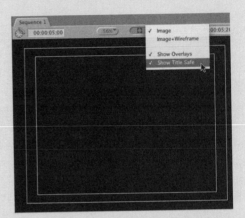

7.9   Safe Action and Safe Title areas with View pop-up menu

viewed at an angle. Titles should remain, if possible, within the **Safe Title Area**. This is not important for graphics destined only for web or computer display, but for anything that might be shown on a television within the course of its life, it would be best to maintain them. That said, more often you're seeing titles that are well outside the STA and lying partially outside even the SAA.

the screen as you might expect, with left as the left edge of the STA, and right as the right edge of the STA (see sidebar on "Safe Areas").

Font Color includes a color picker and a color swatch as well as a disclosure triangle that twirls opens to show the **HSB** sliders and **Value** boxes.

The small icon between the eyedropper and the color swatch serves no function in FCE.

Because of the limitations of television's color and brightness capabilities, it's important that you try to keep your luminance and chrominance values within the correct range. Oversaturated colors or video levels that are too high will bloom and smear on a television set. Set the HSB value so that brightness is no more than 92 percent. This may look pale gray on the computer screen, but as far as NTSC video is concerned, this is white, and it will look white on a television screen.

This is often a problem with using artwork that hasn't been designed specifically for video. All sorts of issues affect images used in video: interlacing, limitation in how saturated a color can be and how bright it can be, the chrominance and luminance range limitations of NTSC, moiré patterns, and compression. Unless the artist makes the necessary adjustments while creating the work, it often looks unsatisfactory when incorporated into a video production.

You can set the origin with a **Crosshair** button or with *x,y* values. You can use the crosshairs by clicking on the button and clicking wherever in the **Canvas** you want the center point of the text to be. The value windows are more precise, of course. The first window is the horizontal, or *x* value; the second window is the vertical, or *y* value. The default is the center of the screen. This is centered on the baseline of the first line of text, in this case somewhere under the **b** in **Kabuki**.

You can also position the text by moving it about the screen in the **Canvas**. If you change the **View** pop-up menu at the top of the **Canvas** to **Image+Wireframe** (or use the **W** key to toggle it on or off), you can grab the text block, or any other image for that matter, and move it about the screen and position it wherever you like. Make sure the text block in the **Timeline** is selected, and a

Fonts and Size

Not all fonts are equally good for video. You can't just pick something you fancy and hope it will work for you. One of the main problems with video is its interlacing. Video is made up of thin lines of information. Each line is switching on and off 60 times a second. If you happen to place a thin horizontal line on your video that falls on one of those lines but not the adjacent line, that thin, horizontal line will be switching on and off at a very rapid rate, appearing to flicker. The problem with text is that a lot of fonts have thin horizontal lines called serifs, the little footer that some letters sit on (see Figure 7.10).

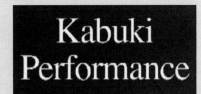

7.10 Serif Fonts

Unless you're going to make text fairly large, it's best to avoid serif fonts. You should probably avoid small fonts as well. Video resolution is not very high, the print equivalent of 72dpi. You can read this book in 10-point type comfortably, but a10-point line of text on television would be an illegible smear. I generally don't use font sizes below 24 point and prefer to use something larger if possible.

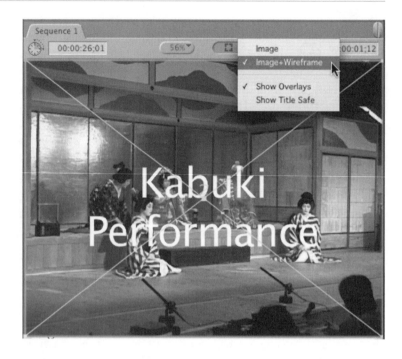

7.11   Image + Wireframe in the Canvas

large **X** will appear through the image with a blue border (see Figure 7.11). This is the image with its wireframe outline. You can move the text block about the screen. If you hold down the **Shift** key, you can constrain it to moving vertically or horizontally.

Tracking is the spacing distance between the letters in a word, not to be confused with kerning, which is the spacing between individual letter pairs. The higher the tracking value, the farther apart the letters will get. Small increases in tracking will have a large impact on letter separation. As you move tracking below zero, the letters will scrunch together, and if you go low enough into negative values, the letters will flip over.

Leading (pronounced *ledding*, as in little bits of lead spacing used in hot-metal typesetting) is the spacing between lines. The default is zero. A setting of −100 moves the text up so that it's all on one line. A value of 100 moves the text down a whole line.

Aspect adjusts the vertical shape of the text. Low numbers such as 0.3 and 0.4 stretch text vertically, and higher numbers such as 2 and 3 will squeeze down the text significantly. Be careful with the **Aspect** control. Very little movement from the default of 1 will cause ugly antialiasing (stair-stepped edges) to appear around the text. **Auto Kerning** adjusts the letter spacing based on the letters' shape rather than absolute values. This kerning not as tight as it was in the previous version of the application, and I think it looks much better than it used to be.

➤**Tip**_____

Flickering Text: Interlace flickering caused by serifs and other fine lines can be alleviated somewhat by smearing the image across the interlace lines. It is easiest to do this with text created in Photoshop, where you can apply a one-pixel vertical motion blur. You don't have to soften the whole image like this. If there are particular portions that appear to flicker, you can select them with a marquee or lasso, slightly feathered, and apply the vertical motion blur to just that portion of the image.

Or you can duplicate the **Text Generator** in the sequence and stack one on top of the other. Apply a slight **Blur** or **Antialias** filter to the bottom copy. Only the slightly blurred edge that sticks out from underneath the unblurred copy will be visible, smearing the edge. You can also darken the lower copy to give the text a slightly harder edge.

_____

Lower Thirds

A lower third is the graphic you often see near the bottom of the screen, such as those identifying a speaker or location that you always see in news broadcasts. They're simple to create in Final Cut, though they are fairly limited. If you want to create something more exciting or stylish, you'll probably find it easier to do in Photoshop or in **Title 3D**, which we'll look at later on page 163. Because **Lower Third** is so limited, it's quick and easy to use.

7.12 Lower Third

Click on the **Generators** button, and in the menu drop down to **Lower Third**.

Figure 7.12 shows the simple Lower Third that Final Cut generates. It's set down in the lower-left corner of the **Safe Title Area**.

You can create the graphic in the **Viewer** before you move it to the **Timeline**, but remember that once you've moved it to the **Timeline**, what's there is now a copy. I like to move the graphic to the **Timeline**, because once it's there, you can put the playhead over it and quickly see what you're doing in the **Canvas**. Open the **Controls** tab in the **Viewer** (see Figure 7.13), and you'll see that the **Controls** are quite different for lower thirds. You have some new parameters, and you are missing a property as well. There is no **Alignment** pop-up menu.

You have two lines of text. Unlike the regular text window, each of the two text boxes here can only hold one line of text. Each text box can be set to any font, size, or color. You can make a line

7.14 **Lower Third with bar and background** *(above)*

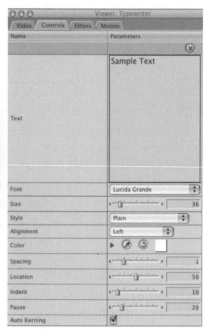

7.13 **Lower Third controls**

7.15 **Typewriter controls** *(right)*

as long as you want—of course, if you make it too long, it will run off the screen. At the bottom of the controls, you have the ability to create a background for the text and to adjust the opacity of the background.

Bar appears as a line between the text blocks. Although it has an opacity of 100 percent, it will show some of the underlying video through it. **Solid** is a block of color that appears behind the two text blocks. You can apply one or the other but not both. You could always add another Lower Third beneath it, with no text, just the background, as shown in Figure 7.14.

Typewriter

Let's look at **Typewriter** next, which is a unique tool. It works especially well if you use a font such as Courier to simulate a typewriter's monospace look.

The controls give you a small degree of flexibility (see Figure 7.15).

Alignment defaults to **Left** so that the typing begins on the left edge of the **Safe Title Area** and works its way across. Be careful with the line layout, because it's easy to type right off the screen.

Because the text doesn't wrap, you have to put in a return wherever you need a line break.

Location sets the vertical height of the typing. The default is 50, the center line of the screen. A setting of about 20 moves the text block to the top of the **Safe Title Area,** which is probably where you should start if you have more than a few of lines to type on.

Indent sets how far in from the edge the text is set if it is either left- or right-aligned.

Center alignment has an odd effect. The typing happens in the center of the screen, and the line of text spreads out from the center. It's unusual and may be worth playing with.

The default **Pause** value of 20 produces the action of a brisk typist, depending on how much text there is to type. The way it works is that the higher the **Pause** value, the longer the text is held on the screen before the end of the clip. So the three variables are:

- The length of the clip
- How long the text holds after the typing is completed (that's the **Pause** value)
- How much you have to type

If you have a lot to type, set the **Pause** value fairly low. If you set the **Pause** value very high—for instance, 100—no typing will occur; the text will just be there and spend 100 percent of the time paused on the screen.

Title 3D

The tools we have used so far in Final Cut Express are text tools. Boris Calligraphy, through **Title 3D** and **Title Crawl,** provides us with a titler. These supersede the FCE text tools and should be the title tool of choice for most of the work you do. These generators give the user great control and flexibility with text. It is a hugely feature-packed tool, an application within itself. I'm going to show you some of its principal tools, but for a thorough look at its capabilities, there is a PDF in the *Extras* folder on the Final Cut DVD that details its operation. Just be warned that it makes much reference to animation of text, capabilities that are not available in Final Cut Express.

Call up **Title 3D** from the **Generators** pop-up menu. It will launch a separate titling window that is part of the Boris interface (see Figure 7.16). This is the first of five tabbed windows that allow

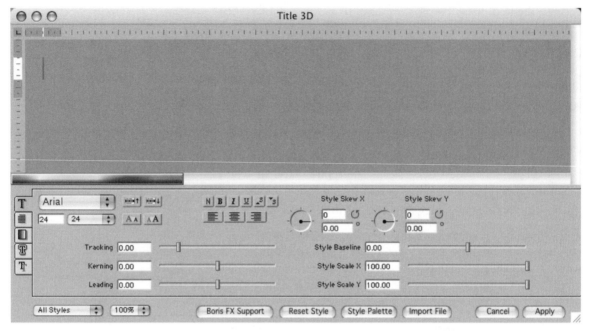

7.16 Title 3D interface

you access to **Title 3D's** powerful and complex tools. In fact, **Title 3D** has so many controls that there seem to be controls for the controls.

The first tabbed window is obviously the text window. Unlike the FCE text box, it is truly WYSIWYG. Most important, each control can be applied to each letter or group of letters separately. So now, with little trouble, you can make a garish combination of colors and fonts, such as I have done in the sequence *Calligraphy*.

7.17 Word wrapping

Before you do anything in this window, you may want to click on the second tab and change the default **No Wrap** to **Wrap** (see Figure 7.17). You can leave the wrap default at 512. At 512 you get a word wrapping that will fit inside a standard 720 video image's **Safe Title Area**. You can set whatever margins you want in this window, just as in a word processor (see Figure 7.18). In fact, many of **Title 3D's** controls are similar to word processors and other graphics applications such as Adobe Illustrator.

7.18 Margins window

The **Top-down Text** and **Right-to-left Reading** checkboxes at the bottom of the same window are great if you want vertical text or if you're doing Hebrew or Arabic text.

After you've set word wrapping and any margins you want, go back to the text window to enter your text. The main window allows you to enter and select text, which you can adjust with the controls at the bottom part of the window.

At the top of the **Text** window is a ruler that allows you to set tabs for precise positioning of text elements (see Figure 7.19). The white area seen in the ruler is the active text part of the screen, and the gray area is beyond the word wrapping. Use the **Tab** key to navigate from one tab indent to the next. After you've set a tab, you can double-click on it to toggle between left-justified, right-justified, and center-justified. This tool is especially useful when making long scrolls such as movie credits, which often use columns and indents for different sections.

Let's look quickly at some of the phenomenal text control in Calligraphy. In the bottom portion of the screen (see Figure 7.20), the first pop-up menu obviously sets the font. The two buttons to the right will move you up and down through your font list. Below the **Font** pop-up is a **Point Size Value** box. The two buttons to the right will incrementally raise and lower your point. To the right of the font controls are six buttons that let you set:

- Normal
- Bold
- Italic
- Underline

> **➤Tip**
> **Text Control Shortcuts:** If the Kerning, Tracking, or Leading value box is active, you can make the values go up or down by holding down the **Option** key and tapping the Up and **Down** arrow keys to raise and lower the values. With the text selected and holding down the **Option** key, you can tap the **Left** and **Right** arrow keys to increase the tracking. Or with the cursor positioned between letters, you can adjust the kerning of individual letter pairs.

7.20 Text controls

Bitmap or Vector

When you scale text created with the FCE titler, the image quickly becomes jagged around the edges, yet in Title 3D you can scale the text, twisting and skewing the letters, and you'll see no apparent anti-aliasing or stair-stepping on the edges of the letters. This is possible because Calligraphy works with vector graphics, but FCE text creates bitmapped graphics.

When a bitmapped graphic is created, the color and position of each pixel in the image is defined. If you scale that image, you have to scale the pixels, trying to create pixels where none previously existed. When a vector graphic is created, no pixels are defined. Only the shape, based on lines and curves, is defined. So if you scale a vector graphic, you're just redefining the shape; no pixels need to be created until the image is displayed on the screen.

Figure 7.21 shows what happens when a bitmapped text file (Helvetica 72 point) is scaled 300 percent and when a vector-based text file is scaled the same amount. The scaling for the vector graphic has to be done within **Title 3D** and not by using the **Scale** slider in the **Motion** tab.

7.21   Left: Bitmapped text; Right: Vector-based text

- **Superscript**
- **Subscript**

Below that, three **Paragraph** buttons let you set justification:

- **Left**
- **Center**
- **Right**

The **Tracking** slider adjusts the letter spacing globally, across the all the letters.

Kerning adjusts the spacing between individual pairs or groups of letters, as opposed to tracking that controls the whole block of words. Kerning is important for many fonts, especially when you are writing words such as AVE, where you need to slide the *A* and *V* closer together than fonts normally place them.

The **Style** controls allow you to skew the text on the *x* and *y* axis. These were primarily designed to be used as animation controls, but because that capability is not available in FCE, these controls can do little more than create interesting letter patterns by tilting letters in various ways.

Style Baseline will allow you to raise and lower letters separately, but **Style Scale X** and **Style Scale Y** will let you scale individual characters on the *x* and/or *y* axis independently from each other, allowing you to create interesting and unusual letter arrangements, as in Figure 7.22.

7.22 Skewed, Scaled and Baseline-shifted letters

The row of buttons and pop-up menus along the bottom of the window (see Figure 7.23) have a variety of functions. The **All Styles** pop-up menu at the far left lets you change to **Basic Style**. You see basic limits in the text window. It does speed up preview, which can get quite slow with long and complex text windows.

7.23 **Pop-up menus and buttons in the Title 3D window**

The **Percentage** pop-up menu lets you change the display size of the text window, a useful feature if you have a lot of text and want to quickly move around in it.

Boris FX Support will connect you to Boris's online web support system.

The **Reset Style** button will reset all the parameters for the words in the text window. It will not, however, reset wrapping, tabs, justification, or margins.

The **Style** palette is a great tool (see Figure 7.24). It allows you to create your own text style and to name and save it. This way you can replicate styles from file to file and even project to project simply and efficiently. The **Import File** button allows you to bring into the **Text** window a previously created plain text file or RTF (Rich Text Format) file. All the justification and styles applied there will be honored in **Title 3D**.

Cancel and **Apply** are self-explanatory.

This is only the first couple of tabs in **Title 3D**.

The third tabbed panel, **Text Color**, lets you set the text fill and opacity (see Figure 7.25). Notice the little checkbox in the upper-left corner that lets you turn off the fill, so that you only have the text outline if you want. The **Text Fill** pop-up menu lets you choose to fill the text with a color or with a gradient. If you choose **Color**, the **Style Color** swatch allows access to the system color picker that we saw earlier. If you choose **Gradient**, you will

Boris FX Style Presets

A great variety of wonderful preset styles can be down-loaded from the Boris FX web site. You have to fill out a simple registration form, and although the information is for Final Cut Pro users, entering Final Cut Express information still seems to be accepted.

The procedure to get the style presets into FCE2 is a little complicated but very well worth the effort.

1. Begin by navigating to *Library/Application Support*. Inside you will find either one or two folders called *BorisFX* and *Boris FX* (one with a space and one without).

2. Delete the contents of these two folders, which should be *Title 3D* and *Title Crawl*.

3. Download and run the Boris Calligraphy 1.1 updater from the Apple web site. It's currently at http://docs.info.apple.com/article.html?art-num=120118.

7.24 **Style palette**

4. Download and install the Calligraphy preset styles, which are currently at http://www.borisfx.com/download/freebies.php.

Your **Style** palette will look like Figure 7.24, and the top pop-up menu will be full of custom style categories such as **SeeThrus**, **Bevels**, **Outlines**, **3Ds**, **Metallic 3D**, **Fuzzy Colors**, and **Glow Colors**.

get access to an incredibly powerful gradient editor (see Figure 7.26), which allows multiple color points as well as transparency. To add color points, click below the gradient-bar display.

7.25 **Text Color** *(above)*

7.26 **Gradient editor** *(right)*

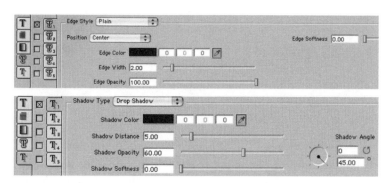

7.27 Text Edge

7.28 Drop Shadow

The fourth tabbed window lets you set the width and opacity for the **Text Edge**, and not just a single edge, but up to five separate edges for each letter (see Figure 7.27). Each edge can be **Plain, Bevel**, or **Glow**, and can be **Center, Inside**, or **Outside**. The slider on the right controls the softening blur for each edge. The variations possible with five edges are nearing infinite. More than anyone could need. To turn on an edge you have to make sure that the checkbox for the panel you're working in is switched on.

The fifth panel sets up to five separate **Drop Shadows**. These can be either a standard **Drop**; a **Cast** shadow, which slopes away from the text; or a **Solid** shadow with sides (see Figure 7.28). **Drop** and **Cast** shadows don't have **Highlight** or **Shade** color, but they have a **Softness** control that appears when the shadow pop-up menu is changed. Each shadow also has controls for color, distance, opacity, and angle. As with edges be careful to turn on the checkbox for each of the shadows you want to include.

One major drawback of working with Boris Calligraphy is that while you're working in **Title 3D**, you cannot see the text composited on top of the image. Once you've created your text, drag it to the **Timeline** or **Superimpose** it over a clip that's already there.

If you need to change or adjust the text, double-click the **Title 3D** file in the **Timeline** to open it into the **Viewer**. Then click on the **Controls** tab to open all the controls for **Title 3D** (Figure 7.29).

To access the text window to change the letters or styles or any of the other controls, click on the **Title 3D** logo at the top of the controls panel.

Many of the features in **Title 3D's** controls panel were designed primarily as animation controls. Unfortunately these features are not available in FCE. Nonetheless the controls panel can be used to change the shape and position of the text.

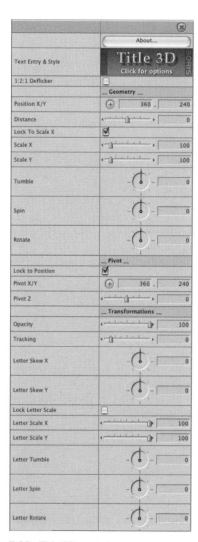

7.29 Title 3D controls

The **Geometry** section controls the text overall, changing:

- **Position**
- **Distance**
- **Scale**
- **Tumble**
- **Spin**
- **Rotate**

Although **Position** places the text in the screen, **Distance** makes the text appear nearer or farther away. The **Scale** value in this panel will allow you to get clean, large fonts. When working with **Title 3D**, scale your text here in this panel, not with **Scale** in the **Motion** tab.

Tumble, **Spin**, and **Rotate** will turn the entire text block around on the *x, y,* and *z* axes respectively. A nice thing about Calligraphy is that if you have a real-time capable system, most of these motion settings, including drop shadow, will preview in real time.

The **Pivot** section controls the point around which the text tumbles, spins, and rotates. If the **Lock to Position** box is checked, the controls have no effect. With the box checked, the text will rotate around the selected pivot point, which can be set with numeric values or with the crosshairs button. Neither the **Tumble** nor **Spin** controls function with the **X/Y** controls, but their movement is affected when the **Z** slider is activated.

The **Transformation** sections affects all of the letters in the text block, but it affects them individually. In Figure 7.30 the image on the left has its **Geometry** tumbled –45 and spun 50, and the image on the right has its **Transformation** tumbled –45 and spun 70. Notice that on the right each letter is moving, but on the left they are moving together.

Title Crawl

Title Crawl is accessed from the bottom of the **Generators** pop-up menu and shares many of the same controls as **Title 3D**. The text window that's evoked when **Title Crawl** is called up functions identically in both Calligraphy title tools. The difference is seen in

7.30 Geometry versus Transformation

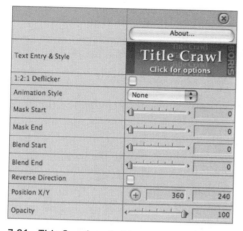

7.31 Title Crawl controls

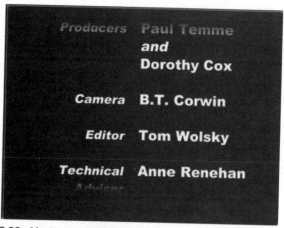

7.32 Masking and blending in scrolling title

the **Controls** tab of the **Viewer** (see Figure 7.31). Here there are far fewer options: no **Geometry**, no **Transformation**.

The **Animation** pop-up menu lets you set:

- **None**, the default
- **Roll (Scroll)**
- **Crawl**

Mask Start, Mask End, Blend Start, and **Blend End** are interesting controls. These allow the scroll to fade in as it comes in off the bottom of the screen and fade out as it disappears off the top (see Figure 7.32). **Mask Start** and **End** controls where on the screen the fades start and end. The **Blend Start** and **End** allows you to separately control the amount of fade at the top and bottom of the screen.

The **Reverse Direction** checkbox does just that, makes a roll reverse from the default bottom-to-top direction to top-to-bottom, and reverses direction of the standard right-to-left crawl to left-to-right.

To do a **Crawl,** a horizontal stream of text across the screen, first make sure **Word Wrap** is switched off.

The speed of the **Roll** or **Crawl** is determined by the amount of text in the text window and the duration of the text block in the **Timeline**: the longer the block, the slower the motion. You should be aware that thought that **Title 3D** is vector based, but **Title Crawl** is not. It produces bitmapped graphics.

🐾 **Note**

Interlace Flickering: If you're doing text animation on interlaced video, check the **1:2:1 Deflicker** box to reduce interlace flickering.

Outline Text's Background

Outline Text for the most part has been superseded by Title 3D, but it has one quite useful feature that can be used to created additional text elements for your graphics. In the lower portion of the **Outline Text** tool is a section to create a background, which defaults to being off (see Figure 7.33). You turn it on by increasing the horizontal and vertical size. The horizontal size acts in relationship to the amount of text you have—the less text, the less effect the horizontal value has; the more text, the farther the background extends. If you don't want any text but you do want to use the **Background** effect, type into the text panel a number of blank spaces, and press the spacebar a dozen or more times.

7.33 Outline Text background control

Horizontal and **Vertical Offsets** set the screen position relative to the text. If the text is set high in the screen, so is the background. On the other hand, with the text high in the screen and the **Vertical Offset** set to negative numbers, the background will be pulled down lower in the screen.

You can set the **Color**, **Softness**, and **Opacity** of the background. Notice also that you can put an image in here as a background using the **Well**, which we saw in Lesson 5 on page 122.

Nesting

The power of FCE's titling tools is in their great flexibility and the great amount of control you have over your graphic elements. In the project **Browser** is a sequence called *Title and Background*, which is made up of a number of FCE titling tools. The output appears in Figure 7.34, but if you open it in FCE, you'll see it in color. I'll show you how it was built up.

If you open the sequence *Title and Background*, you'll see that it is made up of two layers. On **V1** is a video clip twice, and on **V2** is a text block called *Title Composite* and another called *Title Composite Japan*. These are nests. Nesting is an important concept to understand in Final Cut. Because you can have sequences within sequences in FCE, you can also group layers together into nests to form a sequence of their own. You'll notice in the **Browser** there are sequences called *Title Composite* and *Title Composite Japan*. These are the elements that appear on **V2** in *Title and Background*. Let's build these nests together.

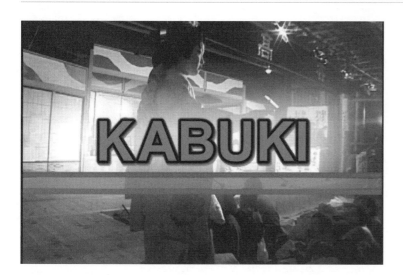

7.34 Title and Background

Text

1. Start by duplicating *Sequence 1* in the **Browser**. Select the sequence and use **Edit>Duplicate (Option-D)**.

2. Rename the sequence *Title Composite 2*, to distinguish it from the one that's already in the **Browser**.

3. Open the duplicate *Title Composite 2* by double-clicking on it or by selecting it and pressing **Return**. Delete anything that may be in the sequence.

4. In the **Viewer**, from the **Text Generator** pop-up menu select **Title 3D**.

5. Go to the second tab in the **Title 3D** window and change the pop-up menu to **Wrapping**.

6. Return to the first tab and type in *KABUKI*.

7. You can, of course, use whatever text, color, or settings you want, but this is how I built this image:

Font	Arial
Style	Bold
Point Size	96
Color Fill	muted red: R 200, G 68, B 88
Edge Style	Plain, Outside, Black
Edge Width	7
Edge Softness	2

8. When you've finished making the text, click the **Apply** button.

9. Immediately drag your newly created text block from the **Viewer** onto **V2** of your sequence, leaving **V1** empty for the moment.

10. Because the edge color is black, you won't be able to see it for the moment in the **Canvas'** blackness.

Background

1. In the **Viewer** create an Outline Text block selecting it in the **Generators** from **Text>Outline Text**.

7.35 Two text blocks in the Canvas

2. Drag it to **V1** and open the new Outline Text clip from the **Timeline** back into the **Viewer**. In the **Canvas** you'll see *Sample Text* behind *Kabuki* as in Figure 7.35.

3. Double-click on the Outline Text block in the **Timeline** to bring it back into the **Viewer**.

This is going to be the background white glow.

4. Go to the **Controls** tab and in the text block, press the spacebar 13 or 14 times; that is, type in 13 or 14 empty spaces. Use the default font size, which is fine.

We've now made a blank area of spaces for the background to work with. If we left the text area empty, there would be nothing for the horizontal and vertical background controls to be applied to.

5. Scroll to the **Background** controls and set the following:

7.36 Text and Background layer

Horizontal Size	200
Vertical Size	200
Back Soft	50 (blurs the background considerably)
Back Opacity	80

Your **Canvas** should like something like Figure 7.36.

6. Placing the cursor at the head of the **V1** track, anywhere near the locks or auto select buttons, hold down the **Control** key, and from the shortcut menu, select **Add Track** (see Figure 7.37).

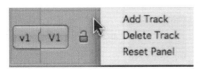

7.37 Adding tracks

7. Do this three times so that you have a total of three empty tracks between the two layers with the text blocks.

8. In the **Viewer** from the **Generators** button, select **Matte> Color,** as we did to make the color backing for the **Page Peel** transition in Lesson 5 on page 121. Again this will fill the screen with midtone gray.

9. Drag it to **Timeline** and place it on the empty **V2** you created.

10. Double-click the Color Matte in the sequence to open it back into the **Viewer.**

11. Go to the **Controls** tab and set the color to the same dark rose as the KABUKI title. Use the color picker if the title is visible in the **Canvas.** It should be if the playhead is sitting over the clips.

12. After setting the color, go to the **Motion** tab and twirl open the **Crop** controls (see Figure 7.38). I used these settings:

Top	66
Bottom	32
Opacity	75

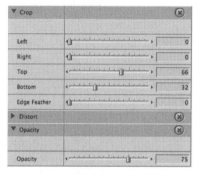

7.38 Crop and Opacity settings in Motion tab

We'll look at the other controls in the **Motion** tab in detail in the next lesson.

13. Open another **Color Matte,** and place it on the track above the red bar you just created.

14. Make the color of this matte green (**R** 20, **G** 96, **B** 19). You can access the system color picker by clicking on the swatch and choosing the **RGB** sliders to set your color values.

15. In the **Motion** tab set these **Crop** values:

Top	60
Bottom	38

16. We have one more color matte to make. Generate the matte and bring it to the sequence below the **Title 3D** block.

17. Set the same green color and these **Crop** values:

Top	70
Bottom	32

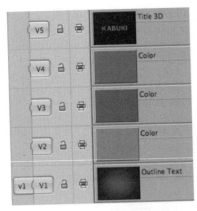

7.39 Timeline after making text and matte layers

Your sequence should have five layers in it (see Figure 7.39):

- Outline Text block on **V1**
- Three color mattes on the layers above
- At the top, the Title 3D block, the one that holds the text KABUKI.

Putting It All Together

1. Duplicate *Sequence 1*.
2. Open the duplicate and delete anything that may be in it.
3. Set **V1** as the destination track in the patch panel, and deselect the patching so there are no audio tracks.
4. From the **Clips** bin select the clip called *Kabuki3*. Use **Overwrite** in the **Canvas** or drag it directly onto **V1** of the empty sequence.
5. Move the playhead so that is over the clip on **V1**.
6. Drag *Title Composite 2* from the Browser to **Superimpose** in the **Canvas** to place it above the video clip.

Drop Shadow

You thought I forgot the drop shadow on KABUKI. Here is the beauty of nested sequences.

1. Double-click the nest. It opens as a whole separate sequence in a new tab in the **Timeline** window.
2. Double-click on the **Title 3D** block at the top to open it in the **Viewer.**
3. Go to the **Controls** tab, and open the text window by clicking on the **Title 3D** logo.
4. In the **Drop Shadow** tab check on the first box, select all the text, and in the panel enter these settings:

Color	Green: **R** 62, **G** 139, **B** 54		
Distance	4	Softness	3
Opacity	100	Angle	55°

5. Click the **Apply** button.

The drop shadow is done. Click back on the parent sequence, *Sequence 1*. You'll see the drop shadow there as well. This change will appear in every iteration of that sequence wherever it appears anywhere in my project.

Here's what else makes this beautiful: Suppose I've built this complex text block, and I want to change the actual text but nothing else.

1. Duplicate *Title Composite 2* in your **Browser**.
2. Change the name of the duplicate to *Title Composite Japan 2* and open it by double-clicking on it.
3. Double-click on the top Title 3D block to open it into the **Viewer**, and in the text window replace the word *KABUKI* with the word *JAPAN*.

Nothing else changes, just the text block and its drop shadow. Easy, isn't it?

A nested sequence is like a clip in a sequence. If you want to apply an effect to a nest or reposition the block—lower in the frame for instance—you can do this without adjusting each layer individually. We'll look at applying effects in a later lesson, as well as animating images about the screen.

Photoshop Titles

If the capabilities of these text and title tools aren't enough for you, there is always Photoshop or its younger brother Photoshop Elements. What great titlers these are, infinitely malleable, allowing you to create many additional graphical elements such as banners and bars and gradients. Although it could be done, it would be far more difficult to construct these items in FCE than in these great graphics applications. It seems that anything you can imagine is possible with these Adobe products.

What you should first know about working in Photoshop is that you should use only the RGB color space—no CMYK, no grayscale, no indexed color. They don't translate to video.

One problem with using Photoshop is the issue of square versus rectangular pixels. Because Photoshop is a computer program, it works in square pixels exclusively, but digital video uses rectangular pixels, tall, narrow pixels that allow for greater horizontal resolution. This presents a minor problem in the earlier versions of Photoshop, but it has been corrected with the release of Photoshop CS (version 8), which allows you to preview images with rectangular pixels and has guides for both Title and Action Safe areas. The important point is to understand how FCE2 handles still image files. It handles different types of images in different ways. Single-layer files are treated one way; Photoshop files with multiple layers or transparency are treated another way. Single-layer files are treated as graphics files, and FCE understands that they've come from a square-pixel world. Multilayer files are treated as sequences, and FCE would not presume to alter the dimensions of a sequence you created. It assumes that you did it correctly.

1. Because you're working in the DV format using rectangular pixels based on a frame resolution of 720×480 pixels, you should create your PSD (Photoshop) files at 720×540 to start with. This is a change from the previous version of FCE.

2. After you've made your graphic, go to **Image Size** and, making sure **Constrain Proportions** is deselected and **Bicubic** is selected, change the height of the image to 480.

This squashes the image down, distorting it, changing it to a file that FCE recognizes as using rectangular pixels.

3. Save your file.

I save a separate PSD file that has been converted to DV format and keep the original so I can correct the typos I usually make.

There are templates for these formats as well as for the 16:9 format in the *Extras* folder of the book's DVD. They have guides for the Safe Action Area and the Safe Title Area.

Format	Start Size	End Size
DV NTSC 4:3	720×540	720×480
DV NTSC 16:9 (anamorphic)	853×480	720×480
DV PAL	768×576	720×576
DV PAL 16:9 (anamorphic)	1,024×576	720×576

You're not always making a graphic that needs to fit in the video format. Sometimes you're making a graphic that is much larger, one you want to move around on to make it seem as you're panning across the image or zooming in or out of the image. To do this, you need to make the image much greater than your video format, perhaps 2,000×2,000 pixels or more.

If you are working with a Photoshop layered image, you still should squeeze the image down to rectangular pixels before you bring it into FCE. To do this, use percentages instead of pixel values, and reduce the height of the image to 90 percent or, if you want to be anally precise about it, 89.886 percent.

Again, you should not resize these images if they are single-layer images without Photoshop transparency. FCE understands that these are square-pixel images brought into the DV world and will handle them appropriately. If they are layered files with transparency, FCE treats these as separate sequences and does not adjust for square pixels. The rules of the road are probably unnecessarily complex, but the bottom line is that if it's a single-layer file, let FCE do the resizing; if it's a file with multiple layers or transparency, squeeze it before you import it.

➤ *Tip*_____

Bringing in the Layers: If you do bring your Photoshop sequence into Final Cut as layers and you decide you'd rather work with it as a single-layer file, use this easy trick: open the Photoshop sequence, and with the playhead over the layers, go to **Modify**＞**Make Freeze Frame** (**Shift-N**). That will make a still image of all the layers. You can drag that still image into the **Browser**, rename it, move it wherever you want, and use it again and again. What's nice about this technique is that it preserves the transparency of the Photoshop file; all the layers will be merged, but the transparency will remain intact. If you want to preserve the layers as individual images, select all the layers and drag them to the **Browser**. They will appear as individual images with their Photoshop layer names as in Figure 7.40. All the colored layers have been pulled out of the sequence *Multilayer.psd*.

7.40 **Layers pulled from inside a multilayer Photoshop file**

When you import an oversized Photoshop file and place it inside a sequence, FCE will scale the image. If the still is smaller than the image resolution—say, a 500×200 image in a 720×480 DV sequence—the application will place it in the center of the screen with blackness around it. If the image is 400 pixels wide but 800 pixels tall, FCE will scale it to fit inside the window, as in Figure 7.41. If you do want to use the image at its full size so that you can move across it, the first step you'll have to do is return it to its full size.

1. Select the image in the **Timeline** and press the **Return** key. Or **Option**-double-click on it to open it into the **Viewer**.

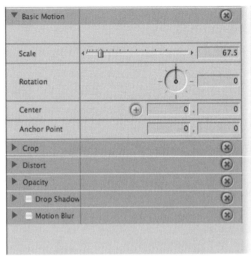

7.41 Large image in the Canvas showing scale in the Viewer

2. Click on the **Motion** tab in the **Viewer**.

3. Set the **Scale** value back to 100.

Resolution

For people who come from a print background, the important point to note is that video doesn't have a changeable resolution. It's not like print where you can jam more and more pixels into an inch of space and make your print cleaner, clearer, and crisper. Pixels in video occupy a fixed space and have a fixed size, the equivalent of 72dpi in the print world, which happens to be the Macintosh screen resolution. Dots per inch are a printing concern. Forget about resolution. Think in terms of size: the more pixels, the bigger the picture. Do not think that you can make an image 720×480 at a high resolution such as 300dpi or 600dpi and be able to scale it up and move it around in FCE. Certainly you'll be able to scale it up, but it will look soft, and if you scale it far enough—to 300 percent, for instance—the image will start to show pixelization. FCE is good at hiding the defects by blurring and softening, but the results are not really as good as they should be. FCE is a video application and deals only with pixel numbers, not with dpi.

Scanners, on the other hand, are designed for the print world where dpi is an issue. Because scanners generate lots and lots of pixels, this is very handy for the person working in video. This means that you can scan an image at, let's say, 300 or 600dpi, which is a quite small image, and your scanner will produce thousands and thousands of pixels, which will translate into video as a very large image. You now have an image that's much larger than your video format of 720×480 pixels. If your scanner can generate an image that's 2,880 pixels across, it's making an image four times greater than your DV video frame. You can now move that very large image around on the screen and make it seem as if a camera is panning across the image. Or you can scale back the image, and it will look as if the camera is zooming back from a point in the image. Or reverse the process and make it look as if the camera is zooming into the image. We'll look at these in Lesson 8, "Animation Effects," on page 197.

Working with a single-layer file within FCE has one advantage: it's simpler. One of the issues that arise with Photoshop sequences in Final Cut is the problem of doing transitions between them (see "Transitions between Sequences" on page 183).

➢**Tip**

Transitions with Still Images: If you want to put together a group of still images with transitions between them, you can simplify the process in a couple of ways. When you import the files, make sure you leave enough room in your **Still/Freeze Duration** preference to accommodate the transitions. Sequentially number the stills you want to import and place them into a separate folder on your hard drive. Next import all your stills as a single folder using **Import > Folder** so that they come in as a bin. Then drag the bin from the **Browser** straight to the **Edit Overlay** and drop on **Overwrite** (or **Insert**) with **Transition**. All the stills will miraculously dump out of the bin and appear in the **Timeline** with a cross dissolve between them. The technique works beautifully with flattened PSD files or other image formats such as PICT files.

Fading

Very often you'll want to fade in the graphic and fade it out again. Take another look at the sequence called *Title and Background*.

1. Click on the **Clip Overlay** button (**Option-W**), the button in the far lower-left corner on the **Timeline** window.

The files now have lines in them near the top. This is the opacity value of the clips. With the lines all the way to the top, their values are 100 percent. You'll notice that the line ramps down at the beginning and end of each of the graphics clips in the lesson sequence. This will fade in and fade out the **Opacity** from 0 to

Pulling Photoshop Effects

One problem many users encounter with Photoshop images is with effects applied in Photoshop, such as drop shadows to text layers or any of the hundreds of image effects the application can do. None of the effects seem to appear when the file is imported into FCE. The problem is that the effects are not applied to the image but exist as code attached to the file so they can be changed at any time without having to recreate the layer. It's like nondestructive editing in Final Cut. There is a way around this, however. Merge the layer with the effect into an empty layer. Make a new blank layer beneath each layer you want to rasterize; then

7.42 Merge Down

from the **Wing** menu of **Layers** palette choose **Merge Down**(see Figure 7.42). This fixes the effect with the image onto the empty layer. Of course, now the layer effects are no longer editable.

Another method, if you only have a few layers that you don't mind merging together, is to use **Merge Visible**. Create a blank layer at the bottom of the layer stack and press **Command-Option-Shift-E**. Unlike the normal **Merge Visible** from the Photoshop **Layer** menu, this keyboard command will not collapse the layers into a single layer but will copy the content of all the visible layers and merge them into the single blank layer. With this method you still have the editable layers in the Photoshop file. If you switch off the visibility for the upper layers in Photoshop, when the file is imported, the merge layer will be visible and the other layers will be present, but their track visibility will be switched off as it was in Photoshop.

This is something you should do at the very end: merge the layers as needed, and squish the file to its DV format, while keeping an original PSD file copy in its original format with the original images, text layers, and effects, separated and still editable.

100 and back again. This works exactly like the control we used for audio levels.

2. Grab the level line and pull it down. The overall level will change.

3. Use the **Pen** tool (**P**) to make opacity keyframes on the level line and to pull down the opacity as needed.

Also, the global **Levels** tool, **Sequence>Levels** (**Command-Option-L**), will also affect the levels of multiple video or title clips. We

Transitions between Sequences

Because FCE allows you to place sequences within sequences, such as these nested Photoshop or graphics sequences we've been working with here, it sometimes becomes necessary to create transitions between them. This presents some problems. FCE treats each sequence as a complete piece of media. So as we've seen, if you have used the media to its limits, you can't create a transition.

Though each layer in a Photoshop sequence can be any length you want, when the sequence is laid into another sequence, the final sequence assumes that the limit of the media is the limit of the nested sequence. It will not go burrowing into the nest to extend the media for each layer to make room for the transition.

So if you want to create a transition between sequences, you have to ripple the outgoing sequence and the incoming sequence to allow room for the transition.

saw this feature in Lesson 6, "Controlling Audio Levels" on page 136. Unlike audio keyframes, though, you can also smooth the opacity keyframes to ease into the fade by **Control**-clicking on the keyframe. In the sequence *Title and Background*, the first clip has had the fade smoothed, while the second has not.

➤ Tip

Fading Graphics: Another way I like to do a fade in or a fade out from a graphic is to lay a cross dissolve just before the edit point. If you place it too close to the edit, it will drop in as a one-frame dissolve, but if you place it slightly away from the edit, it will drop in as dissolve to the edit point, as in Figure 7.43. This only works if there aren't two graphics inline with each other, butted up one to the other.

7.43 Cross dissolve to fade out graphic

Summary

In this lesson we've looked at FCE's title tools, gone through Boris Calligraphy's **Title 3D** and **Title Crawl**, and brought Photoshop title files into Final Cut. But that isn't all there is to titling. There are still some issues with graphics images in FCE, particularly images in motion, that we'll look at in the next lesson on creating animation in Final Cut Express.

Lesson 8

Animating Images

Final Cut Express has considerable capabilities for animating images. It allows you to enhance your productions and create exciting, interesting and artistic scenes. In this lesson we will concentrate on FCE's motion capabilities.

Loading the Lesson

One more time, begin by loading the material you need onto your media drive.

1. Drag the *Media 6* folder from the DVD to your media hard drive.

2. Eject the DVD and launch the *Lesson 8* project which should be in the *Projects* folder on your hard drive.

3. Reconnect the media as in previous lessons.

Motion Window

Let's first take a look at how to create motion in Final Cut.

1. Open *Sequence 1*, which is, of course, empty.

2. We're going to deal only with video tracks for much of this lesson, so the first step, as we did in the previous lesson, will

be to switch off the destination tracks for **A1** and **A2**. In the patch panel click on the **a1/a2** buttons at the head of each track.

3. Next drag a clip—let's say *Archers1*—from the **Clips** bin and drop it onto **Overwrite** or **Insert** in the **Edit Overlay**.

Because the audio tracks were untargeted, only the video portion of the clip will appear in the **Timeline**.

4. Use the **View** pop-up menu at the top of the **Canvas** to select **Image+Wireframe** (see Figure 8.1).

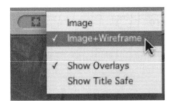

Select the clip in the **Timeline**, and the image in the **Canvas** will appear with a wireframe indicator. The large **X** through it defines the corners and boundaries (see Figure 8.2).

8.1   Canvas View pop-up menu

5. Double-click on the clip in the **Timeline** to open it in the **Viewer**, and then click on the **Motion** tab at the top to open it (see Figure 8.3).

Here are the motion elements that can be keyframed. Most of them, with the exception of **Opacity, Drop Shadow,** and **Motion Blur,** can be keyframed in the **Canvas**. We saw how to keyframe **Opacity** at the end of the last lesson. Once you start twirling open the little triangles, which the FCE manual calls *disclosure triangles,* you might need to stretch down the window.

Notice that each of the control panels—**Basic Motion, Crop, Distort, Opacity, Drop Shadow,** and **Motion Blur**—has a button with a red **X** on it. This allows you to reset the values for that parameter.

8.2   Image+Wireframe clip in the Canvas

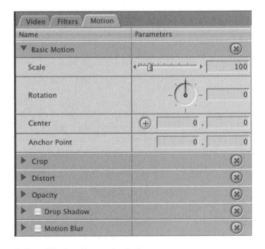

8.3   Motion Control window

Keyframing

The basic concept of keyframing is that you mark the properties for a clip at a particular frame. You mark it by setting a *keyframe*. If you go further forward or backward in time by moving the playhead and change the parameter values for the clip, another keyframe will automatically be set. The application calculates how fast it has to change the values to go from one state to the other. If the keyframes are far apart in time, the change will be gradual. If the keyframes are closer together, then the change will be more rapid.

It's easy to set a keyframe in FCE. With the clip selected in the **Timeline**, click the **Keyframe** button (the little diamond at the bottom right of the **Canvas**), or press the keyboard shortcut **Control-K** (see Figure 8.4).

8.4   Keyframe button

This sets an initial keyframe for those properties in the **Motion** tab that are keyframeable. It will not set keyframes for **Opacity** or for **Drop Shadow**. When a keyframe is set, the wireframe for the clip turns green in the **Canvas**. The wireframe will also display a number that indicates the track number of the track where the clip is.

To delete a keyframe that you've set, **Control**-click on the image in the **Canvas** and select **Delete** point from the shortcut menu (see Figure 8.5).

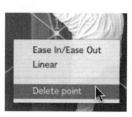

8.5   Keyframe shortcut menu

Let's look at the parameters in the **Motion** tab that can be keyframed and what you can do with them.

Scale

The first keyframeable property in the **Motion** window is **Scale**, a simple slider and value box that lets you set a size. Because FCE deals exclusively in bitmapped images, stills, video, and text files made up of pixels, it's generally not a good idea to scale upwards, not much above 110–120 percent.

➤**Tip**

Controlling Sliders: Because there is so little travel in the slider's useful range, I usually use it while holding down the **Command** key, which gives smaller increments of movement. The **Command** key works like this in many drag movements in FCE, such as dragging clips to lengthen and shorten them in the **Timeline**. If you hold down the **Shift** key, you'll get increments up to two decimal places.

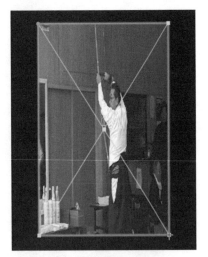

8.6 Image scaling distorted

While the sliders and value boxes in the **Motion** tab give you precise control, the easiest way to scale or control the other motion parameters is in the **Canvas**. With the **Canvas** set to **Image+Wireframe**, grab one of the corners and drag. The image will, by default, scale proportionately. If you want the image to be distorted, hold down the **Shift** key while you drag (see Figure 8.6).

If you hold down the **Command** key while you drag an image's corner to scale it, you add the **Rotation** tool so that you can scale and rotate at the same time.

Rotation

Rotation is controlled with the clock dial or with values.

There is a limit on how far you can take rotation. No more than 24 rotations seems possible. To get there, you can either:

- Keep dialing in more and more turns of the screw or
- Type in a value

Each notch of the "hour" hand is one revolution. It would be nice if separate value boxes for revolutions and degrees had been included. At the moment, you either have to:

- Twist the dial around and around lots of times or
- Calculate, such as 22 revolutions times 360 degrees equals 7,920 degrees

By the way, 24 revolutions are 8,640 degrees.

As with **Scale**, **Rotation** can be created in the **Canvas**. As you move the cursor near one of the edges of the image, it changes into a rotation tool (see Figure 8.7). You can grab the image and swing it around the anchor point, which we'll see in a minute. For the moment, rotation is happening around the middle of the image. It's a little easier to rotate the image if you grab nearer the corner, but don't get too close or you'll grab the **Scale** point.

8.7 Rotation tool

> **Tip**_____
> **Rotation Tip:** Holding down the **Shift** key will constrain the dial to 45-degree increments, and holding down the **Command** key will give you a little finer control over the movement of the dial.

Center

Center is the position of the clip, where the image is on the screen. FCE counts the default center position, 0,0, and counts outwards from there, minus x to the left, plus x to the right, minus y upwards, plus y downwards. The crosshairs allow you to position an image with a click in the **Canvas**.

Straight Motion

Let's set up a simple motion for a clip. You should have the clip *Archers1* at the beginning of an empty sequence.

1. If you have done any movement to the clip, reset the parameters by clicking on the red **X** buttons in the **Motion** tab.

2. Make sure that the **Canvas** is in **Image+Wireframe** and that the playhead is back at the start of the sequence.

We're now going to move the clip off the screen.

3. If you need to position an image outside of the **Canvas**, first reduce the size of the display in the **Canvas** with the **Zoom** pop-up menu (see Figure 8.8) to something like 25 percent. You might want to stretch out the **Canvas** a little. This will show you the grayboard around the image.

4. Grab the image and move it off the screen (see Figure 8.9). Or use the Center crosshairs to click on a point out in the grayboard.

5. Once the clip is positioned off the screen, use **Control-K** to set a keyframe or click the **Keyframe** button in the bottom right of the **Canvas**.

6. Go forward five seconds in time. To move the playhead exactly, make sure the clip in the **Timeline** is deselected (**Command-Shift-A**) and type **+5.** and press **Return**. You'll see the playhead in the **Timeline** move. You can also hold down the **Shift** key and tap on the **Right** arrow key five times to move forward five seconds.

7. Drag the clip across the screen to the other side, creating a line with a string of dots on it.

You have created a straight linear motion of the image across the screen (see Figure 8.10). Notice that while at the first keyframe the wireframe was green, at the second keyframe only the dot in the center of the wireframe is green. This is because only the **Center** position value has changed.

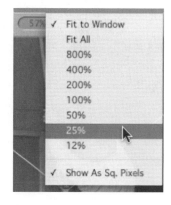

8.8   Zoom pop-up menu

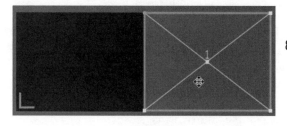

8.9   Moving an image off the screen

> **Tip**
>
> **Straight Lines:** If you hold down the **Shift** key while you drag the image, its movement will be constrained to right angles, either straight horizontally or straight vertically, depending on which direction you drag the clip.

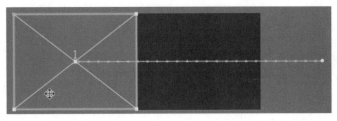

8.10 Linear motion path

8.11 Curved motion path

➤**Tip**
Navigation Tips

Tip 1: In the **Canvas**, the center point turns green when the playhead is on the keyframe. It's visible only when the clip is selected. When the clip isn't selected, there is no indicator.

Tip 2: If you are moving a clip or multiple clips off the screen, it's handy to use **Fit All** from the **Zoom** pop-up menu. This will adjust the **Canvas** to include all the clips off the screen.

Tip 3: The spacing of the little dots along the motion path indicates the speed of the motion. If the dots are bunched together, the motion is slow, whereas if they're more separated from each other, the motion is fast.

Curved Motion

There are two ways to create a curved path:

- Pull out the path from the linear motion.
- Create a curved path by using Bezier handles.

In the first method, when you place the cursor on the line, it changes from the regular **Selection** tool into the **Pen** tool. You can drag out the line so that it's a curve (see Figure 8.11). This creates a new keyframe.

Notice also the two bars sticking out from the dot on the curve. The bars have two handles each, represented by little dots, one slightly darker than the other. These bars are the Bezier handles.

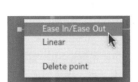

8.12 Ease In/Ease Out menu

The second method doesn't create an intermediate keyframe. There are normally no handles to adjust the arc on either the start point or the end point of the motion. You can quickly add these by **Control**-clicking on the point and selecting **Ease In/Ease Out** from the shortcut menu (see Figure 8.12).

When you select **Ease In/Ease Out,** the handles appear. These can be used to pull the line into an arc (see Figure 8.13). Unfortunately, the handles are quite small, and minor adjustments can have a major impact on the motion path. The outer handles allow you to adjust the arc of the curve. Each side of arc can be adjusted separately to make complex movements.

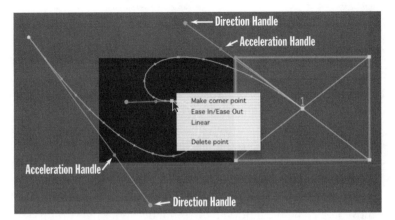

8.13 Curved motion with Bezier handles

Changing Speed

Normally objects don't arrive at speed instantly, nor do they stop instantly; so if your image is starting or stopping on the screen, you probably want it to accelerate or decelerate rather than jerking into motion. In graphics animation this is called *easing*: you ease into a motion, and you ease out of a motion. This is what the darker set of points, halfway along the Bezier handles, do. These are the ***acceleration handles***. They control the speed at which the image moves through the keyframe, the rate of deceleration as it approaches the keyframe, and the acceleration as it leaves the keyframe. If you want the motion to smoothly pass through the point without changing speed, make sure those handles are not moved, or **Control**-click on the keyframe and choose **Linear**. If you pull the handles apart, the motion will be faster. If you push the handles inward toward the keyframe point, the motion will slow down. The image will decelerate as it comes to the keyframe and then accelerate away. In the sequence in your **Browser** called *Curved Motion Path* I have created a simple motion path that shows this. On a slower computer you might have to render this out, depending on your **RT** settings.

You'll clearly see the deceleration and acceleration as the image passes through the intermediate keyframe. Notice that the image moves much quicker in the first part of the movement and slower in the second portion. This happens because the first portion of the movement is shorter both in time and distance.

➤Tip
Adjusting Bezier Handles: If you want to make the curves or the motion even more complex, you can adjust each end of the Bezier handles independently. If you hold down the **Command** key and grab a handle, it will move separately from the other (see Figure 8.14).

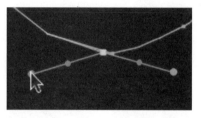

8.14 Separate Bezier control handles

8.15 Using the Hand tool to move a motion path

8.16 Anchor point moved with the Distort tool

One great feature of FCE is the ability to move the entire motion path you've created. You can move the whole path as a single entity to whatever position on the screen you want. This can be very useful if you've made a horizontal movement—say, left to right across the screen—that slides a clip through the upper portion of the screen. Later you decide it would be better for it to slide across the lower portion of the screen. Rather than resetting all the motion path keyframes, simply move the entire path. To do this, make sure the **Canvas** is in **Image+Wireframe** mode. Hold down **Command-Shift,** and when the cursor is over the clip, it will change to the **Hand** tool (see Figure 8.15). Grab the clip and move it. The whole motion path will move as a single group.

Anchor Point

The anchor point is the pivot point around which the image swings. It's also the point around which scaling takes place. For some reason that escapes me, **Anchor Point**, unlike **Center**, does not have crosshairs for positioning it. Fortunately there is a way to move it in the **Canvas** (see Figure 8.16).

1. Select the **Distort** tool (keyboard **D** for distort) and grab the center point of the clip. Drag it to where you want to position the anchor point. The point you're moving with this tool is actually the anchor point.

We'll look at the **Distort** tool on page 194.

➤Tip
Anchor Point Keyframe: If the clip is deselected, the anchor point keyframe is not indicated in the **Canvas**. If the clip is selected, however, the track number will turn green to show that the playhead is over an anchor point keyframe.

2. Apply a rotation to the image.

Notice that it doesn't swing around the center of the image but around this new point. If you pull it out to the upper-right corner, that's where the image will pivot. Take a look at *Anchor Point Sequence.* Two images swing through the frame with opposing anchor points.

Notice also that on the second clip, I have animated the center as well as repositioning the anchor point. It moves slightly differently, more tumbling than simply rotating. Be careful with animating multiple parameters: once the anchor point has been moved, it can lead to unexpected results.

Other Motion Controls

Crop

Crop allows you to cut the image from the sides. This can be done with the controls hidden under the twirly disclosure triangle (see Figure 8.17) that we used in the previous lesson.

If you have specific values, or if you want to reduce the image by precise amounts—such as equally from all sides—then this is place to do it. To crop in the **Canvas**, you'll need to use the **Crop** tool. The **Crop** tool is in the tools and can be called up with the letter **C**, just as in Photoshop (see Figure 8.18). As with the other motion controls in the **Canvas**, it will work only while you're in **Image+Wireframe**.

The **Crop** tool in Final Cut doesn't work very much like Photoshop's. You can't simply drag a marquee across the image to define the section you want to keep.

1. Select the image, and with the **Crop** tool grab one edge of the image.

As the tool gets near the edge, it changes into the **Crop** icon, indicating that the cursor is acting in **Crop** mode.

2. Grab the edge and pull in the image to crop (see Figure 8.19). Or you can grab the corner and crop adjacent sides at the same time.

Notice at the bottom of the **Crop** control panel the slider for **Edge Feather**. This softens the edges of the image and can be very attractive, particularly when there are multiple images on the screen (see Figure 8.20).

➤ *Tip*_____
Double Crop: If you hold down the **Command** key while you drag one edge of the image with the Crop tool, the opposite side will be cropped equally. And if you use the **Command** key and drag from one of the corners, you can crop all four sides proportionately and simultaneously.

➤ *Tip*_____
Crop Line: If the clip is selected in the timeline, then when the playhead reaches a Crop keyframe, the crop line shows as mauve. If the clip is not selected, no indicator appears in the **Canvas**.

8.17 Crop controls

8.18 Crop tool

8.19 Cropping the image in the Canvas

8.20 Two clips in the Canvas cropped and feathered to 80 *(left)*

8.21 Distort control panel *(below)*

▼ Distort		⊗
Upper Left	−360 ,	−240
Upper Right	360 ,	−240
Lower Right	360 ,	240
Lower Left	−360 ,	240
Aspect Ratio	◄—————▯—————►	0

Distort

This tool allows you to squeeze or expand the image, either maintaining its shape or pulling it apart. Be careful, though. Remember that these are pixels you're dealing with, and making pixels bigger will make them blocky and ugly. What's remarkable is how much you can distort the image and still get away with it. As with other tools there are two or more places to do everything. We already saw one way to distort the image by grabbing a corner with the Selection tool and dragging the image around while holding down the **Shift** key. This distortion alters the aspect ratio of the image but maintains its rectangular shape. This can also be done with the slider at the bottom of the **Distort** control panel (see Figure 8.21).

Moving the **Aspect Ratio** slider to the left, into negative numbers, will squeeze the image vertically so it mashes down into a narrow slit. Pulling the slider to the right into large positive numbers will squeeze it horizontally, so that it's a tall, thin image. The slider ranges from −1,000 to 1,000. The image can't be squeezed until it's gone, but it does come close.

You could dial in values into the corner-point boxes, which will move the corner points to any position you want, but the easiest way to use **Distort** is with the **Distort** tool, which is underneath **Crop** in the tools. Select it with the D key.

The **Distort** tool lets you grab a corner in the **Canvas** and pull it around and really mess the image up (see Figure 8.22).

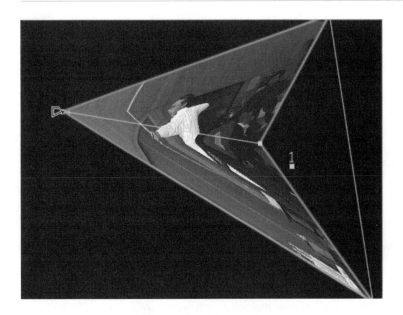

8.22   Distorted image in the Canvas

Anything becomes possible with these kinds of tools. Now that images are digital, they can be twisted and distorted, shaped and sized, and blended any way you can imagine. I hope you see the potential for creating almost any transition you can imagine.

I've made a simple one using **Distort, Scale,** and **Center** animation. Look at *Transition Sequence.* That's only the beginning. A few pulls on **Distort** tool, a little scaling, and the image shoots off. If you apply motion or any other effects to a clip, the whole clip has to be rendered out, even if for the greater part of its duration, all the values remain at default.

The simplest way to get around this problem is to cut the clip—**Control-V** or **Blade**—and separate the normal section from the twisted section. You can see what I did in *Transition Sequence.* Just be careful you don't move elements around so that the two parts get dislocated from each other.

There are still a few more elements to look at in the **Motion** panel. **Opacity** is next.

Opacity

This effect is pretty obvious. The transparency of the image decreases from a 100 percent opaque to zero opacity. It's a useful way to do simple fades, as we saw in the **Timeline** with titles in the previous lesson on page 181. Whatever is adjusted in the

> **➤Tip**
>
> **Proportional Distortion:** If you use the **Distort** tool and grab one corner while holding down the **Shift** key, you will distort the image proportionately. Dragging the upper-left corner in, for instance, will make the upper-right corner move inward the same amount. It's a easy way to create perspective. It's also an easy way to bend the image inside out so half of it is flipped over on itself.

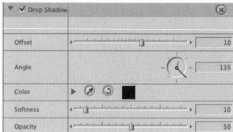

8.23 Drop shadows against white matte *(left)*

8.24 Drop Shadow control *(below)*

Timeline with the **Pen** tool will also appear reproduced here. Using the **Pen** tool, you can fade video in and out the same way you can audio.

Drop Shadow

Drop Shadow gives a multilayered image a three-dimensional appearance. It gives titles and moving images some depth and separation (see Figure 8.23). FCE's **Drop Shadow** is pretty basic, but it works fine. The control panel has all the expected features of **Offset**, **Angle** of offset, shadow **Color**, **Softness**, and **Opacity** (see Figure 8.24). Note that **Drop Shadow** has to be activated with the little checkbox in the upper-left corner of the control panel.

What might seem puzzling about the **Offset** slider is that it goes into to negative numbers. Just ignore those and use **Angle** to set the direction of the shadow.

The **Angle** control lets you change the direction in which the shadow drops onto the underlying layers.

Softness lets you control the amount of blurring on the edges of the shadow. Though the slider goes up to 100, I'm quite disappointed in how little effect it has. Shadow softness in FCE reaches no more than about 10 percent into the shadow area, so you're forced to rely on **Opacity** to soften the shadow area, which is not the same look. It lacks the subtlety of other compositing applications.

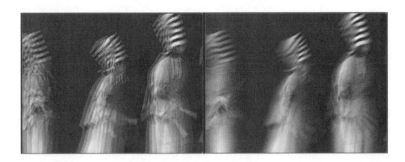

8.25 Motion Blur set to 1,000 with four samples on the left and 32 samples on the right

The default drop shadow settings work well for stills and other large images, but not so well for text. If you're using this drop shadow with the basic **Text** tool, you should bring down the **Offset** value and push up the **Opacity** value. For thin objects such as text, the first is too high and the second too low. Better yet, use **Title 3D** and make your drop shadow there.

Motion Blur

Motion Blur is also activated with a checkbox in the upper left of its control panel. Figure 8.25 shows FCE's **Motion Blur** at a setting of 1,000 with four samples and with 32 samples. This was created by applying **Motion Blur** to a panning shot. It gives the clip the appearance of great speed because of the added blur. Sampling goes down to 1, which produces no **Motion Blur** at all. The stepping that occurs in the lower sampling rates is ugly and best avoided. The low sample settings can be used, though, to produce interesting effects in images that contain fast-moving objects. You will see a ghosting effect as the object moves through the screen.

Use **Motion Blur** if you're trying to make it look as though your animations are moving very quickly, but be warned that **Motion Blur** adds considerable time to all renders. It's a very long and slow calculation for each frame. If you are going to apply it, always add it last, just before you're finally going to render out your sequence.

Animation Effects

Pan and Scan

Pan and scan, or the Ken Burns effect, are slang terms for doing motion on large-size images such as stills. I have set up a sequence that illustrates some of the problems. If you open *Pan Sequence*,

> **Tip**
> **Moving between Keyframes:**
> Because keyframes aren't visible in the application, it's sometimes difficult to find them. In addition to keyframes being sticky if you have **Snapping** turned on, you can also use keyboard shortcuts to move between them. **Shift-K** will take you to the next keyframe, and **Option-K** will take you to the previous keyframe.

you'll see that it contains four copies of a still image. It's a PICT file called *Pict*, but it could as easily be a Photoshop file, Targa file, or TIFF. I try to work with PICT files for single-layer images because they're simpler to deal with in FCE. *Pict* is a very large image, much larger than our **Canvas**. It's 1,494×1,098.

In the previous lesson, I said you should forget about image resolution as far as video is concerned and think only in numbers of pixels. In the print world for which scanners are designed, resolution is critically important. If you're scanning images such as this one to use in FCE, you can scan it at a high resolution, like 300 or 600dpi. Ideally you'd want to calculate the area you're going to zoom into based on an image that's a multiple of 720 pixels across at 72dpi. Often it's simpler just to scan more than you need and adjust it in Photoshop or even leave it to Final Cut. By scanning at high resolutions, the scanner will make lots of pixels. FCE will translate this into a very large image, not a small image at high resolution as a print system would do.

In *Pan Sequence*, I've panned and scanned *Pict* four times. Look at them one at a time. On real-time systems, these movements will not need rendering to play back on the computer screen.

1. In the first, the image starts out center in the screen and zooms into a point in the upper-right corner of the image.

A couple of problems are apparent:

- The image jerks into motion; acceleration is not smooth.
- The zoom-in seems to get slower and slower as it progresses.

This latter is a difficult problem and pretty much impossible to deal with when using the **Motion** controls in FCE. It is totally unnatural and the bane of trying to create motion that looks like a camera moving over an image and zooming as it goes.

2. To try to solve the jerking problem, I applied **Ease In/Ease Out** to the keyframes in the second copy of *Pict*.

This obviously isn't going to work. The smoothing rate of **Scale** and the **Ease In/Ease Out** rate of center-point animation are different so that the image shoots off the **Canvas** and slowly comes back into frame.

3. The third version of *Pict* compromises by limiting how far into the corner the keyframes allow the motion to go. By leaving room for easing to overrun and swing back, the move is more acceptable. At least it doesn't shoot off the **Canvas**.

Scaling takes place around the anchor point, so if you scale to zoom and pan off to one corner at the same time, the image is moving farther and farther away from the point on which the scale is changing.

4. In the fourth animation, to try and get around this problem and the problem of the mismatched animations, another animation is added, the anchor point, which is not normally animated. Using the **Distort** tool I dragged out the anchor point so that rather than moving farther and farther off the screen as the image moved, it remained centered in the screen. This produces a different result, not great, but acceptable, still sometimes subject to overshoot, especially on very large images.

The bottom line is you have three basic choices:

*   Live with the jerky motion and lack of acceleration and deceleration.
*   Apply easing to the center keyframes and leave room for the overshoot on the zoom in.
*   Or animate the anchor point as well to try and compensate for the overshoot.

Which one you use probably depends on the situation. Sometimes one might work better rather than another.

Animating Text Files

The problems of pan and scale apply equally to animating text files, such as titles created in FCE. As with graphics files, you don't want to scale images up, because the text becomes pixelated (see Figure 8.26).

8.26 Text at 48 point scaled to 300

So use a larger size and scale down, you say. That works up to a point. But what if the point size is larger than the screen and you scale down? Figure 8.27 shows what happens.

The text is cut off. So how do you solve this? There is unfortunately no good way to do this with the tool set FCE provides. You can't animate the text so that it's larger than the screen and scales down. The only way to do this is to generate a large text image in Photoshop or Photoshop Elements or some other imaging application and bring that into FCE and animate the scale there.

8.27 Text at 200 point scaled to 70

Split Screen

This is a common request for all sorts of purposes, for showing parallel action such as two sides of a phone conversation or to show a wide shot and a closeup in the same screen. It's easy to do if the video was specifically shot for a split screen. For a phone conversation, for instance, it should be shot so that one person in the phone conversation is on the left side of the frame and the other person on the right side of the screen.

Take a look at *Split Screen Sequence* in your **Browser**. Don't bother rendering it out; they're just still frames. In the first clip, Rich was shot on the left of the screen and Anita on the right. I had to crop the picture of Anita from one side, and because neither image left enough space for the other person, I had to move Rich farther to the left and Anita farther to the right.

8.28 Split Screen with bar

Some people like to add a bar that separates the two images as in Figure 8.28. That's easy to do. Use the **Generators** to create a color matte and place it on the top track, as in *Split Screen Sequence*. Crop the matte left and right so that only a narrow stripe is visible over the join of the two frames.

Picture in Picture

By now you've probably figured out how to make a PIP, a Picture in Picture. You just scale the image down to the desired size and position it wherever you want on the screen.

One note of caution about PIPs: many video formats, such as DV, leave a few lines of black on the edges of the frame, as we saw when doing transitions. These are normally hidden in the overscan area of your television set and never seen. However, as soon as you start scaling down images and moving them about the screen, the black line becomes apparent. The easiest solution is to take the **Crop** tool and slightly crop the image before you do your PIP so as not to get the black lines, which give the video an amateur look. You might also want to add a border to the PIP to set it off, but that's for Lesson 9 when we look at "Bevel Border " on page 217.

A nice touch to add to PIPs is to give them a drop shadow from the **Motion** tab. This will help to separate it from the underlying image and give a screen a sense of three dimensionality.

Brady Bunch Open

This is one of the classic opens on American television. It's relatively easy to reproduce in Final Cut Express using the techniques we've learned here.

In the **Browser** is a clip called *BB.mov*. Play through it. This is the sequence we're going to build. It's based on the timing of the original show's open. If you know the Brady Bunch song, sing along. In building this sequence, we'll use still images rather than movie clips to conserve storage space.

1. Open the *Brady Bunch Sequence*.

2. You'll probably have to render it out to play it at real speed, but it shouldn't take very long. Or use **Option-P** to play through the sequence as quickly as your computer can.

We're going to replicate this sequence. Look through it closely to get an idea of where we're going.

3. Make a copy of the *Brady Bunch Sequence* and open it. This sequence has markers set in where events will occur.

4. Use **Command-A** to select everything in the sequence and delete it.

5. To begin, you might want to lay *BB.mov* on **V1** in your **Timeline** and lock the track. That way, it can act as a guide.

Sliding White Bar

The first step we have to take is to create the white bar that slides across the screen. Easy enough.

1. Make a color matte. In **Controls,** change the color from the default gray to full white.

2. This bar moves across the screen very quickly. So set the duration to about two seconds. You'll need even less than that, but if you make it too short it may be difficult to work with in the **Timeline**.

3. Crop the top and bottom with the **Crop** tool in the **Canvas**. In the **Crop** controls, the **Top** value is 48.75 and the **Bottom** value is 47.92, creating a narrow bar. You could bring it into the **Timeline** first and then bring it back to the **Viewer** to crop it, but we know we're going to create a thin white line, so we may as well do it before loading it into your work sequence.

4. Drag the bar onto **V3,** leaving a video track free below it.

I'm assuming that you've placed *BB.mov* on **V1** as a guide and have locked that track.

5. Slide the bar off the screen to the left so that you start in black. Its coordinates should be *x* –720, *y* 0.

6. Keyframe the white bar with the **Keyframe** button at the bottom of the **Canvas.**

7. Move the playhead to about 22 frames into the sequence.

8. Using *BB.mov* as a guide, slide the bar across the screen to its end position, which is when about half the bar is off the screen on the right side. Hold down the **Shift** key as you slide it to constrain the movement to horizontal. Its **Center** coordinates should now be *x* 360, *y* 0.

9. Use the **Pen** tool on the **Opacity** overlay in the **Timeline** to fade out the white bar over three or four frames.

10. When you're done with the **Pen** tool, return to the **Selector** (**A** for arrow).

Remember that although keyframes are invisible in the **Timeline**, if **Snapping** is turned on as you drag the playhead through the sequence, it will snap to keyframes inside the clips.

Fixing the Headshot

1. Open the bin in your **Browser** called **Graphics.**

It's probably best to leave it open. In the **Graphics** bin are the headshots of this sequence and the image for the pan and scan sequence we dealt with earlier. These are mostly PICT files and a few titles made with Title 3D. We'll get to those later on page 209.

2. Drag *HeadshotPink.pct* to **V2** to the point where the bar stops and begins fading out (see Figure 8.29).

Obviously at this point the headshot will fill the frame with the white bar over it. What we have to do is scale down and reposition the headshot.

3. Grab one corner of the headshot in the **Canvas** and pull it in.

4. Grab the image and slide it to the right so it's positioned under the bar (see Figure 8.30). I scaled it down to 52.3 percent and positioned it to *x* 166, *y* 0.

Next we have to crop the image.

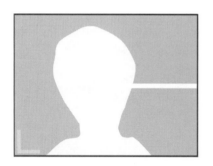

8.29 Headshot and white bar

8.30 Scaled and positioned headshot

5. Select the **Crop** tool from the tools (keyboard shortcut **C** for crop). With the **Crop** tool, pull in the left and right edges a little bit.

6. Crop the top and bottom until the headshot is a narrow slit hidden underneath the bar. Or hold down the **Command** key as you drag with the **Crop** tool to proportionately crop the image from both top and bottom. The settings used in the sequence are:

Left	6.38	Top	50
Right	11.28	**Bottom**	50

7. Select the clip and set a keyframe in the **Canvas**.

8. Go forward about 14 frames in the timeline. With the **Canvas** active, type *+14* and press the **Return key**.

Be careful you don't do this in the **Timeline**, because if you don't drop any selected clips, you'll move them 14 frames in the **Timeline** rather than moving the playhead 14 frames.

9. Pull open the top and bottom crop lines to the full height of the image or in the **Motion** tab set the **Top** and **Bottom** crop values to 0.

You've made the first part of the animation: the bar slides across the screen, stops, and fades out, and the headshot wipes open to reveal the picture. Don't worry about the lengths of the clips yet. We'll fix that later.

Middle Headshots

Now we're ready to bring in the next set of headshots.

1. Go down to Marker 1 in the timeline.

Shift-Down Arrow takes you to the next marker; **Shift-Up Arrow** takes you to the previous marker. This is where the three headshots of the girls appear on the left.

2. From the **Graphics** bin, drag in the image *HeadshotGreen.pct* and place it on **V3**, the track above the pink headshot.

3. Again, first we have to scale and position it so that it's in the lower-left corner of the screen. The settings I used are:

Scale	29.59
Center	x –231, y 147
Crop Right	3.85

4. Then we need to fade in the image in the **Timeline** with the **Pen** tool (**P**).

This again is a fairly quick fade-in, about 14 frames.

5. Select the clip in the **Timeline**.

6. Now **Option-Shift**-drag from **V3** to **V4** to make a copy of the clip on the track above.

7. Repeat to place a third copy on **V5**.

At this stage, all three copies of *HeadshotGreen.pct* are on top of each other.

8. Select the clip on **V4** and in the **Canvas** drag it upward, holding down the **Shift** key to constrain direction, and position the image about the center line of the screen.

9. Repeat for the clip on **V5**, dragging it up vertically to the top third of the screen. I used these **Center** position settings for the three layers:

V5	x –231, y –148
V4	x–231, y –1
V3	x –231, y 147

At Marker 2, where the fade-ups on the green headshots end, the screen should look like Figure 8.31.

Extending

So far so good. Next you should extend the image files in the timeline all the way down to Marker 3. You could drag them out to Marker 3 with the **Selector** tool (**A**), or you could do an Extend edit.

1. Position the playhead at Marker 3.

2. **Command**-click on the edit points at the end of each clip in the **Timeline**.

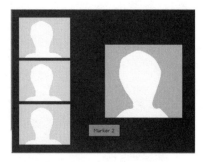

8.31 Four headshots on screen, Marker 2

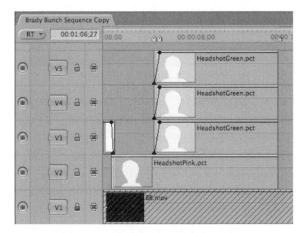

8.32 Timeline at Marker 3 *(left)*

8.33 Auto Select buttons *(right)*

3. Press **E** to do an Extend edit.

Voilà. All the clips will be extended to Marker 3, as shown in Figure 8.32.

At Marker 3, all four shots end, and we cut to black, but not for long. Next we have to bring in a new white bar from the right side.

4. Copy the white line from the beginning and paste it at the next marker on **V3**. To do this, make sure that the **Auto Select** buttons for **V1** and **V2** are switched. The easiest way to do this is to **Option**-click on the **Auto Select** button on **V3**. The buttons should look like (see Figure 8.33).

The line will appear with all its motion and opacity just like the first time you made it. The only problem is that it's moving in the wrong direction.

5. Open the copied clip at Marker 4 into the **Viewer**.

6. Holding down the **Shift** key, slide the clip in the **Canvas**, which should still be in **Image+Wireframe** mode, across the screen to the other side.

This is the bar's new start position at *x* 720, *y* 0.

7. Go to the point where the fade-out begins, which should also be the bar's second Center keyframe. Scrub in **Timeline** until the playhead snaps to it.

8. Slide the bar to the left to its end position, mirrored from the first time you did it. The Center position should be *x* –360, *y* 0.

8.34 Paste attributes

9. Select the clip *HeadshotPink.pct* that's on **V2** and copy it.

10. From the **Graphics** bin, drag *HeadshotBlue.pct* onto **V2** in the **Timeline,** placing it at the point where the bar begins its fade-out.

11. With *HeadshotBlue.pct* selected in the **Timeline,** go to the **Edit** menu and choose **Paste Attributes (Option-V)**. This brings up the dialog box in Figure 8.34.

12. Select **Basic Motion** and **Crop** from the dialog box. Because we've lengthened *HeadshotPink.pct*, make sure that the checkbox at the top of the window for **Scale Attribute Times** is deselected. The default is for the box to be checked.

This duplicates the position and animation of the earlier shot. This ability to copy the attributes of a clip and to paste these attributes to one or more clips, pasting the copied clip's motion, filter, and audio settings is a very powerful tool in Final Cut Express.

Now all we have to do is reposition the clip to the left side of the screen.

13. Holding down the **Shift** key, slide the image in the **Canvas** to the left so that it's underneath the white bar.

Adding More Headshots

1. Jump down to Marker 5 and bring in the clip *HeadshotRed.pct* from the **Graphics** bin and place it on **V3**.

2. Copy the green headshot that's earlier on **V3**.

3. Select the new red headshot and again use **Paste Attributes (Option-V)**.

4. Apply **Basic Motion, Crop,** and **Opacity** with **Scale Attribute Times** deselected, as previously.

Now reposition its center so that it's on the opposite side of the screen.

5. Again, **Option-Shift**-drag the copies of the clip from **V3** to **V4** and **V5**.

6. Holding down the **Shift** key to constrain movement, reposition the clips so that they appear one above the other on the

right side of the screen. The **Center** values I used for these three shots are:

V5	x 215, y –148
V4	x 215, y –1
V3	x 215, y 147

7. Again, extend the green headshots and the blue headshot all the way down to Marker 7.

Again the screen cuts to black.

New Headshots

1. Go down to Marker 8 and bring in the clip called *Head-PinkSmall.pct* and place it on **V2**.

2. The image is the right size for the start of this section, but it's in the wrong place.

3. In the **Canvas,** drag it straight up to the top of the frame so that the top edge of the image is at the top edge of the screen. My setting for the **Center** was *y* –129.

4. Go to Marker 9 and set a keyframe.

It's often easier to work backwards in animation, to start with the end position on the screen and then animate the wipe on.

5. Now go back to Marker 8 and with the **Crop** tool (**C**), grab the bottom crop line and pull it upward off the screen.

This is why it's easier to make the end position first, because the two crop lines are now right next to each other, and they're much harder to separate. That's your start keyframe position. It will give you a quick wipe on of the picture.

Marker 10 is where the next image comes in.

1. Place *HeadBlueSmall.pct* on **V3**.

2. Reposition to the bottom center of the screen. My **Center** value was *y* 125.

3. Go to Marker 11 to set a keyframe.

4. Go back to Marker 10, and this time take the top crop line and drag it down to hide the image.

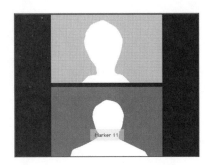

8.35 Two headshots on screen at Marker 11

At Marker 11 both pictures should now be on the screen as shown in Figure 8.35. We're ready now to bring in the rest of the headshots.

Final Headshots

At Marker 12 we'll first have to place a keyframe on both the pink and blue headshots. Both images need to scale down slightly and have the left and right sides cropped so the images fit into their final position.

1. With the playhead at Marker 12, select both headshots and click on the **Keyframe** button in the **Canvas** to set a keyframe for the two headshots.

2. Change the scale of the **Timeline** window so that you can see most of the **Timeline**.

3. Position the playhead at Marker 13 to place the next headshots. **Shift**-select the three green headshots from near the beginning of the sequence and copy them.

4. Make sure **V4** is autoselected and that none of the tracks below it are. Paste the clips into the **Timeline**. It doesn't matter if the other tracks aren't selected. The clips will stack on top of each other based on the lowest autoselected track, **V4** in this case.

The three duplicate green headshots should be on **V4**, **V5**, and **V6**, leaving **V2** and **V3** for the pink and blue headshots. Next do the same for the red headshots in the **Timeline**.

5. Select the red headshots and copy them.

6. Set **V7** as the lowest autoselected track and paste the clips into the **Timeline**.

Between Marker 12 and Marker 14 where the green and red headshots reach full opacity, the pink and blue headshots scale, crop, and slightly reposition to their final locations.

For the pink headshot, my values at Marker 14 are:

Scale		Crop Right	5.23
Center	x 1, y –148	Crop Top	4.29
Crop Left	2.83		

Note: Scale value is 58.08

8.36 Eight headshots on screen, Marker 14

For the blue headshot, my values at Marker 14 are:

Scale	66.5	Crop Left	8.23
Center	*x* 0, *y* 139	Crop Right	11.22

When you've positioned the clips about the screen, you should end up with the **Canvas** looking like Figure 8.36.

One more step needs to be taken before we put in the titles: extend the headshots down to the end of the sequence.

1. Move the playhead all the way down to Marker 24.
2. Then **Command**-click on the edits at the ends of all the headshots: pink, blue, the three greens, and the three reds.
3. Now do an Extend edit to stretch them out to the playhead.

Titles

We're finished with almost all the headshots. Next we have to get the titles on the screen. I've prebuilt them for you using Title 3D. They are made with the *Marker Felt* font, which the closest in the current Apple font collection to the original title style.

1. Lay the first title, *Main Title* in the **Graphics** bin, at Marker 15 on the topmost track, **V10**.

You'll see that it's at its full size. In fact, there is a small scaling of the title in the open.

2. Go to Marker 16 and set a keyframe. This will be the end point of the main title animation.

3. Go back to Marker 15 and set the **Scale** value in the **Motion** tab of the **Viewer** back down to 47.83.

4. Go down to Marker 17 and with the **Blade** tool (**B**), cut the title and throw away the rest of it.

At Marker 18, the next title, *Starring Title*, appears.

5. Drop *Starring Title* onto the same track as the main title.

6. Cut this title off at Marker 19.

7. At Marker 20 introduce *Mom Title*. Because it overlaps with the final headshot we're going to bring in, it needs to be placed on a higher track, **V11**.

8. At Marker 21 set an Opacity keyframe with the **Pen** tool for *Mom Title*. *The frame before* Marker 22 set the **Opacity** down to zero. This will fade it out quickly.

9. Blade *Mom Title* at Marker 22.

Final Polishing

We're on the home stretch, just a few more steps to take. At Marker 21, while *Mom Title* is fading out, one more headshot is fading in.

1. Drag one more copy of the green headshot into the center of the screen. Place it on **V10** underneath *Mom Title*.

2. The final green headshot needs to be positioned, scaled, and cropped top and bottom to fit the center square in the screen. The values I used are:

Scale	33	Crop Top	5.12
Center	x −5, y 0	Crop Bottom	6.11
Crop Left	1.6		

3. Set an Opacity keyframe for the green headshot at Marker 21 and set the value to zero. Ramp up the **Opacity** to 100 at Marker 22.

At Marker 22 the last title, *Alice Title*, just cuts in. Place it on **V11**.

4. Cut off both *Alice Title* and the center headshot at Marker 24.

Fade to Black

The last step we want to do is to fade to black. We could keyframe and ramp down the opacity on each of 10 layers now on the screen, but there's an easier way.

1. Make a short slug and place it on the topmost video track at Marker 23.

2. Set its **Opacity** down to zero.

3. At Marker 24 use the **Pen** tool bring its **Opacity** up to 100 percent so that black fills the screen.

Congratulations. You've made the Brady Bunch open. The original open was made with a good deal more precision than I invested in it, but if you want, you can precisely align and shape the images using exact values in the **Motion** tab.

Summary

In this lesson we've looked at Final Cut's animation capabilities. These are tools you can use to composite images one on top of another, using FCE's multilayer capabilities. We'll look at more compositing techniques in a later lesson, but first let's see how to use Final Cut's filters.

Lesson 9

Adding Special Effects Filters

In this lesson we're going to look at and work with Final Cut's filters to create some special effects. FCE offers a great variety of excellent effects. Unlike transitions that go between clips, filters are applied to single clips or parts of clips. In addition to the filters included with the application, other programmers are creating effects using Final Cut's scripting software FXBuilder, such as the collection of filters written by Christoph Vonrhein, Graeme Nattress, Klaus Eiperle and others. In the *Extras* folder of the DVD is a folder for *CHV-FCE Plugins*, which includes demo versions of some of Vonrhein's *Keyframe-collection*. These include the ability to be keyframable using a display built into the **Canvas**. There are 130 demo filters from Klaus Eiperle's *CGM DVE's Vol.1+, CGM DVE's Vol. 2+, and CGM DVE's Vol.3+*. Check out the HTML files and the demo movies that explain them. Klaus wrote the FXScript DVE's that were part of the first version of FCE. There are also demo versions of the G-Filters, an outstanding collection of image-control filters. And if you want a variety of film-look effects, including an excellent bleached color effect, the G Film Effects are outstanding. Read the PDF that accompanies them to learn how to fully use them. Also included is the demo version from John Wainwright of Lyric Media's

213

Drawing Tools generators, which are very handy. Lyric also make useful Motion Tracking plugins.

To add new filters to FCE, place them in the *Plugins* folder while the application is closed. Drag the plugins into *Library/Application Support/Final Cut Express Support/Plugins*.

Loading the Lesson

One more time, let's begin by loading the material you need onto your media drive.

1. Drag over the *Media 7* folder from the DVD.

2. Eject the DVD, open the *Projects* folder that should be on your hard drive, and double-click the project file, *Lesson 9*, to launch the application.

➤**Tip**
Navigating Video Filters: To quickly get to any filter in the **Video Filters** sequence, **Control**-click in the Timeline Ruler of the Timeline, and from the shortcut menu select any one of the markers by name. Above each marker is the name of the filter that was applied to the shot.

Inside your project copy, you'll find in the **Browser, Clips** bin, a master clip called *Dance,* and other files. One of the sequences is called *Effects Builder.* This demonstrates some of the filters we'll see in this lesson. As we go through the lesson, I'll show you how the effects in this sequence were made. There is also a sequence called *Video Filters.* In it each filter has been applied with its default settings to a two-second portion of *Dance1,* except for the two **Color Smoothing** filters, which we'll see later in the lesson. These have no controls that you can adjust anyway. For quite a few filters, such as the color correction filters, the default settings do nothing, but having them laid out like this lets you easily look at any filter and twiddle its knobs to see what it does.

You may have thought there were a lot of transitions. There are even more filters—84 of them, in fact—some of which aren't very useful, but there still quite a few that allow you to do amazing things with video. Because there is so much redundancy in the filters, different filters that do basically the same things, as well as filters that don't function well in FCE, I'll only go through some of the important ones.

Applying a Filter

It couldn't be simpler to apply an effect in Final Cut Express.

1. Select the clip in the **Timeline** or in the **Browser** and from the menu bar select **Effects>Video Filters**.

2. Pick a submenu and pick an effect.

If they're applied in the **Browser**, then every time that clip is used, the filter will go with it. If the effect is applied in the **Timeline**, it's applied only to that one copy of the clip. It is immediately applied with its default settings to the clip. If you prefer, you can drag the effect from the **Video Filter** bin inside the **Effects** panel of the **Browser**.

It's just as easy to remove an effect. Open the clip into the **Viewer**, go to the **Filters** tab, select the effect by clicking on its name, and press the **Delete** key (see Figure 9.1).

Any number of filters can be added to a clip. The order in which the filters are applied can be important. The filter order can be changed by dragging the filters up and down to new positions in the order. Filters can also be turned on and off with a little checkbox. This allows you to leave a filter in place yet toggle its effect on and off to see what it's doing to the picture.

Filters can also be copied and pasted. If you select a clip that has a filter applied, you can copy the clip and use **Paste Attributes** (**Option-V**) to paste that filter or filters and their settings to any number of other clips simultaneously (see Figure 9.2).

You can also select a clip or a number of clips in the **Timeline**, and from the **Edit** menu choose **Remove Attributes** (keyboard shortcut: **Command-Option-V**). Make sure the **Filters** box is checked in the **Remove Attributes** dialog box, and the filter or multiple filters will all be removed.

Filter values cannot be keyframed so that they can be altered over time, but you can often split a clip, apply different filter values to the two parts, and connect them with a long cross dissolve. This gives the appearance of the filter values changing over time. Look at the set of clips at Marker 1 in the sequence *Effects Builder*. The middle portion of the clip *Dance2* has the effect applied to it. By slowly cross dissolving to itself, the illusion is created that the image becomes more blurred and then less blurred.

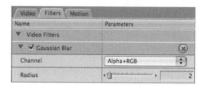

9.1   Selected effect in Filters tab

9.2   Paste filter attributes

Favorites

Favorites are a great way to save effects, because you can not only save them as their default settings, but you can also save them as an effects pack, a number of effects that work together to produce a result. It's simple to do. Apply the effects and adjust them as you as you want them, and then with the **Filters** tab of the **Viewer** open, drag them to the **Favorites** bin, where you can rename them (see Figure 9.3). Notice that I created a bin within the **Favorites** bin, in which I put the filters, and that the stack order in which the filters were created is maintained in the bin.

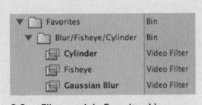

9.3 Filter pack in Favorites bin

The **Favorites** bin sounds great, but it has a serious downside, which is that **Favorites** are part of the application's preferences. So if you have to trash your prefs file, your favorites are gone with it. See "Favorites" on page 124 for one good solution to this problem.

Let's begin looking at the filters by opening the empty *Sequence 1* and dragging one of the clips from the **Clips** bin into it. We'll start with *Dance1*. We'll apply some filters to this clip to see how they work.

Some Useful Filters

Gaussian Blur

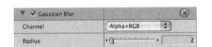

9.4 Gaussian Blur controls

Gaussian (pronounced *gousian*), named after the 19th-century German mathematician Karl Friedrich Gauss, produces a smooth blurring of the image. This blur does more, though, than softening the picture. It allows you to blur channels separately through a pop-up menu (see Figure 9.4).

Selecting different channels can produce some interesting and unusual effects. Try applying the filter. With the clip in the **Timeline** selected, choose **Gaussian Blur** from the **Effects>Video Filters>Blur** menu. If you want to blur a couple of channels, apply the effect twice.

The order in which the effects are applied often makes a difference. Don't assume that because you apply **Luminance blur** and **Blue blur** you get the same effect by applying them the other way around. FCE processes the filters from the top down as they're stacked in the **Filters** tab. If you blur **Luminance** first, the color values smear, and you'll get less impact than if you blur the color value first.

The clip at Marker 2 in the *Effects Builder* sequence shows **Gaussian Blur** applied twice, first with the **Blue** channel blurred and then with the **Luminance** blurred. A word of caution: be careful with blurring the **Luminance** value of an image. It can produce nasty blotchiness.

Bevel Border

Bevel Border is a nice touch to Picture-in-Picture effects (PIPs) and can be used to mask those nasty black edges we talked about in the previous lesson.

Bevel creates a nice edge for scaled images (see Figure 9.5).

The color picker is called **Light Color,** like the color of a gel a lighting director might put over a light that's falling across the beveled edges. You can, of course, also set the angle the light is falling from.

9.5   Bevel border with a width of 15

Channel Arithmetic

The **Channel** filters allow you an amazing degree of control of color and compositing. We'll look more closely at compositing in the next lesson on page 235, but here the channel effects allow you to combine clips and apply color effects to them combined with compositing modes.

Arithmetic is a basic **Channel** effect. It composites a color to any one of the color channels **R, G,** or **B,** or all three combined, using one of the compositing modes on a pop-up menu (see Figure 9.6).

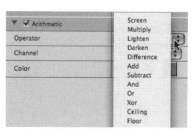

9.6   Arithmetic channels pop-up menu

FCE calls them *operators,* but they are really compositing modes. We'll look at compositing modes in the next chapter. In the *Arithmetic* sequence in your **Browser,** I have laid out a short clip of *Dance1* 12 times. Each clip has a different operator mode applied to its RGB value using the default color, gray. Look through these to get a basic idea of how the operators work. Most of the operators such as **Add, Subtract, Darken,** and **Lighten** are commonly known, but there are a couple of unusual ones, **Ceiling** and **Floor,** that produce interesting results.

9.7 Channel offset three times with Large Offset and Repeat 8i *(loft)*

9.8 Compound Arithmetic controls *(below)*

▼ ✓ Compound Arithmetic	⊗
Layer	
Operator	Difference ⬍
Channel	Alpha+RGB ⬍

Channel Offset

Channel Offset is a cool filter, although you can easily take it to great extremes where strange effects will happen, especially if you use the **Repeat Edges** pop-up menu. The clip at Marker 3 in the *Effects Builder* sequence shows you **Channel Offset** as applied in Figure 9.7.

Compound Arithmetic

Compound Arithmetic is based on an image placed in the **Well** (see Figure 9.8). Without an image there, the **Operator** pop-up menu produces little effect. It does not change by compositing with the layer below, only with itself. If an image is in the **Well**, the operator will apply to the image. Try it with text such as that on the clip at Marker 4 in the *Effects Builder* sequence.

Color Correction

Good exposure and color begins in the shooting. It's easier and always better to do it right to start rather than trying to fix it in post. That means lighting the scene well, correctly exposing it, setting your white balance correctly, and not leaving the camera's auto exposure and white balance to guess. If you're producing work for output on a television set, it is essential that you view your color correction work on a properly set-up production monitor, not the computer monitor. The color and luminance values on television sets are very different from computer monitors. Do not trust the computer screen to display the colors and luminance values the way they will appear on TV. Watch your video monitor while you work, or at least a TV set. Don't try to rely on your computer monitor.

The color correction tools are professional-strength tools, so use them carefully. In FCE2 all the color correction tools are real-time-capable, which can really speed up your workflow. **Broadcast Safe** is the perfect tool to use if you suspect your video is too bright for television. Just drop it on a clip, and you'll immediately see if it reduces the video level. It will have no effect if the image does not need correction.

Though **Broadcast Safe** can be used as a magic bullet, you do have quite a bit of control on the filter to set it to whatever parameters you want (see Figure 9.9). The default is **Conservative**. The values controlled by the sliders are based on luminance value standards from zero to 100. A value of 100 is considered peak white, and 0 is pure black. In practice, most cameras, especially consumer camcorders and prosumer equipment, shoot at levels much higher than 100, up to 120 and beyond, what's called superwhite. Televisions are designed to accept a video signal with peak white at 100, although they too have a good deal of tolerance, and most newer TV sets can readily accept values around 110 and 120.

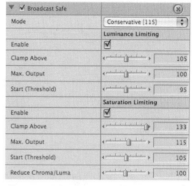

9.9   Broadcast Safe controls

Notice that as the default you limit both the luminance values and the chrominance values. If you want to keep the luminance in an acceptable range but do something outrageous with the color, you have to make sure **Custom—Use Controls Below** is selected from the pop-up menu. Then uncheck the **Saturation Limiting** checkbox and go to town.

Color Corrector

Unlike most filters, **Color Corrector**, as well as the **Chroma Keyer** in the **Key** submenu, has two panels in the **Viewer** (see Figure 9.10). One marked **Filter** has sliders and numerical controls to adjust the values (see Figure 9.11), and a useful button at the top that lets you switch to the **Visual** display. The second panel with the name of the filter has the visual interface that you are most likely to use (see Figure 9.12).

9.10   Top of the Viewer window with Color Corrector tab

Some important functions are on the **Filter** panel only. One is the little button with the red **X** to reset the entire filter. The other items are the whole group of controls for **Limit Effect Control**, **Edge Control**, and **Mask Control**.

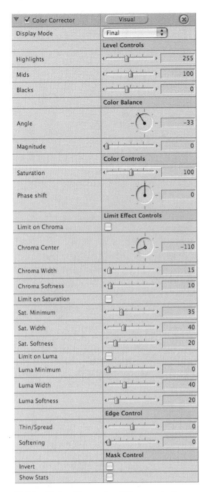

9.11   Color Corrector filter controls

Let's take a look at the visual controls for **Color Corrector.** At the top is a grouping of useful buttons (see Figure 9.13). The **Numeric** button takes you to the **Filter** panel. There is also the little checkbox that allows you to toggle the filter on and off. The eye icon tells you that you're in the **Visual** panel, if you didn't realize that already. There is a small timeline that has the basic timeline controls and timecode reference.

There is the grab handle, which lets you pull the effect onto a clip, similar to the grab handle in the **Audio** panel. On either side of the grab handle are some very useful buttons. The first to the right, with the number 1 on it, allows you to copy your **Color Corrector** settings to the next clip in the **Timeline.** The second button to the right, marked with the number 2, can be even more useful. This copies the settings not to the next clip in the **Timeline,** but to the second clip down the **Timeline.** For instance, if you have a two-camera setup for a wedding or a theatrical performance that basically switches back and forth between the two cameras and you want to color-balance one camera to the other, you need to color-correct every other shot in the **Timeline.** Clicking the **2** button will copy the settings to the next shot for that camera. You can quickly copy the settings to every other shot in the **Timeline.**

The two buttons marked with a **1** and **2** to the left of the grab handle act similarly. They let you copy the **Color Corrector** settings to the clip you're working on from either the shot before, the **1** button, or from the shot before last in the **Timeline,** the **2** button.

Let's take a look at the central control panel in **Color Corrector,** which has two color wheels, four sliders, and a few buttons.

9.12   Color Corrector visual display

9.13   Top of the Color Corrector visual panel

The left wheel controls the color balance of the image, and the right changes the hue, just like the hue knob on a television set. Below are four self-explanatory sliders. The first controls the white levels; the second, the midtones; and the third, the black level. The fourth slider adjusts the **Saturation** or amount of color in the image. The three buttons stacked together on the right are auto setting buttons. These are the best place to start with any image. From the top the buttons are **Auto White, Auto Contrast,** and **Auto Black.** To the right of that is an eyedropper, a color swatch, and a white **Reset** button; these functions are not fully operational in this version of FCE.

In the *Color* sequence, take a look at the pair of images at Marker 2. The first is probably a bit darker than it should be. The image right after it has the **Color Corrector** filter applied.

To use the filter you should begin by clicking the **Auto Contrast** button, the middle of the three-button stack. Do not click on it repeatedly. You'll just keep shifting the contrast. Just click once. Next set the **Auto Black** and then the **Auto White.** Again, just one click for each button. Always adjust the luminance, whites, mids, and blacks before you start adjusting the colors. I usually start with the mids. A little adjustment there will spread the contrast levels nicely and brighten the image without increasing the overall level. Remember, as with almost all FCE sliders, if you hold down the **Command** key, you'll "gear down" the drag, giving you finer control.

The image at Marker 3 in *Color* has been overexposed. With it is an attempt at fixing the problem. As you can see, you'll usually get a better result fixing an image that's been underexposed than one that's overexposed and washed out.

Color Corrector obviously is for color as well as luminance and contrast. At Marker 4 in *Color* is another still image. Something's certainly gone wrong here. It looks like the white balance hasn't been set correctly. **Color Corrector** is the easiest tool to fix this. To correct it, start with the **Auto Contrast** button and set your luminance levels to what looks correct to you. It's not going to take much work. The exposure is correct; just the color is wrong.

What we're going to do is pick white in the picture and use that to set the correct color balance. There are a couple of tricks to this.

➤**Tip**

Limiting Color Effect: Without having the visual interface for the **Limit Effect Controls** and the other functions, they are very difficult to use, although with some care you can effectively limit color control to only particular portions of the image. Take a look at the two stills at beginning of the sequence called *Color.* The color effect is changing the color of the woman's jacket. I did this by turning on the **Limit Effect Controls** and isolating the color of the jacket. I could do that by turning down the color saturation to zero and turning the **Chroma Center** dial until I found the color that was being desaturated. Then by increasing the color width, I was isolating just that area of color. Turning the **Phase Shift** in the upper portion of the controls changed the jacket color from its original lime green to a more conservative tan. Notice that there are two clips stacked in the *Color* sequence. That's because I used another filter, the **Four-Point Garbage Matte,** to limit the area that I had to color select.

➤*Tip*_____
Color Balance: If you want to color-balance two cameras or two shots that have a slightly different color cast, open one shot into the **Viewer** and go to its **Visual** control panel. Select the shot you want to match it to and open it into a new **Viewer** (Shift-Return). You can use the **White Balance Eyedropper** to pick white out of the second shot in the new **Viewer**. You're balancing the white of one shot to the white of the other. It's a good first step in color matching.

1. First, take the **Saturation** slider and crank it way to the right, terribly oversaturating the image.

What this does is emphasize any color cast in the image, making it easier to pick out what's wrong. The second trick is to find the right bit of white. The temptation is to use something that's very bright, but the problem is that what's very bright often is quite washed out and has almost no color information in it. Look for something that's white but not at full luminance or something that's neutral gray. Here's how you do it with **Color Corrector**.

2. Just to the bottom left of the **Balance** wheel is a tiny eyedropper. (Not the eyedropper next to the **Auto Contrast** button.) Use this to pick something in the scene that should be white or gray. In this image there isn't anything that's very oversaturated, so I'd pick something off the white roof of the van.

This will immediately pull the color back toward a truer representation of the image. You'll also notice that the button in the center of the **Balance** wheel has shifted toward the red direction. When I pulled the white, it gave the image a slightly more magenta tinge than I would have liked. Again, this was apparent because the Saturation was turned up. You'll want to fine-tune the color more toward the yellow-red direction of the **Balance** wheel.

3. Before you do that, slide the **Saturation** slider back down to normal, and you'll see that the image is close to looking correct.

4. Push the **Balance** button in the center of the **Balance** wheel a little farther to yellow-red.

There's a little gotcha here. All the color wheels are geared down by default. So you have to move the button a lot to get any effect. In the color wheels, as with **Balance**, you use the **Command** key to gear up. This is the only place in FCE that this occurs.

The little white buttons to the lower right of the **Balance** wheel and the **Hue** wheel are **Reset** buttons.

Desaturate and Sepia

Desaturate

This is the quickest, easiest way to remove color. The default **Amount** of 100 is a fully desaturated image, pure black and white. I find it makes a somewhat flat-looking black and white.

Desaturate does not only *de*saturate, it will also *over*saturate. **Desaturate** can go into negative values, which overchromas the image. It won't take much of a push into the negative numbers to get excessively colorful, especially if the scene already has a lot of color, particularly reds. To do anything other than desaturate quickly, you should use FCE's **Color Correction** filters.

Sepia

The default setting generates a rich brown color without being too orange (see Figure 9.14). Bringing down the **Amount** slider to around 60, blending in the underlying color, makes an interesting look.

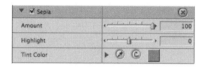

9.14 Sepia controls

Although the filter is called **Sepia**, the color picker allows you to tint the image any color you'd like. **Sepia** also has a **Highlight** slider, which increases the brightness in the highlight areas, punching them through the tint color. Pulling the **Highlight** slider into negative numbers will deepen the shadow areas.

Keying

Keying is used to selectively cut out areas of the image. The most efficient way to do this is chromakeying, the technique of removing one specific color from an image. It's how weather reporters stand in front of weather maps. The two commonly used colors are blue and green. Because of the way the DV format works, it's easier to chromakey green than blue. On the other hand, if your subject has to wear green for St. Patrick's Day, you'll have to use blue.

The key to keying is to shoot it well. Poorly shot material just will not key properly. For chromakeying, the background blue or green screen must be evenly lit and correctly exposed so that the color is as pure as possible. Video, of course, and DV even more so, have many limitations of color depth and saturation that make good keying difficult.

FCE has tools to do keying, the best of which is the **Chroma Keyer**, in my opinion.

In your **Browser** is a bin called **Keying**, which holds the elements we'll work with in this part of the lesson. Open the *Keying* sequence. This has a couple of still images to work with. On **V1** in the sequence is a still of the Stanford University clarion tower called *Background.pct*, and on **V2** is the image to chromakey called *Blue.pct*. We're going to work with a quite difficult bluescreen image.

Color Smoothing – 4:1:1

Color Smoothing – 4:1:1 and **Color Smoothing – 4:2:2** are new to FCE2. Because Final Cut Express is a DV-resolution application, you will probably only need the 4:1:1. These filters are designed to reduce the effects of pixelization in digital video. You should apply **4:1:1** first to any clip that you want to key. The filter has no controls. You just drop it on the clip first and apply the **Chroma Keyer** filter to remove the green or blue that you want to key out off the image.

Chroma Keyer

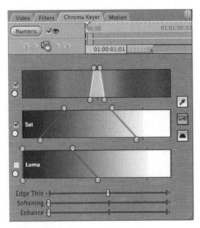

9.15 Chroma Keyer controls

If the material is properly shot and lit, there is no trick to chromakeying in FCE. I would ignore the **Blue** and **Green Screen** and **Color Key** filters and just work with the **Chroma Keyer**. Let's start by examining some of the controls in this perhaps daunting-looking filter.

1. Begin by applying **Color Smoothing – 4:1:1** to *Blue.pct* on **V2**.

2. Apply **Chroma Keyer** to the same clip.

3. Open the clip into the **Viewer** and go to the **Chroma Keyer** panel (see Figure 9.15).

The controls show a **Color Range** slider at the top, the rainbow-colored bar. Below that is the **Sat** (saturation) control and **Luma** (luminance) control. Each has a round radio button that allows you to reset the parameter and a square checkbox that lets you toggle the parameter on and off. Each of the controls has handles that can be adjusted. Pulling the buttons on the top of the sliders will increase or decrease the range of the effect, and pulling on the buttons at the bottom of the slider will control the tolerance, how widely the parameter will be applied to adjacent colors or saturation or luminance values.

9.16 Chroma Keyer buttons

➤*Tip*_____
Important: The key icon toggle does not function when the **Canvas** is in **Image + Wireframe** mode.

On the right are three important buttons (see Figure 9.16). At the top is the critical eyedropper. Below that, in the middle, is a three-way toggle switch with a key icon. Its default position is colored gray, which shows the final output of the image. Click it and it will change to white, which will show you a black-and-white representation of what you're keying. Click it again and the button goes blue, which shows you the original source material. The bottom button with the keystone icon will invert the key, which can be useful in some instances.

4. Click on the eyedropper, click in the blue screen behind the flowers in the **Canvas**, and you're practically done.

Almost instantly the bulk of the blue has disappeared.

5. Check the matte by clicking on the **Matte/Key** icon. You'll see most of the background has been keyed out, as in Figure 9.17. This is a grayscale representation of transparency. What is white is opaque in the *Blue.pct* clip, and what is black is transparent.

6. Widen the **Color Range** slightly with the button pulls at the top and broaden the **Luma** controls a bit, and you'll have a pretty good key.

If you look closely at your key in FCE, you'll probably see a rather unnatural color fringe around the edges of the flower. This can be a little tricky to get rid of.

7. Push up the **Edge Thin** control a bit.

8. At the very end of the **Softening** control is a tiny little triangle. Give it a few clicks. This will move **Softening** incrementally.

9. Try adding a little **Enhance**, but not too much, or the edges will start to turn yellow.

Spill Suppressor-Blue and Spill Suppressor-Green

The **Spill Suppressors** are used if there is a blue or green cast on the edges of the image (see Figure 9.18). This often happens when you get reflected light for the blue screen wall falling on the edges of a curved object, like a person's shoulders. The **Spill Suppressor** takes the blue in the image and replaces it with black, like a shadow area. This is fine on the object you want to leave, but if the background color has not been keyed out sufficiently, it can leave a dark edging on the screen.

Lower the **Suppressor** slider substantially. Usually only a small amount will be sufficient to do the work.

➤Tip

Color Selection: If you hold down the Shift key you can click on multiple points, and the **Chroma Keyer** controls will extend the range of values, color, saturation, or luminance as needed. Also, if you hold down the Shift key and drag a line through the area you want to sample, the tool will use the range of values along the line to set up the controls.

9.17 Matte Display

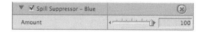

9.18 Spill Suppressor control

Matte Choker

Adding another tool in the mix here may be helpful. The **Matte Choker** is useful, but it isn't in the **Key** package. It's in the **Matte** package, which we'll see in a moment. The **Matte Choker** is mostly commonly used as a keying tool, however, and adding it to the key will improve the image.

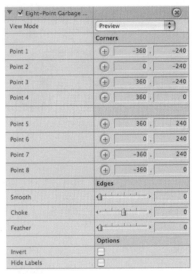

9.19 Matte Choker

The controls (see Figure 9.19) are basically the same as the **Edge Thin** and **Softening** controls in the **Chroma Keyer**, but adding a second line of choking to the key's edges will make it easier to get a tight, sharp line between the edges and the background. If you find that your keying is cutting too much into the image, the **Matte Choker** can also be applied again. By pushing the slider down into negative numbers, you can bring back some of the cut-off image.

Mattes

Eight-Point Garbage Matte

A garbage matte allows you to roughly cut out a section of the image by selected points on the screen that define corners of the picture. In addition to the **Eight-Point Garbage Matte** there is a **Four-Point Garbage Matte** as well, the only difference being the numbers of points available (see Figure 9.20).

> **➤Tip**
> **Matte Preview:** If you want to see how the image will look while you're trying to apply a garbage matte, click one of the points' crosshairs in the **Filter** panel and then mouse down in the **Canvas**, which will update as soon as it can. If you hold the mouse down and drag the point around the screen, the image will be pulled around on the screen as quickly as your computer can manage it. The faster your computer, the sooner this will happen.

9.20 Eight-Point Garbage Matte controls

The controls in **Eight-Point Garbage Matte** allow you to set eight points on the image, beginning with Point 1 in the upper-left corner. The points go clockwise around the screen starting with that corner (see Figure 9.21). It's best to try to keep the points in those relative positions. Because lines connect the points to each other, it's important to avoid having the lines cross each other. Bizarre shapes can be created with your image if the lines cross.

In the controls there are eight points that can be placed anywhere on the screen using the **Crosshairs** button. Click in the crosshairs for Point 1 and click in the **Canvas**. The point will be placed there. It's as simple and as difficult as that.

9.21 Garbage Matte Canvas display

The three **View Modes** can be selected from a pop-up menu at the top of the controller.

- **Final** is the output as seen on the screen along with the underlying layers, but without any point markers.

- **Preview** is the same as **Final**, only with the points indicated and with the point numbers. The number display can be toggled with the checkbox.

- **Wireframe** shows you the matte outline but only on the layer on which you're working, without cutting away the rest of the image to reveal any underlying layer.

Below the points are some important tools. The first is **Smooth**. This rounds out the corners in your matte. You can combine it with **Feather** to create soft-edged mattes with interesting organic shapes (see Figure 9.32).

Without **Smooth** applied, **Choke** is a subtle adjustment of the matte shape. Moving **Choke** into negative numbers will slightly reduce the matte, and pushing the value up will increase the size of the matte.

Finally, an important but often overlooked checkbox is **Invert**. This feature allows you to create a matte around an object that you want to remove, and then rather than keeping the area you defined, by checking the **Invert** box, you'll cut it out.

Extract

Extract is a real beauty of a filter. It's a little unpredictable to work with, but with luck it will create interesting combinations of

➢*Tip*

Do it First: It's a good idea to apply your garbage matte before you reposition or scale your image. The points are based on the image frame. So if you move the image before you apply the garbage matte, it's hard to pin down where the points should be because they're not referring to the new shape and position and scale of the image, but to its original position in the frame. So apply your garbage matte, make it the shape you want before you scale, center, or rotate the picture about the screen.

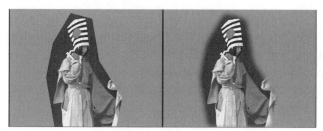

9.22 Matte without Smooth, and with Smooth and Feather at 20

9.23 Extract controls

Matte Boundaries: Although you can extend the points out into the grayboard, the matte doesn't extend out there. If only it would. The matte is still bound by the edges of frame. So if you hope that extending the points out from the screen so that **Feather** will not affect one edge of the image, give up. **Feather** will unfortunately occur around the frame edges.

matte shapes, especially when used with a garbage matte to define a core area.

Extract gives you deceptively simple controls together with a three-up display in the **Canvas,** if needed (see Figure 9.23).

A pop-up menu lets you select if you want the extraction applied to RGB or to the alpha channel of the image. Applying it to RGB will make a high-contrast black-and-white image. By adjusting **Threshold, Tolerance,** and **Softness,** you can vary the image substantially.

It gets really interesting when you apply it to the alpha channel instead of the RGB value. Then you cut through to an underlying layer with a great amount of control. It's useful for pulling an alpha channel from an image that doesn't have one.

Look at the file in the **Browser** called *TIFF.tif.* Apply the **Extract** filter to it with **Copy Result to Alpha Channel,** and you'll see that with hardly a tweak of the sliders, the white will disappear from around the word. It's set up at Marker 5 in the *Effects Builder* sequence.

Tip

NightScope: If you apply **Color Corrector** to a clip, taking down the black level a bit, then use the **Extract** filter, followed by **Color Corrector** again with a green tint and the white level brought down considerably, as well as the mids choked down, you can create quite a credible NightScope look for your image. Look at the clip at Marker 6 in *Effects Builder.* A touch of **Gaussian Blur** softens the hard edge look of the **Extraction.** It needs a little fiddling, depending on the image, but it's fun, especially if you can add a little blurred glow to it with a composite mode, which we'll talk about in Lesson 10.

Mask Shape

Mask Shape is a useful filter that lets you easily control the shape the image. The controls allow basic shapes (see Figure 9.24) and have **Horizontal** and **Vertical** sliders that let you adjust the default shapes. I'll show you a practical application.

An interesting use for **Mask Shape** is to create borders using color mattes. It's simple to do. Look at the clip stack at Marker 7 in *Effects Builder.* On **V1** is the *Dance3* clip with **Mask Shape>Round Rectangle** applied. On **V2** is a color matte in pale yellow. The color also has **Round Rectangle** applied to it twice. The first time it's applied inverted. This leaves the matte with the picture showing through and fills the rest of the screen with the color. Applying the shape again, only slightly larger and not inverted, will cut the color outside in the **Round Rectangle**. I also used **Anti-alias** to soften the stair-stepping around the mask.

9.24 **Mask Shape controls**

Widescreen

This filter lets you to take a standard 4:3 video and crop it to one of seven standard cinema shapes (see Figure 9.25).

This is a crop, not an overlay, so the area outside the image is empty. If you want to place a color there, you should put a color matte underneath it.

9.25 **Widescreen controls**

The **Offset** slider allows you to move the image up and down without altering the position. Negative numbers drag the image downward; positive numbers move the image upward, the opposite of the way the *y* axis functions in the **Text** tool.

Making a Sequence Widescreen

If you want to make a whole sequence widescreen—which is probably the point, rather than applying it to individual clips—nest the whole sequence, and apply the filter to the nest.

1. Make a new sequence, naming it something useful, such as *Final Widescreen.*

2. Drag your edited sequence into the new open **Timeline** window. This is now a nested sequence, with the edited sequence nested inside the new sequence.

3. Select the nested sequence in the **Timeline** and apply the **Widescreen** filter.

4. To access the settings for the filter, simply select the nest in the **Timeline** and press the **Return** key or **Option**–double-click to open it into the **Viewer.** You can now go to the **Filters** tab to change the settings.

If you need to use **Offset,** you may not want to do it here because it will offset all the clips in the nest. Better would be to open the nest, use the **Motion** tab of any shots you want to offset, and move them up or down in the frame as necessary.

There are other ways to create the widescreen effect. You can use **Four-Point Garbage Matte.** Create the shape you want for the masked area, and use the **Invert** button. Or for a simple widescreen without the border, you could also use the **Crop** tool. Remember to drag with the **Command** key to get opposite sides to move equally. Or you could make a mask in Photoshop, a black area at top and bottom with transparency in the middle. I like this way best, particularly for projects such as commercials, because it lets me create interesting effects with the mask edges, such as graphic elements that overlap the widescreen line, different color masks, text, and logos.

➤**Tip**
Constraining Dials: Holding down the **Shift** key will constrain the **Basic 3D** dials to 45-degree increments.

Perspective

Basic 3D

Basic it is, but it does the job and can be used effectively for making customized effects such as bow ties. The controls for the x,y,z axes are self-explanatory (see Figure 9.26).

Notice the **Center** and **Scale** controls. Set these functions here and not in the **Motion** window. If you scale or reposition in **Motion,** the 3D will be cut off by the bounding box, as in Figure 9.27.

A bow tie is broadcasting term for two images on the screen at the same time, often tilted toward each other to create the illusion of perspective (see Figure 9.28). Take a look at the stack at Marker 8 in *Effects Builder.* That's a bow tie, most commonly used in two-ways (interviews from a remote site).

Both clips are tilted backwards on the y axis, one by 45 degrees and the other by −45 degrees. The center points are shifted to move the images left and right, and both are scaled down to 60 to

9.26   3D controls

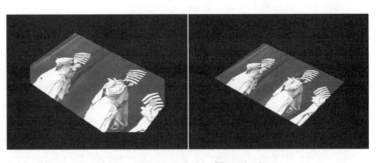

9.27   3D scaled in Motion tab and scaled in 3D controls

9.28 Bow Tie

fit the screen. You can add all sorts of graphical embellishments such as borders, bars, and logos across the bottom and top.

Flop

This filter can be a real lifesaver. If you ever shot something in which someone is looking right to left and they really should be looking left to right, **Flop** is what fixes it. It reverses the direction of the image. Just be careful and watch out for words that might appear backwards, or hair parting that swings from side to side, and similar telltales that would give you away. The only controls are a single pop-up menu, which lets you flop the default **Horizontal** and also allows you to reverse the image vertically or both horizontally and vertically at the same time.

QuickTime

Color Tint

Color Tint has one feature that is difficult to duplicate with any other tools. It allows you to create an X-ray negative effect (see Figure 9.29). It also has a subtle sepia tint, even less orange than FCE's **Sepia**.

Color Tint also has **Other,** a wonderful tool. It allows you to set extremely different colors for light and dark. You can have a warm light color and a cold dark, a very nice duotone effect.

The **Brightness** and **Contrast** controls really help with the duotone, letting you put in rich color while keeping the luminance from looking too washed out. Take a look at Marker 9 in *Effects*

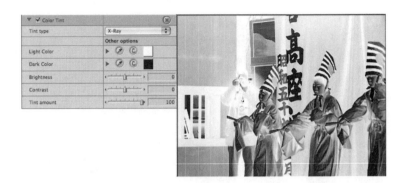

9.29 Color Tint controls with X-ray image

Builder. It shows you the type of duotone effect that **Color Tint** can create.

Stylize

Find Edges

Find Edges is a neat filter that gives you a nice, stylized look (see Figure 9.30). Try it with the **Invert** checkbox on, which puts a hard, black outline on the edges. Both ways have their uses and can work well. **Find Edges** can be used to create interesting effects, especially when composited over other images, or blended over itself.

Replicate

Replicate is a cool filter (see Figure 9.31). The default output produces only four images on the screen, but if you push the sliders, you can get 16 horizontal and 16 vertical. That's 256 very small images on the screen. It's a nice effect when it steps back 2, 4, 8, 16.

Look at the strings of clips in *Effects Builder* at Marker 10. This was made up by blading a clip and changing the replicate values up and then back down again.

Video

De-interlace and Flicker

This has to be one of the most-used filters in FCE, if for no other reason than that it's used to remove video interlacing when making freeze frames. If you place a freeze frame of a clip with a lot of motion in it, the freeze will twitch horribly as the interlacing

9.30   Find Edges *(left)*

9.31   Replicate Controls *(below)*

▼ ✓ Replicate		⊗
Horizontal	◄ ▯——┴——┴——┴——►	2
Vertical	◄ ▯——┴——┴——┴——►	2

switches between the lines. The way around the problem is to apply the **De-interlace** filter to the freeze frame. The de-interlaced freeze frame will play back smoothly when edited into video.

The **De-interlace** filter has only a single control, a pop-up menu that lets you select a field. Choose whichever looks better.

You can also use the **Flicker** filter to do this, which gives you three separate settings, letting you choose how much flicker removal to apply if there is only a minimal amount of jittering in the freeze frame. Flicker is also used to overcome that horrible shimmering effect you get when there are thin, horizontal lines across the screen, such as serifs in text, thin lines of newsprint on the screen, stripes in a shirt, Venetian blinds in the distance, and a host of other possible causes. These are all caused by interlace flicker, and **Flicker**, which probably should be called De-Flicker, helps to remove it. It's particularly useful for minimizing flickering that can occur during scrolling titles as serifed fonts run up the screen.

De-interlace or **Flicker** should also be used before you export a still frame with motion. In that case, the frame will look like Figure 9.32. If you don't remove the interlacing on an image with movement, you get a still that looks like Figure 9.33.

The other use for the **De-interlace** filter is to help make video look more like film. The high temporal resolution of NTSC video, giving 60 discrete fields every second, is one of the reasons that video looks like video; but film, which has a lower frame rate and no interlacing, produces a more blurred motion, a softer look which we associate with film. Removing interlacing is the first step

9.32   De-interlaced still frame

9.33   Interlaced still frame

toward trying to recreate that ever-popular film look. The best way to create a film-look effect though is to use the G Film Effects filters from Graeme Nattress.

Summary

This is just the tip of the iceberg of the some of the filters in FCE. I urge you to look through them and use the *Video Filters* sequence to explore its capabilities. By now you should have a fairly good idea of what you can do with this application and should be well on your way to creating exciting, interesting, and original video productions.

We need to explore one more aspect of FCE before we're ready to put our creations out on tape, the web, or some other delivery format, and that is compositing, the topic of our next lesson.

Lesson 10

Compositing

Compositing is the ability to combine multiple layers of video on a single screen and have them interact with each other. This capability adds great depth to FCE. Until now we have been looking primarily at horizontal editing. In compositing we're dealing more with vertical editing, building stacks of layers. Compositing allows you to create a montage of images and graphics that can explain some esoteric point or enhance a mundane portion of a production. This kind of work has become the staple of wedding video production, for instance. Good compositing work can raise the perceived quality of a production. Compositing is used for a great deal of video production work on television— commercials, of course—but also on news programs and for interstitials, the short video that appears between sections of a program. Be warned, though, that compositing and graphics animation is not quick and easy to do. Most compositing is animated, and animation requires patience, skill, and hard work.

Loading the Lesson

Let's load the material you need onto your media drive.

1. For this project you will need the *Media 3* and *Media 7* folders from your DVD as well as the *Media 8* folder.

235

2. Eject the DVD, open the *Projects* folder on your hard drive, and launch the project *Lesson 10.*

3. Reconnect the media.

Inside your copy of the project *Lesson 10,* you'll find the **Clips** bin, three master clips (*Village, Dance, and Ceremony*), and a number of sequences.

As in the previous lesson, a couple of sequences contain examples of effects used in the lesson. They're called *Composite Stacks* and *Composite Modes.* Before we get into compositing, we should take a quick look at the **Generators,** because these provide us some useful compositing tools.

10.1 Generators

Generators

We used the **Generator** pop-up menu to create text files as well as color mattes, but let's take a moment to have a look at what else is under that little **A** (see Figure 10.1). There's **Bars and Tone, Matte, Others** (which are more video test signals) **Render, Shapes,** and **Slug.** We're going to look at a few of the **Generators.**

Render

The **Render** generators are a great tool and a hidden secret inside FCE's **Generators.** They allow you to create compositing tools that will alter the shapes and textures of video and graphics images. Be aware that the blackness you see in **Render** items and in the **Shapes** is not the emptiness you normally see in the **Viewer** or **Canvas** around text or animated images. What you see in the gradients and shapes is actual opaque black without any transparency, such as in the highlight in Figure 10.2.

10.2 Default highlight

Custom Gradient

Custom Gradient lets you create gradient ramps or radials, either from the default black and white or from two colors (see Figure 10.3).

As with titles, you can create one in the **Viewer** and pull it into the **Timeline,** double-click on it, and use the controls in the **Viewer** while seeing your work updated in the **Canvas.**

The default is a white-to-black gradient. The crosshairs let you pick where the white point or start color begins, and **Gradient Direction** obviously controls the angle at which the gradient

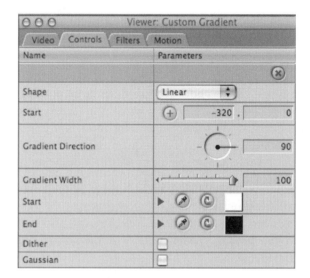

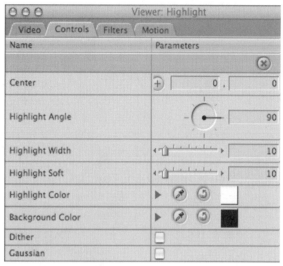

10.3 Custom Gradient controls   10.4 Highlight controls

proceeds, the default being pure white on the left and going to pure black on the right. In a **Radial Gradient** only the crosshairs have effect; there is no direction, of course. Generally you should leave **Dither** off. However, when a gradient shows *banding*— when what should have been a smooth transition from one color to another instead appears as sections of color with a clear edge where one color changes to another—then **Dither** should be turned on. Dither will add some noise to the image to break up the banding, which is usually due to the way codecs compress the video. They often are not able to make the fine distinctions in color and tone needed to produce smooth gradients. **Gaussian** makes the gradient tighter looking and seems to have less of a ramp.

Creating gradients allows you to make wonderful, complex layered images using traveling mattes, as we shall see on page 243. By animating the motion of the gradients, you can make opacity vary and change over time, revealing and fading out layered images and graphics.

Highlight

The **Highlight** render is great for generating quick highlights that race across images or text (see Figure 10.4).

The default sets the highlight to 90. I usually use it at 45 and with a much narrower highlight width than the default 10. When you combine it with a compositing mode, it produces effects that give a quick sparkle to your images. We'll work with it a bit later.

Noise

Using composite modes, this **Render** generator can be used to create film grain–type noise that blends with your video (see Figure 10.5). It's perhaps a bit too "noisy" for most film grain, but it helps to enhance the illusion. Small quantities of noise can also be used to break up banding, similar to the effect of **Dither** in the **Custom Gradient**.

Noise defaults to black and white, but the checkbox at the bottom of the controls can set color noise as well. You can also randomize it, which you probably want. Otherwise the noise looks stuck on top of the image.

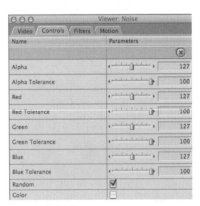

10.5 Noise Controls

Compositing Modes

One of the best ways to combine render elements with images is to use compositing modes. If you're familiar with Photoshop, you probably already know that a compositing mode is a way that the values of one image can be combined with the values of another image. Final Cut has 13 compositing modes, including two traveling mattes, which we'll look at on page 243. For the moment, we'll deal only with the first 11. These can be accessed from the **Modify>Composite Mode** menu. The composite modes are:

- **Normal**, the way clips usually appear
- **Add**
- **Subtract**
- **Difference**
- **Multiply**
- **Screen**
- **Overlay**
- **Hard Light**
- **Soft Light**
- **Darken**
- **Lighten**
- **Travel Matte—Alpha**
- **Travel Matte—Luma**

Compositing Exercise

1. Open up the sequence *Composite Modes*.

This sequence contains 11 iterations of two clips, one on top of the other. Each clip on **V2** is composited onto the clip on **V1** using a different compositing mode. There's an extended marker on each clip that identifies the compositing mode applied to the clip stack.

No two compositing modes are the same, although the differences are sometimes subtle. Some will make the output darker; some will make it lighter, but all in a slightly different manner. It's a wonderful tool for controlling image quality.

The two last composite modes, **Travel Matte—Alpha** and **Travel Matte—Luma**, have special uses that we'll look at shortly.

2. To change the compositing mode of a clip, select the clip on **V2** and from the **Modify** menu choose **Composite Mode**, and choose a type.

You can also select the clip in the **Timeline** and with the **Control** key bring up the shortcut menu and select **Composite Mode**.

One very useful composite mode is **Screen**, which will remove black from an image. It screens out portions of the image based on luminance values. Pure black will be transparent, pure white fully opaque. Any other shade will be partially transparent. This is great for creating semitransparent shapes that move around the screen, very useful for making animated backgrounds.

Instant Sex

Let's look at some of what you can do with composite modes.

1. Begin by opening the blank *Sequence 1*.

2. Again, we won't be working on the sound, so let's switch off **a1/a2** in the patch panel.

3. Let's open a clip from the **Clips** bin into the **Viewer**. We'll use *Ceremony2* because it has some nice highlight areas that will show off the effect.

4. Set the clip's duration down to five seconds and edit it into your sequence.

5. In the **Timeline** move the playhead back over the top of the clip that was laid in.

Note

NTSC Warning: If you are going to output to NTSC analog to be seen on a television set, be careful in using compositing modes, particularly **Add**. It will brighten the image, often beyond the luminance and chrominance values allowable for broadcast transmission. If the image is too bright or overchromaed, especially in red, it may bloom objectionably and smear easily when analog copies are made, particularly VHS copies.

6. Drag the same clip from the **Viewer** to **Superimpose**, making identical copies on **V1** and **V2**.

You can also **Option-Shift**-drag the clip from **V1** to the space above to make a copy of the clip and create **V2**.

7. To the top layer, apply a generous amount of **Gaussian Blur**, something like 30. The image looks very out of focus now.

8. Turn down the **Opacity** of the clip on **V2** to something like 40 percent.

9. Go to **Composite Mode** and change the clip on **V2**'s setting to **Add**. I prefer **Add**, but try some of the others, such as **Screen** or **Lighten**.

10. Try adjusting the **Blur** amount and the **Opacity** levels to different settings.

This is a recipe for Instant Sex from the great After Effects artist Trish Meyer. Although it was created for After Effects, it adapts readily to Final Cut. The soft, blooming highlights make a wonderful, dreamy, romantic effect.

Noise Exercise

Next let's bring up the noise. We can use **Noise** to add a film-grain effect.

1. Go to the **Generators** pop-up, and from **Render** select **Noise**.

2. Drag it onto **V3**, above the Instant Sex stack, or set **V2** as the destination and use **Superimpose** to bring it into the **Timeline**.

3. Change the Noise layer's compositing mode to **Screen**.

4. Remember, the piece in the **Timeline** is a copy of the one you created in the **Viewer**, so double-click it to bring it back into the **Viewer**.

5. Double-click on the *Noise* clip on **V3** and go to the **Controls** tab in the **Viewer** to make sure the **Random** box is checked and the **Color** box unchecked.

In **Color** mode, **Noise** is too strong and generates too many sparkling bits to be useful for our purposes.

Toning It Down

At this stage the **Canvas** should look like a very snowy television picture (see Figure 10.6). Now we need to reduce the effect of the **Noise**.

1. In the **Noise** controls set the **Alpha** level all the way to zero and pull down the **Alpha Tolerance** to something around 10 or 20, depending on how much graininess you want to introduce.

2. Try also using the **Soft Light** composite mode, but with **Alpha** turned up to around 120.

3. To see the effect the Noise layer is having, toggle the track visibility on and off with the green button at the head of the track.

Text

Let's not stop there. On top of your video, which should still have strong, glowing highlight areas, as well as a sprinkling of grain, let's add a text element.

10.6 Snowy Noise

1. Use the standard **Text** tool to create the word *JAPAN* in any font you like, fairly large size and a nice, bright color.

I used Optima, bold and italicized, with a size of 168 in a fairly bright red, **R** 200, **G** 18, **B** 18. Create whatever text block you like, using any available font.

2. Place your text block on **V4**. I also used **Image+Wireframe** to move it lower in the frame.

3. **Option-Shift**-drag the *Text* clip to the space above to create a copy on **V5**.

Your stack should look like Figure 10.7.

4. Go the controls for the text file on **V5** and change the color to bright yellow, something like **R** 223, **G** 223, **B** 18.

5. Next, apply a **Gaussian Blur** filter to the text, maybe something in the 30 range. This will make it quite wispy-looking.

6. Change the composite mode for the text on **V5** to **Add** so that it combines with the layers beneath.

10.7 Two video layers, noise layer, and two text layers

Making the layer blurred out and composited will make it look like a glow over the image (see Figure 10.8). But you may not want that top glow layer on the image all the time.

7. Ramp up the **Opacity** on the glow layer quickly over a few frames.

8. Hold the **Opacity** at full level for four or five frames.

9. Quickly ramp it down again. When you play it back you should just get a quick flash of yellow glow.

10.8 Composited layers and effects

10.9 Drop Shadow Glow layer behind

Look at the sequence *Composite Stacks*. I've build the five-layer stack with the quick opacity animation at the beginning of the sequence at Marker 1. For some reason the render output will show a much more pronounced effect than the wispy glow you see in the **Canvas** before rendering.

Drop Shadow Exercise

Another variation is to use a composite mode to create a different kind of drop shadow, using this type of glow layer technique, only behind the text rather than on top of it (see Figure 10.9). Rather than using yellow in the glow layer, we'll simply keep the same color as the text layer.

1. You should still have in your *Sequence 1* the five-layer stack we created. Let's start by deleting the top text layer that became our glow.

2. Once again **Option-Shift**-drag the text on **V4** onto the empty **V5** to make two copies of the text stacked on top of each other.

This time, rather than working with the upper text layer, let's work on the lower text layer.

3. Double-click the lower of the two text layers on **V4** to open it into the **Viewer**. In the **Motion** tab, change the value **Scale** up to about 110 percent.

4. With the **Viewer** still active, go to **Effects>Video Filters>Gaussian Blur**. Set the blur value to something around 20.

5. At this point the color will be too rich, so change the composite mode to **Multiply** or **Darken**.

The drop shadow glow layer stack is built in the *Composite Stacks* sequence at Marker 2. This is a different-looking shadow than you usually see. Instead of being directed to one side, it flares out from the text as though the light is coming from the front projecting the text onto the background.

Travel Mattes

Technically these are compositing modes as well, though they function in a special way. The two travel mattes are **Luminance** and **Alpha**. In a travel matte the layer to which it's applied will take its shape from either the **Luminance** value or the **Alpha** (the transparency) value of the layer directly beneath it. Because it tracks the layer, any animation or change in the layer below will be reflected in the tracking layer. This makes **Travel Matte** an extraordinarily powerful tool.

Area Highlight

A travel matte allows you to highlight and isolate a specific area of the screen. To do this we're going to begin by creating a sandwich of three layers in *Sequence 1*.

1. On **V1** place the image to be highlighted. I used the first five seconds of *Dance1*.

2. Drag the same image and drop it onto **V2** empty. It's important that the two clips on **V1** and **V2** are lined up exactly.

3. Making sure the playhead in the **Timeline** is over the clips and that **V1** is set as the destination track.

4. From the **Generators** pop-up choose **Shapes>Oval**.

5. Drag the Oval to **Superimpose**. This will edited it onto **V2**, pushing the second video clip up to **V3**.

6. To the clip on **V3**, apply **Composite Mode>Travel Matte—Luma**.

At the moment you're not going to see anything happen because the two layers are identical. Whatever is removed from the clip on **V3** will be visible in the clip on **V1**.

7. To the clip on **V1**, apply **Brightness and Contrast (Bezier)** from the **Image Control** submenu **Video Filters**.

8. In the **Filters** tab adjust the **Brightness** value down to about –60.

10.10 Highlight area using oval shape

The Oval should now be clearly visible in the center of the screen.

9. Open the **Oval** controls and set the **Aspect** down to about 0.6 and the **Size** to 35 percent, which will make a tall narrow oval.

10. In the **Motion** tab for the Oval shape, move the *x* point so that it's off toward the left, around –140, and the *y* value to 50.

You will now have a highlight area of normal exposure spotlighting the photographer while the rest of the image is darker and obscured (see Figure 10.10). In the *Composite Stack* sequence at Marker 3 I have laid out the three-layer stack. Notice that the Oval on **V2** is animated. As the camera pans, the Oval moves with it to keep the photographer highlighted as he goes off the screen. Because you can't animate filters in FCE, on **V1** I cut the video clip and did a short cross dissolve to the same clip without the filter applied. That makes the clip seem to fade up from its dimmed state to full brightness as the highlighting Oval moves off the screen.

Highlight Matte

Next we're going to create a **Highlight Matte**. Let's set up a simple animation. We'll use the two layers of *Ceremony2* that we used earlier. You can copy them out of *Composite Stack* and then fine-tune them in your own sequence.

10.11 Video tracks in the Timeline

1. Use only the first five seconds of the clips for these layers that are just background to the title. The layer on **V1** is normal; the layer on **V2** as before with **Composite Mode Add, Gaussian Blur** about 30, and **Opacity** about 40.

2. Add two tracks of video to your sequence above **V2**. **Control**-click at the head of the sequence and select **Add Track** from the shortcut menu.

3. Create a text block using a large font in a bright red as we did earlier. Make it the same five-second duration as the other clips.

4. Instead of placing it on **V3**, place it on **V4** as in Figure 10.11.

I've set V2 as the destination track because I'm going to superimpose the next element into the empty track above it.

5. Select **Highlight** from the **Render Generator** pop-up menu and superimpose it above **V2** onto the empty **V3** between the text and the background, which will disappear, of course.

Let's work on the highlight.

6. Double-click the Highlight to bring it into the **Viewer**. Go to its **Controls** tab and move the **Highlight Angle** around to 35 degrees.

7. Set the **Width** and **Softness** to about 20 and 10, respectively.

8. Leave off **Dither** and **Gaussian**; the latter only tightens the sharpness of the fall-off.

Your **Canvas** should look something like Figure 10.12.

Animating the Highlight

The next step will be to animate the Highlight.

1. Put the playhead at the start of the clip.

2. In the **Motion** controls tab of the Highlight, set the **Center** x axis to –640, which should take it off screen left, at least away from the text file on **V4**.

3. Make sure the Highlight clip is selected in the **Timeline** and create a keyframe with the **Canvas Keyframe** button.

4. Move to the end of the clip (**Shift-O**). Now set the **Center** x point to 680.

Over the five seconds of the clip, the **Highlight** bar will sweep slowly across the screen. Of course, we still don't see the background layer.

5. Next set the **Composite Mode** of the text file on **V4** to **Travel Matte—Luma**.

If you're at the start or end of the clip, everything except the background will suddenly disappear. As you scrub through the sequence, you'll see the text will softly wipe onto the screen and then wipe off again as the Highlight layer slides underneath it. The text file's transparency is being directly controlled by the luminance value of the layer beneath it. The matte layer, the Highlight in this case, is itself invisible.

6. Try applying a drop shadow to the text layer in its **Motion** tab. It should look Figure 10.13.

✎ Note

Auto Select: If you copy and paste the text block from an earlier sequence, remember that the **Auto Select** buttons control where the clip is pasted. If you want to paste the text onto **V4**, you have to switch off **Auto Select** on the video tracks below the track you want to paste on. Use **Option**-click on the **Auto Select** button on **V4** to select only that track for pasting. Use **Option**-click again afterwards to reset the **Auto Select** buttons to their default condition.

10.12 Highlight under text

10.13 Highlight text with Drop Shadow

Notice that the drop shadow wipes on and off with the text file. The stack at Marker 4 in *Composite Stacks* uses a **Drop Shadow Offset** of 6, with **Softness** at 80 and **Opacity** at 80.

Glints

We've seen how we can put a glow on an image and how to use a traveling matte to highlight an image. Next we're going to do something a little more complex, creating a traveling highlight, but one that goes only along the edges of a piece of text, a highlight that glints the edges.

1. We'll begin again with our two base layers, two copies of *Ceremony8*, stacked as before with the top layer blurred, the **Opacity** turned down and composited with **Add** mode.

2. Next we add the text to **V3**. Make it big, a fat font, such as Optima in bold, with a font size of about 180, right to the edges of the **Safe Title Area** and beyond. Set it a little below center in the frame. For my font I used a *y* value of 70.

Next we'll create a moving highlight area.

3. Use FCE's **Custom Gradient** from the **Generators** pop-up menu, **Render>Custom Gradient**.

4. Set the **Duration** for the Custom Gradient to five seconds, because that's how long the animation will be, and drag the Custom Gradient into the **Timeline** onto **V4**.

5. Open the Custom Gradient from the **Timeline** and use the **Control** tab of the **Viewer**; change the **Shape** pop-up menu to **Radial**.

6. Change the gradient's **Start** coordinates to 0,0, centering the radial in the screen.

7. Set the **Gradient Width** to 35.

8. Make sure both **Dithering** and **Gaussian** are not checked.

10.14 Radial Gradient in the Viewer

Animating the Radial

We want the glint to run along the top edge of the letters, so we'll position the radial gradient higher in the frame.

1. First let's move the start position of the Radial Gradient to *x,y* of 0,–100 in the **Controls** tab as in Figure 10.14.

To animate the gradient, we want it to move from left to right across the screen and then back again, staying at its current height. At the start you want the gradient off one side of the screen.

2. Make sure you're at the beginning of the **Timeline**. In the **Custom Gradient's Motion** tab set the Center x point to −450, leaving y at −100, and keyframe it with the **Canvas Keyframe** button.

3. Deselect it and type *215* to go forward 2:15 (two and one-half seconds), about halfway through the clip.

4. Set the **Center** x point way over on the opposite side of the screen, about 500.

5. At the end of the five-second clip, set the x value back to its start position of −450.

Over the five seconds of the clip, the radial gradient will sweep across the text and then back again. So far so good.

6. If you scrub the timeline, or play through with **Option-P**, you should see the gradient swing from left to right and back again.

We now have to get rid of the black and just leave the gradient across the text. We could do this by changing the composite mode of the gradient layer to **Screen**. This gets rid of the black and is useful when you want to use these kind of gradient elements on a picture.

Here, though, the gradient appears not only on the text, but on the background image as well. In this case, we want to confine the gradient to affect only the text portion of the image, so we'll leave the radial gradient layer at normal, not composited.

7. To make the glow appear only on the text, start by copying the text layer on **V3** and placing the copy on **V5**, on top of the gradient. You can do this with **Option-Shift-Drag**.

Your stack should look like Figure 10.15.

8. Open the top text layer into the **Viewer** and use the controls to change its **Color** to white, pale yellow, or whatever glow color you want to use.

This layer will be the glow on top of the text; the radial gradient will be the matte it follows.

9. To the top text layer, apply **Composite Mode>Travel Matte— Luma**.

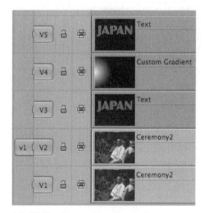

10.15 Five-layer video layers in sequence

10.16 Text with Glow Composite

Immediately the gradient will disappear and the glow will be composited on top of the bottom text layer. Figure 10.16 shows the text with the glow but with the underlying video switched off.

Polishing the Glow

That's a nice effect. You could be happy with it and stop there, with the glowing layer animated across the screen with the Custom Gradient layer.

What we really want, though, is for the glow not to race across the whole text, but to run just along the top edge of the text. It's not hard to do. We just need to add a few more layers.

1. **Option-Shift**-drag two more copies of the text layer on **V3** up to the top of the stack onto **V6** and **V7**.

These will, of course, completely hide the glow, so what we want to do is create a mask that will hide most of the text except for the very edges.

2. Open up the controls for the topmost layer and set its Center point slightly to one side, away from the side the glow starts from.

3. Also set it slightly lower on the screen if the glow is traveling above the text or slightly higher if the glow is traveling below the text.

I increased the values of both x and y by 6. This will make the text look slightly fatter than it is, so what we want to do is make a matte that cuts off the bits of text that protrude beyond the correct shape of the text. That's what the layer beneath is for.

4. To the top layer, apply **Composite Mode>Travel Matte— Alpha**.

The Travel Matte layer disappears, and you're left with just a glint that travels along the edges of the text (see Figure 10.17).

10.17 Glint on text

One More Touch

At the moment, the glint brushes across the upper-left edge of the letters as it moves back and forth across the screen. If you want to be really crafty and add a little something special, you can shift the glint side as it swings back and forth.

1. For the first pass of the Radial Gradient, leave the settings as they are.

2. When the glint reaches the far right side of the screen at 2:15, set a keyframe on the uppermost offset text layer on **V7**.

3. For the next frame, while the Radial Gradient is still off to the right, change that offset text layer's Center *x* value to –6, leaving the *y* value as it is.

Now when the glint passes back from right to left, the glint will be on the upper-right edge of the letters.

The glint stack is at Marker 5 in *Composite Stacks*.

Soft Edge Split Screen

Let's see one more thing we can do with gradients. Sometimes when doing a split screen effect, you like to have a soft, blurred edge, instead of the hard edge the **Crop** tool gives you, which we saw in Lesson 8. The **Crop** function does have an **Edge Feather** function; unfortunately this feathers all the edges, not just the edge that splits the two images. That's where gradients with composite modes come in. At Marker 6 in *Composite Stacks* I've created a soft-edged split screen. One clip is on **V1**, another on **V3**, and sandwiched in between is a custom gradient.

1. To build this start out by laying the clips into the **Timeline** on **V1** and **V3**.

2. Offset each to left and right so the heads are separated enough to leave room for the soft-edged split. You'll have to toggle the **Visibility** of the top layer on and off as you make this adustment.

3. From the **Generators** select **Render>Custom Gradient** and put it on **V2** between the clips.

4. To the clip on top, apply **Composite Mode>Travel Matte—Luma**. You will immediately start to see that much of the image has become transparent.

What we need to control is the shape of the gradient, how quickly it falls off from white to black, and where that fall-off happens.

5. Double-click the Custom Gradient in the **Timeline** to open it into the **Viewer** and go to the **Controls** tab.

6. To make things easier, grab the **Video** tab and pull it out of the **Viewer**, positioning it to the left. Now you can see the gradient on the left, its controls in the center and the output of the effect on the **Canvas** to the right (see Figure 10.18).

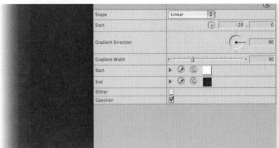

10.18 Viewer, controls and Canvas

7. Begin by setting the **Start** *x* value to 0, 0, and pull down the **Gradient Width** to about 40.

That's about it; you just need to adjust the *x* value at it so the gradient doesn't bleed too much into the right image. Perhaps even tighten the gradient some more. Turning on the **Gaussian** checkbox will make it easier to get a tighter gradient fall-off from white on the left to black and transparency on the right.

Video in Text

I hope you're getting the hang of this by now and are beginning to understand the huge range of capabilities that these tools make possible. Next let's try an even more complex animation with traveling mattes, the ever-popular video-inside-text effect, the kind of technique that might look familiar from the open of another old television program.

To look at what we're going to do, open the *Composite Stacks* sequence and go to Marker 7. If you click on the clip on **V2** called *Damine Nest* and press **Command-R**, you will render out the section of sequence defined by the length of the clip. That's what we're going to build.

If you want to make really enormous letters that fill right to the top and bottom edge of the screen, you will have to create this in Photoshop or Photoshop Elements. As we saw earlier, we can use Photoshop to create oversized sequences that we can work in FCE. This would become a stage sequence. The stage sequence is an intermediary sequence, usually larger than your final output, that lets you work with a very large text file without cutting it off. The problem usually is that the word will extend beyond the edge of frame, so you need to make an image that is as tall as your final but a lot wider. For this project we'll use a sequence that's

1,220×480, 500 pixels wider than the normal frame but the same height.

Start out by creating the multilayer text file in Photoshop or use the one called *Stage.psd* in the **Graphics** bin. You may want to duplicate the graphics file before you start working with it.

Making Text

We need to start with really big blocks of text.

1. In Photoshop I started with a 1,220×540 pixel image at 72dpi.

2. I created the text with the **Text** tool using the word *DAMINE*, the name of the mountain village in Japan where the clips were shot.

3. Pick a chunky, broad font. Don't use a thin, wimpy, serif font. I used Arial Black, but you can use whatever you have at hand.

4. Make the type size large, something in the 270-point range.

We're going to not only move images in the text, but we're going to move a different image in each letter of the text.

5. You can make this easier by kerning the text a little. I opened up the space between the *D* and the *A*. Don't worry about the text going outside the **Safe Title Area**. As long as it stays within the confines of the screen, it will be okay.

6. Because text starts in the center of the screen, a large text block such as this will stretch right off the top of the image, so set the text low in the frame, fairly close to the bottom edge.

7. To make the letters taller, I used Photoshop's **Transform** function, dragging out the top of the letters until they were as close to the top of the image as from the bottom (see Figure 10.19).

8. Finally, I squeezed the image down to 1,220×480 and imported the Photoshop file into FCE with a duration of five seconds.

If you don't have Photoshop or Photoshop Elements available, use a duplicate of *Stage.psd*.

10.19 Large title block in Photoshop

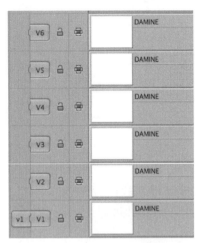

10.20 Six-layer stack of text blocks

10.21 Cropped text layer

Separating Letters

The text file will be the matte for the video that's inside it. Because we want different video in each letter, we need to separate the word into its individual letters. We also don't need the background layer, which is only there to create the multilayer image.

1. Begin by deleting the black background and dragging the text block onto the bottom layer.

2. **Option-Shift**-drag the text layer from **V1** onto the layers above again and again, until you have a stack six text layers tall, or one for each letter (see Figure 10.20).

After you've created the layer stack, then you need to crop each letter so that only it is visible.

3. If the **Canvas** is not already in **Image+Wireframe** mode, switch to it now.

4. Select the text on **V1** and use **Control-S** to solo it, so that none of the other layers are visible.

5. Use the **Crop** tool to pull in the right side of the text layer that's in your sequence. Crop it between the *D* and the *A* until only the *D* is visible (see Figure 10.21).

6. Select the text layer on **V2** and solo it with **Control-S** to make only that layer visible.

The number in center of the **Canvas** will tell you which layer is selected.

7. With the **Crop** tool, move the right crop line from the right until you are between the *A* and the *M*.

8. Move the left crop line so that it's between the *D* and the *A*.

9. Select the text on **V3** and repeat, moving the right crop line to the right until all of the *M* is visible.

10. Move its left crop line so that it's between the second and third letters, *A* and *M*.

11. Repeat for the other four layers until each layer has one letter visible on it.

12. When you're done, be sure to switch off **Soloing** on the last layer with **Control-S** so that all the letters are visible again.

Adding Video

We're ready now to put in some video. We'll work only with video here.

1. Set **V1** as the destination track, and make sure the playhead is at the beginning of the stage sequence.

2. Find a clip in the **Browser** you want to place above the text on **V1**.

I used *Ceremony1*.

3. Drag the clip to the **Canvas** to **Superimpose**, slotting the clip into a new V2 between the *D* on V1 and the *A* now on **V3**.

4. Roughly position the clip in the **Canvas** so that it's sitting on the left side of the frame over the letter *D*.

The next step will be to apply a **Composite Mode**.

5. With the clip on **V2** selected, use the **Control** key to see the shortcut menu, and choose **Composite Mode>Travel Matte—Alpha**.

The image doesn't have to be the whole size of the frame or positioned in the center of the frame. It can be placed anywhere at any size, so long as it covers the letter.

6. Grab a corner of the image and resize it. Hold the **Shift** key and distort the image shape if you want (see Figure 10.22).

Next we need to add some more video to the other layers.

7. Set **V3** as the destination track and find a clip in the **Browser** to superimpose over it.

I used *Village 3* for this one.

8. **Superimpose** it onto **V4** and change its **Composite Mode** to **Travel Matte—Alpha**.

9. Scale the image in the **Canvas** and position it so that it covers the letter *A*.

The next clip will take its matte from the text now on **V5** and fill the letter *M*. I used *Dance3* beginning about three seconds into the shot.

10. Find a clip to use and **Superimpose** it above **V5**.

11. Set the composite mode to **Travel Matte—Alpha**.

12. Scale and position in the **Canvas**.

I used the beginning of *Ceremony2* to super above **V7**.

13. Repeat the process, which will create a new **V8**, above the letter *I*.

I used *Village1* for the next track.

14. Repeat the process to create a new **V10** to be matted by the letter *N* on **V9**.

10.22 Distorted image composited over text

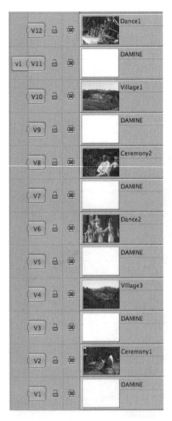

10.23 Twelve-layer stack

Finally, I used *Dance1* to super above **V11**.

15. Repeat the process for the new **V12**, taking its **Travel Matte—Alpha** from the letter *E* on **V11**.

Your 12 layers in the sequence should now be made up of six layers of text interspersed with six layers of video scaled and positioned to fit the text layer below it (see Figure 10.23).

Nesting

So far we've created the text in a stage sequence with very large letters, and we've placed moving pictures inside each letter. Next we need to animate the whole composite over another image so that the stage sequence itself moves across another image. The stage sequence we created is a nest of material. The one I've created, called *Damine Nest*, is in your **Browser**.

1. Open a copy of *Sequence 1* and from the **Generators** make a Custom Gradient that's five seconds long.

2. Bring your Custom Gradient into the sequence on **V1** and double-click on it to open it back into the **Viewer**.

3. In the **Controls** set your gradient to whatever pair of colors you'd like for your background.

4. Place your stage sequence on **V2** above the video on **V1**.

Sequence 1 is, of course, 720×480. So when you place the much larger stage sequence in it, the stage sequence, *Damine Nest*, will shrink to fit into the **Canvas**.

5. **Option**-double-click the nest on **V2**, which will open it into the **Viewer**.

6. Go to the **Motion** tab and reset the **Basic Motion** with the red **X** button. This will reset the motion values and extend the layer beyond the sides of the **Canvas** as in Figure 10.24.

10.24 Damine Nest composited on video

Next we'll want to animate the text so that the whole nest slides across the screen from right to left.

7. In the **Motion** tab, set a Center *x* value at the start of the clip to 968, which will push the nest off the right side of the screen and set a keyframe. 2. At the end of the clip, set a Center position of *x* –970, which will move the nest off the left side of the screen.

Over the course of the five seconds the text will travel from right to left on top of your Custom Gradient. I have built the animation at Marker 7 in *Composite Stacks*.

Variation with Fades

At Marker 8 in *Composite Stacks* is a variation in which each letter fades in one after the other.

1. Place the Custom Gradient background layer on **V1** in a new sequence and your stage sequence on top of it on **V2**.

For this animation we're going to need the text sequence with the word to fit into the **Canvas**. Rather than rebuild all the text files, with all the all the layers and all the cropping, we'll simply rescale the stage sequence so that it fits into the 720×480 sequence.

2. Use the **Zoom** pop-up menu at the top of the **Canvas** and set it to **Fit All**, which should show you the full width of the stage sequence.

3. Grab a corner of the image and pull in to reduce the scale to fit inside the **Canvas** as in Figure 10.25.

4. Double-click the nested sequence on **V2** to open it up with all 12 layers.

5. Make sure the playhead is at the beginning of the sequence, and turn on the **Clip Overlays** (**Option-W**).

6. Take the **Pen** tool, set an Opacity keyframe right at the beginning of the clip, and drag it down to zero.

7. Move the playhead forward half a second, 15 frames, and ramp **Opacity** up to 100.

8. Now go to on the video clip on **V4**. You're half a second into the clip. Set an Opacity keyframe with a value of zero here.

9. Go forward to the one-second mark. Change **Opacity** to the clip in **V4** to 100.

10. Bring **Opacity** on the video clip on **V6** down to zero with the **Pen**.

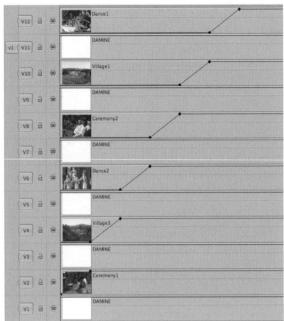

10.25 Resizing the image *(above)*

10.26 Twelve-layer stack with Opacity keyframes *(right)*

11. Bring **Opacity** up to 100 15 frames later.

12. Do the same for the clips on **V8**, **V10**, and **V12**, bringing up **Opacity** for each 15 frames after the one before.

Each letter will now fade onto the screen one after the other, in half second intervals. One last touch will polish it. Your stack in the sequence should look like Figure 10.26.

Drop Shadow Finale

1. Go back to your final sequence, the one with the rescaled stage sequence and your Custom Gradient.

2. **Option**–double-click on the nested sequence on **V2** to open it in the **Viewer**.

3. In the **Motion** tab, set a **Drop Shadow**.

Now as each letter fades on, its drop shadow will fade on with it. This is easier than doing it for each letter in the nested sequence. The finished sequence is at Marker 8 in *Composite Stacks*.

Outline Text

Let's look at a technique for getting video inside outlined text. It's simple to do once you understand the principles behind compositing modes and travel mattes. To do this we're going to use FCE's **Outline Text** tool from the **Generators**.

1. Start off by from the **Generators** pop-up **Text>Outline Text**.

2. In the **Controls** tab, type *DAMINE* in the text box. Use Arial Black or some other fat font, set the size up to about 120 point, leaving the default black and white.

3. Change the **Aspect** to 0.4. This will make the text much taller so that you'll see more of the image through it.

4. In the **Controls** give the text a large amount of **Line Width** and some **Line Softness**.

5. I used a **Line Width** of 180 and a **Line Softness** of 50.

6. Set the **Duration** to five seconds and lay this outline text in *Sequence 1* on **V2**.

7. Put a video clip as a background layer on **V1**. I used *Village1*.

8. The next thing we have to do is **Option-Shift**-drag the outline text from **V2** to **V3** to copy the text.

9. Now open up again the Outline Text layer on **V2** and make the Line Color anything you want. I went for a bright yellow.

10. Put a video clip that you want to appear inside the outline text on **V4**, above the two layers of outline text. I superimposed *Dance2*.

11. The final touch is to apply a **Compositing Mode>Travel Matte—Luma** to the video clip on **V4**.

A travel matte will always hide the matte layer. Therefore the outline text on **V3**, which provides the matte information for the video clip on **V4**, disappears, leaving you to see the outline color on the layer below. The **Canvas** should look something like Figure 10.27. The stack is at Marker 9 in *Composite Stacks*.

Grunge Edges

Next we'll do something different. We're going to grunge up the edges of a clip.

1. Start out in Photoshop, making a new image that FCE will resize for digital video. Start at 720×540. If you don't have Photoshop or Elements, the file I made up is in your **Browser**. It's called *Grunge.psd*.

2. Make the new image completely black.

3. Take the **Rectangular Marquee** tool and draw a rectangle that's about 50 pixels in from the edges of your image.

4. Fill the selection with white.

10.27 Video in outline text

10.28 Grunge.psd

5. Now have some fun. Drop the selection and grunge up the edges of the white box. Start with Photoshop's **Smudge** tool (**R**), with which you can pull the white into the black and black into white. Or you can use one of the PS filters from the **Distort** group, maybe **Ripple** or **Ocean Ripple** set to a small size but a high magnitude. Or combinations of various tools.

I like to smudge up the edges a bit first and then apply the filter so it doesn't come out too repetitive. Do it by mostly pulling the black into the white, because the filter will expand the schmutzing effect. Avoid doing an effect that goes beyond the edges of the frame. It will look cut off when you composite it with the video. You should end up with something that looks like the *Grunge.psd* image in your **Browser** (see Figure 10.28).

6. Import your Photoshop file into Final Cut.

7. In a new sequence place your Photoshop file on **V1** and place a video clip on top of it on **V2**.

8. Apply **Composite Mode>Travel Matte—Luma** to the clip on **V2**.

In the **Browser** is a sequence called *Grunge Sequence* that contains *Ceremony2* on **V2** and the Photoshop file *Grunge.psd* on **V1**. To the video clip I applied **Composite Mode>Travel Matte—Luma**.

Look at Marker 10 in *Composite Stacks*. Here I've laid a gray color matte on **V1**, and on **V2** I placed the nested sequence *Grunge Sequence*. With the **Canvas** in **Image+Wireframe** mode, I scaled and rotated the nested sequence in the **Canvas** (see

Figure 10.29). As you can see, you can work up millions of variations on the basic idea.

Bug

A bug is an insect, a mistake in software coding, and it's also that little icon usually in the lower-left corner of your television telling you what station you're watching. There are lots of different ways to make bugs, but I'll show you one using Photoshop and compositing modes. In your **Browser** is a Photoshop file called *Logo.psd*. Double-click it, and it will open as a sequence with two layers. The bottom layer, which has the visibility switched off, has the bug already made up with the Photoshop effect. The top layer that is visible in the **Canvas** doesn't have the effect applied, and that's the one we're going to work on. If you want to just work with the bottom layer that's made up for you already, you can skip the first section of this tutorial.

10.29 Scaled and rotated grunge-edged clip

1. Make sure in your **User Preferences** that your **External Editor** for still images is set to Photoshop (or Photoshop Elements).

2. **Control**-click on the visible layer in the *Logo.psd* sequence, and from the shortcut menu choose **Open in Editor.**

3. Once Photoshop has launched, select Layer 2, and from the little **F** in the bottom left of the **Layers** palette, add a **Layer Style,** choosing **Drop Shadow** (see Figure 10.30).

4. Change the **Drop Shadow Angle** to 145 and the **Distance** to 15. Leave the other controls the same.

5. Check the **Inner Shadow** checkbox to add the shadow. Set the **Distance** to 5, and the **Choke** and **Size** to 10.

6. Also add a **Stroke.** Set the **Size** to 6. I made the color blue (see Figure 10.31).

7. Click **OK,** and you've built the effect.

10.30 Add Layer Style > Drop Shadow

There is one more step to take before going back to FCE. The effects have to be applied to the layer. The easiest way to do this is to add a layer underneath the effects layer.

8. Add a new layer to your Photoshop composition and in the **Layers** palette drag it below Layer 2, which holds the effects.

9. Make sure Layer 2 is selected. From the **Wing** menu, choose **Merge Down,** or use the keyboard shortcut **Command-E** (see Figure 10.32).

10. Save your file and go back to Final Cut Express.

10.31 Drop Shadow panel with Inner Shadow and Stroke *(right)*

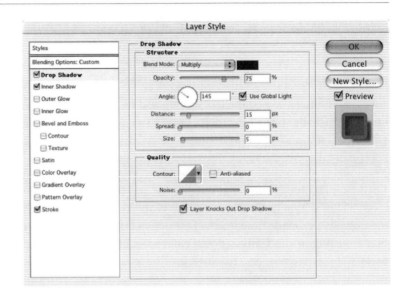

10.32 Merge Down

➤*Tip*

Distinctive Logo: There are any number of different ways to give your logo a distinctive edge by using the power of layer styles. Rather than use the **Inner Shadow** and **Stroke** method, you could also use **Bevel and Emboss**. Change the **Technique** pop-up to **Chisel Hard**, and push the **Size** slider until the two sides of the bevel meet. This will give you maximum effect. Remember that the logo is going to be very reduced in size. Also in bottom part of the **Bevel and Emboss** panel, try different types of **Glass Contour** from the little **arrow** pop-up menu.

If you want to learn more about working with Photoshop, especially for use with digital video, I highly recommend Richard Harrington's *Photoshop for Nonlinear Editors*, published by CMP Books, ISBN 1578202094.

Layer 2 in the PS sequence *Logo.psd* will have been updated and will include your new effects.

11. Open a new duplicate *Sequence 1* and drag some video into it. I used *Village2*.

Now normally you're going to want your bug to run the duration of your sequence, which might be an hour or more. Because you can't drag out still image layers to an unlimited duration once they're in a sequence, you need to set the duration of the bug while it's still in the **Browser**.

12. The simplest way to work with this is to first open the sequence *Logo.psd*. Now drag your newly minted effects layer Layer 2 out into the **Browser** (or the original Layer 1 if you prefer).

This will, of course, be a copy of the *Layer 2* in *Logo.psd*. With *Layer 2* as a single-layer image, before you place the bug into the final sequence, you can change its duration in the **Browser**. Here you can make the duration of the still image anything you want—anything up to four hours anyway, which is the duration limit of any FCE sequence.

13. Set the **Duration** for the bug logo to the duration of the sequence you want to cover. Now you can drag the layer into your final sequence.

14. The first step is to change the logo's composite type.

10.33 Logo with Composite
Mode > Multiply

There are a number of compositing modes that will work for this, but I like to use **Composite Mode>Multiply** (see Figure 10.33). This will make the white of the logo almost transparent. For a slightly brighter look, try **Soft Light,** and for an even more transparent look, use **Overlay.**

15. At the current size the logo is probably a bit intrusive. You might want to scale it down a bit and reposition it in the corner or your choice, bottom right being the traditional location on American television.

It will now be your unobtrusive watermark on the screen. Some people also like to use effects such as displacements or bumpmaps, but for something this small, I don't really think it's necessary. The simple transparency effect of a composite mode is enough. The one I created is at Marker 11 in *Composite Stacks.*

Day for Night

Color mattes don't have to be used only for backgrounds or graphical elements as we looked at in earlier lessons. They can also be used as a color filter. Day for Night is the now seldom-used technique of trying to shoot in daylight and make it look like a moonlit night. Old Westerns almost always used this technique. Basically, you stop down the camera and shoot through a blue or a graduated blue filter. Let's do something similar.

1. Start off by laying the clip you want to affect on **V1** in a new sequence.

I used *Village3* because it presents a typical daylight problem, the bright sky.

2. Darken the image, such as with **Color Corrector.**

I pulled down all the levels—**Whites, Mids, Blacks,** and even **Saturation.** Even with the levels pulled quite far down, the sky remains bright and pale (see Figure 10.34). Next we'll use the **Color Matte** to add the blue night filter.

3. Create a deep, dark blue color matte and lay it on **V3.**

4. Create a **Custom Gradient** and place it between the two layers on **V2.**

5. Set the **Composite Mode** on the color matte to **Travel Matte—Luma.**

All that's left to do is to make the gradient.

10.34 Darkened image with a bright sky

6. Open the controls, leave the default at **Linear** gradient, and change the **Direction** to 180.

Next you need to use the crosshairs to place the start of the gradient. There is a start point but no end point for the gradient. If you start at the top of the **Canvas,** the blue will carry too far down into the image.

7. Scale down the size of the **Canvas** to something like 25 percent.

8. Place the start point for the crosshairs out in the grayboard above the image.

9. Tighten the **Gradient Width** so that it falls off more sharply.

10. Make the end color of the gradient somewhat less than pure black to give the image a cold, blue cast.

10.35 Day for Night gradient filter

The sky should be dark blue, but the center of the image should still show some light and color (see Figure 10.35). The stack is at Marker 12 in *Composite Stack*s.

That brings us to the end of this packed lesson on compositing. We're almost ready to export our material from Final Cut and out into the world, which is the subject of our final lesson.

Lesson 11

Outputting from Final Cut Express

Remember that I said at the beginning that the hard, technical part of nonlinear editing was at the start, setting up and setting preferences, logging and capturing? The fun part was the editing in the middle, and the easy part was the outputting at the end. We're up to the easy part, the output. Because it's so simple this will be a short lesson.

The two basic ways of outputting are:

- Exporting, if you're going to another computer application or CD or DVD or web delivery
- Recording to tape, if you're going to traditional tape delivery

Because it's probably the most common requirement for Final Cut Express users, let's look at outputting to tape first. We'll see exporting later on page 266.

There are basically two ways to get material from your computer to tape:

- **Record to Tape**
- **Print to Video**

Record to Tape

You can get your edited material back out to tape in several different ways. The simplest one, and probably the most commonly used way, is to record to tape. Before you do that you should always

- Make sure everything that needs to be rendered in the sequence is rendered.

- Make sure you are set to **FireWire** in the **View>Video** menu.

- Make sure you mix down your audio. Go to **Sequence> Render Only>Mixdown (Command-Option-R)**.

Mixdown the audio even if you have only a single stereo pair of audio. It's much easier for your computer and your drives to play back a mixdown file than it is to mix your audio on the fly. Also, the default audio quality playback is set to **Low**. If you just record to tape without mixing down, you will get low-quality playback. However, whenever you mixdown your audio, it's always done to high quality, and that's what you want when you record to tape. Put the playhead at the beginning of the timeline, put your camcorder into VCR mode, switch on record with the VCR controls, and press the spacebar. This is a fast, effective, and simple-to-use method.

It's probably a good idea to have some black at the beginning of your sequence and have the playhead sitting on it, so that when you begin recording, you're not recording a still image for a while. You should record at least 10 seconds of black before pressing the spacebar to begin playing back your sequence.

There is one other trap in recording to tape, either manually or with **Print to Video**. If you have set your **Render Controls** in **Sequence Settings** down to low values to speed up rendering, that's the playback quality you'll get. You cannot now switch to high quality and automatically force a re-render. You have to switch to high quality and then reset each effect that was rendered at low resolution to force it to re-render at high quality. There is no force re-render function, unfortunately. This is also true of exporting to tape and can be a significant issue in Final Cut.

Using playback from the **Timeline** has some disadvantages. You don't get to put in bars and tone and neat countdowns and slates and black leaders and trailers, unless you physically add them to your sequence. If you want these features, you can use **Print to Video**.

Print to Video

Print to Video is under the **File** menu. If you have a sequence selected in the **Browser** or an active **Timeline**, you can call up **Print to Video** from the menu or use **Control-M**. This brings up the dialog box in Figure 11.1.

In this dialog you can set any number of options for program starts and ends. You can add bars and tone and set the tone level, depending on the system you're using. A number of different digital audio standards are used, if you can call anything that has variables a standard. Different systems use –12, –14, –16 or –20dB as digital audio standards. Analog uses a variety of other standards around 0dB. If you are going to send your video to a duplication house, check with them before selecting a tone level.

The **Slate** pop-up lets you use the:

- **Clip Name**
- **Text,** which you can add in the text window
- **File,** which is any still image, video or audio file

So if you want to record an audio slate, selecting file and navigating to it with the little **Load** button will play the sound during recording.

You can use FCE's built-in countdown, using a form of Academy leader. Or you can use a countdown of your own by selecting **File** in the **Countdown** pop-up menu.

Notice the checkbox in the bottom left, new to FCE2,which provides the ability to automatically begin recording. When you start **Print to Video**, FCE will write a video, and if necessary, it will write an audio file of any material that needs to be rendered. Every time you use **Print to Video**, it will have to do this, even if you've just used **Print to Video**. After it's finished writing the video and audio files, FCE will prompt you before it begins recording. Accept by clicking **OK**, and the computer will take control of the deck and send it into record at whatever point it's parked on the tape.

You can use either **Record to Tape** or **Print to Video** to make a VHS recording. Connect your DV camcorder or deck to your computer, and connect its analog output to your VHS deck. It's probably a good idea to have the VHS deck in turn connected to a video monitor or TV set so that you can see what you're recording. Then set the VHS deck in **Record**, and use the DV device as a digital-to-analog converter to get your movie onto VHS.

✎ Note

PtV Limits: Although you can loop FCE's **Print to Video** as many times as you want, the sequence had better be fairly short. The duration of any **Print to Video** recording is limited. It can't be longer than four hours, which is probably more than enough for most people.

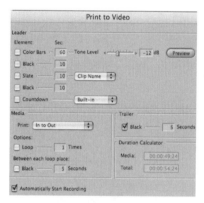

11.1 Print to Video dialog box

➤**Tip**
In to Out: If you want to record only a portion of your sequence, select the portion you want to record by marking it with In and Out points in the Timeline. Then in the **Print to Video** settings window, select **In to Out** from the **Print** pop-up menu in the **Media** portion of window. When you press **OK**, playback will begin at the marked In point and run until it reaches the Out point.

Export

You can access the different formats and ways of exporting from FCE from the **File** menu (see Figure 11.2). From here you can export to **QuickTime Movie**, which in the previous version was called Final Cut Movie, or **Using QuickTime Conversion**, which in the previous version was export to QuickTime.

QuickTime Movie

Let's start with QuickTime Movie, the first of the two **Export** options. When you export a QuickTime movie, Final Cut is listed as its creator type, so that if you launch the resulting movie, it will launch FCE. Because Final Cut is a QuickTime-based application, the exported movie will also play using the QuickTime Player and will work in any other QuickTime-based application, such as iMovie or iDVD.

You can export a sequence as a digital file into a Final Cut movie in several ways:

- From the active **Timeline** window directly from the sequence you're working in
- From an active **Viewer**
- From the **Browser** by exporting a sequence or clip

Click on the item and go to **Export>QuickTime Movie**. This brings up the dialog box in Figure 11.3.

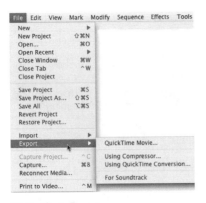

11.2 File > Export

Here you can rename your sequence, and you can select whether you want to export **Audio** and **Video** or **Audio Only** or **Video Only** from the **Include** pop-up menu.

Here you also have the option to export **Markers** through a pop-up menu (see Figure 11.4). To export chapter markers to iDVD4, select **Chapter Markers** from the pop-up.

The checkbox at the bottom of the dialog box, **Make Movie Self-Contained**, is an important one. This checkbox defaults to being on, but if you uncheck it, FCE will generate a reference movie. This is a relatively small file that points back to the original media source files. It will play the contents of the sequence as you laid them out.

11.3 QuickTime Movie export dialog box

The reference movie will play back from the QT player, and it can also be imported into other applications such as iDVD or compression programs such as Sorenson Squeeze. The reference movie is treated just like any other QT clip inside these other applications. FCE and the importing application do not need to be open at the same time for this to work.

The advantages to making reference movies are the speed in generating the file and the comparatively small file size. If anything in the FCE sequence needs to be rendered, it will still have to be rendered for the reference movie, and the audio files will also be duplicated as a mixdown of your tracks. You do, of course, need to have access to all the source media included in the sequence, because a reference movie only points to existing media source files on your hard drives. It's not a complete video clip in itself. Be warned: if you delete any of the media needed for the reference movie, it will not play. It will be a broken QuickTime file. If you send it to somebody on a CD, they won't be able to play it. It will play only on a machine that has access to the media.

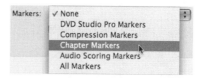

11.4 Exporting Markers pop-up menu

Export to QuickTime Movie is an important tool because it is the only way to export a sequence from FCE without recompressing the video. All other exports, including export Using QuickTime Conversion, will recompress the frames, producing some degradation of the video image, albeit very slight.

🐜 Note

Export to Soundtrack: This export function is the same as exporting to **QuickTime Movie**. The only difference is that exporting to Soundtrack, Apple's music-creation application, is preset to export audio scoring markers. A little thing to watch out for: if you do an export to Soundtrack with scoring markers and then do an export to QuickTime Movie, the preset will still be set to export audio scoring markers. **Export Using Compressor** will launch that application, if you have it. There you can set whatever file-conversion settings you want as well as have access to Compressor's excellent MPEG-2 compression engine if you're going to work in DVD Studio Pro 2. Although you can run Compressor from inside FCE2, it's generally consider better, giving much faster performance, if you export your sequence as a reference file and open that file in Compressor with FCE closed.

QuickTime Conversion

QuickTime Conversion is the catch-all for every form of file conversion and still export from FCE. I would have liked for **Still Image** export to be separated, but it's hidden in here as well (see Figure 11.5).

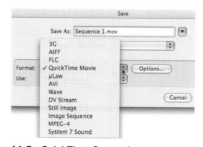

11.5 QuickTime Conversion export

How to Make Chapter Markers

The last thing you should do to a project before exporting is to set up chapter markers to use in iDVD4 or Compressor. It could not be simpler to create them.

First, you need to ensure that the marker is in the correct location. It has to be placed on the **Timeline Ruler** itself, not on a clip. To put a marker in the **Timeline**, make sure nothing is selected in the sequence. Use **Command-Shift-A** to **De-select All**.

Add the marker by pressing the **M** key. Press it again to call up the **Edit Marker** dialog box (see Figure 11.6). To create the chapter marker, click the **Add Chapter Marker** button. **<CHAPTER>** will appear in the **Comment** field. Do not alter this.

If you want to give the chapter a name that will carry over to iDVD, enter it in the **Name** field. That's it. Close the dialog box, and you're done.

11.6 Edit Marker dialog box

Notice that you can also enter scoring markers here in the same way to use with Soundtrack, and compression markers, if you're going to Compressor.

You should bear in mind a few rules about chapter markers:

- iDVD4 will accept no more than 36 chapter markers.

- Chapters markers cannot be closer than one second from each other.

- You can't have a chapter marker within one second of the start or end of the sequence.

- A chapter marker is automatically created for the beginning of the exported material.

It's probably a good idea not to put in chapter markers until after you have completely, positively, and finally finished editing your show. Otherwise you may have to redo or at least reposition all your chapter markers to get them into the right place.

Video export

Final Cut Express has a number of video export choices for QuickTime Conversion. The **Format** pop-up allows you to choose from a variety of formats including:

- **3G,** a format used by handheld devices such as cellphones
- **FLC,** an 8-bit format used for computer animations
- **AVI,** a PC video format
- **QuickTime Movie**

- **DV Stream,** DV audio and video encoded into a single track for use with iMovie
- **MPEG-4,** a format designed primarily for cross-platform web compression

These are the video formats. Some, such as AVI and QuickTime, allow you to use a number of different codecs. DV Stream is used by iMovie, not by FCE. Do not export to DV Stream if you're going to a video-editing application other than iMovie.

In **QuickTime Conversion,** the **User** pop-up is contextual; that is, what is offered here is determined by what's selected in the **Format** pop-up.

If you select **QuickTime** in the **Format** pop-up menu, the **User** pop-up menu offers a number of common Internet settings based on MPEG-4 (see Figure 11.7). This is a good place to start if you want to create a video to show on the Internet or put on your .mac homepage.

If you want more control, choose **MPEG-4** from the **Format** pop-up and then click on the **Options** button to bring up the **MPEG-4 Settings** window (see Figure 11.8). The **Video** and **Audio** tabs give you full control over your media. It takes a great deal of practice and testing to become proficient at compression for the web. Try

Default Settings
Modem – Audio Only
Modem
✓ DSL/Cable – Low
DSL/Cable – Medium
DSL/Cable – High
LAN

11.7 QuickTime Conversion User pop-up menu

11.8 MPEG-4 Settings window

Video will make use of improved MPEG–4 features (known as ISMA Profile 1). This produces files of higher quality, while potentially being incompatible with some MPEG–4 devices. The video will have a data rate of 900 kbits/second and a frame rate of 30.0 frames per second. The resulting movie will be 320 by 240 pixels.

Audio will be optimized for music (known as Low Complexity AAC). The audio will have the current sample rate in stereo. The data rate of the audio will be 128 kbits/second. The audio encoding will be done in better quality mode.

This MPEG–4 file will support ISMA (Internet Streaming Media Alliance) specifications.

various data rates, frame sizes, and frame rates and compare them to the default web settings that come with selecting **Quick-Time** in the **Format** pop-up menu.

Exporting with QuickTime Conversion allows you to use a variety of different codecs for compression, such as, among others:

- Animation
- Cinepak
- DV-NTSC
- Motion-JPEG A
- Photo-JPEG
- Sorenson Video 3

11.9 QuickTime video and audio options

Codec stands for compression/decompression and is the software algorithm that a specific system uses to reduce the file size of the media. To export to other QuickTime codecs, such as the excellent Sorenson Video 3 codec, use the **Options** button and select the correct video and audio settings (see Figure 11.9).

The default compressor is **Video,** but if you click on the **Settings** button, you can choose the codec you want to use. For Quick-Time video on the Internet, you might set the Compressor to Sorenson. Try various data rate settings. 100Kbps will give good results. Set the frame rate to 15fps.

Size should be set to 320×240.

These settings will produce a fairly large file, suitable for use on high-speed connections.

Photo-JPEG is used for file-size reduction. An important codec is Animation, which has a high data rate. Animation is a lossless compression codec often used to transfer material between various applications. One advantage that the Animation codec has is that it can carry alpha-channel information with the video. This allows you to create a sequence in one application and bring it into FCE without loss and with its transparency information. Or you could export an FCE sequence that has transparency and bring it into another application such as After Effects, keeping the transparency you created in FCE. When you export with the Animation codec with an alpha channel, make sure that for **Colors** you select **Millions+**. The plus is the alpha channel.

The **Sound** dialog box allows you to set an audio compression scheme as well as setting the sampling rate you want to use.

To create high-quality web video, you'll need a separate application such as Discreet's Cleaner or Sorenson Squeeze. To create video CDs, you'll need an application such as Roxio's Toast, that allows compression to the MPEG1 codec. This is a heavily compressed codec but a remarkable one in that it can play back off the very low output of a CD and still produce a full-screen, full-motion image. To create a DVD, you need another application such as iDVD or DVD Studio Pro. When exporting to iDVD, you should use either a self-contained or a reference Final Cut movie, and iDVD will do the compression to MPEG2 for you.

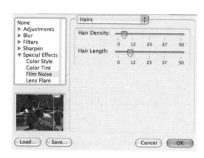

11.10 Film Noise Hairs panel

Exporting to QuickTime Conversion allows you to add filters to your clips or sequences. Most of the QuickTime filters are available directly within FCE, with one notable exception, **Film Noise,** which is under the **Special Effects** submenu (see Figure 11.10).

This filter adds an old-time film look to your video, as if it were scratched and dirty. A small QT movie runs in the bottom-left corner showing you how much schmutz you've added to the picture. Here you can set amounts of **Hair** that appear on your video, from very low to quite furry. Notice the buttons that allow you to **Save** and **Load**, letting you create favorite preferences for the filter that you can access again and again. In addition to **Hair,** the pop-up at the top will take you to another panel to set **Scratches,** where you can set the amount of damage on your video, and another to set **Dust and Film Fading,** which allows you to tint the film. The sepia is quite subtle, and the 1930s color film is suitably garish.

Image sequence export

Two other types of QuickTime Conversion export are often used: **Image Sequence** and **Still Image.** Image sequences are useful for rotoscoping, frame-by-frame painting on the video image, and other animation work, and provide high-quality output without loss. You can set any frame rate, and exporting will create one frame of video for every frame you specify. Make sure you first create a folder in which to put your image sequence because this can easily generate a huge number of files.

Still image export

Finally, **Quicktime Conversion** allows you to export still images. This is how you get frames of video out to your computer for web or print use. Your stills will only be 72dpi, probably not good enough for fine printing. Photoshop plugins such as Lizard Tech's Genuine Fractals can help improve the image's appearance.

The **Options** button for **Still Image** export, which uses the same dialog box as **Image Sequence**, includes a **Frame Rate** box. Don't be confused; leave the **Frame Rate** blank if you want only one frame.

The still you're exporting may very well be in rectangular pixel aspect ratio. This is not a problem if you're going back to a video application, but in print or on a computer display, the stills will look squashed. Photoshop will fix this problem for you. If the still image comes from DV, in Photoshop go to **Image Size**. Switch off the **Constrain portions** checkbox and change the size to 640×480. You'll end up with a 4:3 image in the correct pixel aspect ratio. Check **Resampling** and select **Bicubic** whenever you resize in Photoshop.

If you're going to export stills for web or print work that's come from video, especially video with a lot of motion in it, you'll probably want to de-interlace it. You can do this either in FCE or before you export the frame. As we saw in "De-interlace and Flicker" on page 232 in Lesson 9, you select **Video Filters>Video>De-interlace** from the **Effects** menu. Or you can de-interlace in Photoshop as well. It's in the **Filters** menu under **Video>De-Interlace**. I normally do it in Photoshop because I think its **De-interlace** feature works better than FCE's built-in one, which simply drops one of the fields. In the Photoshop **De-Interlace** filter, you have an interpolation option, which works very well.

Audio Export

FCE can export to a number of different audio formats including:

- AIFF
- μLaw
- Wave
- System 7

If you select **AIFF** in the **Use** pop-up you'll get common audio file settings (see Figure 11.11).

✓ Default Settings
11.025 kHz 16 bit Mono
11.025 kHz 16 bit Stereo
11.025 kHz 8 bit Mono
11.025 kHz 8 bit Stereo
22.050 kHz 16 bit Mono
22.050 kHz 16 bit Stereo
22.050 kHz 8 bit Mono
22.050 kHz 8 bit Stereo
44.1 kHz 16 bit Mono
44.1 kHz 16 bit Stereo
44.1 kHz 8 bit Mono
44.1 kHz 8 bit Stereo

11.11 AIFF Export Use pop-up menu

Notice that the selection does not include any of the DV sampling rates, although AIFF is the most commonly used format for audio files with Final Cut. Instead of the **Use** pop-up, use the **Options** button, which is also context-sensitive and offers a wider range of options, including 32,000 and 48,000, the DV sampling rates. AIFF export options also offers a large number of compressors to reduce the file size of the audio (see Figure 11.12). Generally audio for video is not compressed, except for web use or in DVD creation.

Archiving

Now that you've finished your project you should think about archiving your material. Your original videotapes on which you shot the project should be your primary archive. Using the **Project** feature that we saw in the **Capture** window in Lesson 2 on page 46, you can recapture all the video for your project.

You need to store the project file itself. The best way to do this would be burn it onto a CD. On the CD you should also put on whatever graphics files you created for the project. Not the FCE titles, which are retained in the project file, but any Photoshop or other images you may have used. You should also save any music or separate sound you used in the project. And don't forget to save any Voice Over tracks you created. Everything other than the video clips that made up your movie should be burned onto your archive CD.

To restore the project, copy all the material back from the CD onto your computer. Open the project file and reconnect the existing files. Next run the capture process, clicking on **Project** in the **Capture** window to bring your video material onto the computer. The **Capture** window will prompt you for each tape it needs in turn. When all the material is back on your computer your project will be restored and ready to be re-edited.

Summary

We've now gone through the whole cycle of work in Final Cut Express, starting from tape raw material, either analog or digital, to capturing, editing, transitions, titling, special effects, compositing. Now finally we have returned our finished project to tape. It's been a long road, but I hope one that was exciting, interesting, and rewarding for you.

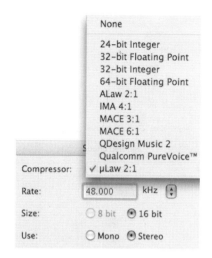

11.12 AIFF Export options

Index

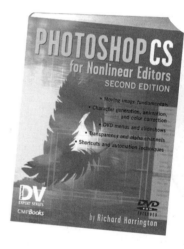

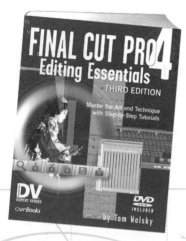

Final Cut Pro 4
Editing Essentials

by Tom Wolsky

Master the craft of editing with Final Cut Pro 4. This editing workshop gives you firsthand experience with the art and technique of editing using eight tutorial lessons that cover the essentials: capturing your material, organizing it, editing, adding transitions, employing basic titling and sound techniques, and outputting from the application. The companion DVD contains tutorial media and plug-ins

$29.95, Softcover with DVD, 284pp, ISBN 1-57820-227-2

Final Cut Pro 4 On the Spot

by Richard Harrington & Abba Shapiro

Learn what you need to know—when you need to know it. Packed with more than 350 expert techniques, this book clearly illustrates all the essential methods that pros use to get the job done. Experienced editors and novices alike will discover an invaluable reference filled with techniques to improve efficiency and creativity.

$27.95, Softcover, 236pp, ISBN 1-57820-231-0

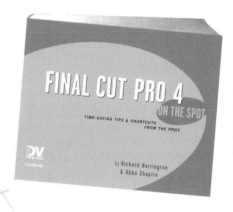

Creative Titling with
Final Cut Pro

by Diannah Morgan

Create compelling title sequences using Final Cut Pro and LiveType. Packed with four-color illustrations, explanations, instructions, and step-by-step tutorials, this book teaches and inspires editors to produce work that is a cut above the rest. Covers conceptualization, design, methodology, and the mechanics of successful title sequences.

$44.95, 4-color, Softcover, 192pp, ISBN 1-57820-225-6
Available in North America only

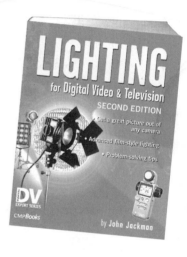

What's on the DVD?

The companion DVD for *Final Cut Express 2 Editing Workshop* is a hybrid DVD. The DVD portion of the disc is a short introduction to FCE aimed primarily at iMovie users making the transition between the two applications. In the video I go through some of the principle differences between the two as well as a few things to watch out for to make the transition easier.

The DVD-ROM portion of the disc includes unedited, raw footage for the tutorial projects, which contain sequences that guide you through the material.

The disc contains:

- Over 11 minutes of DV and audio media files
- 26 graphics files
- Nine FCE2 tutorial project files
- QuickTime preview movies of all FCE's transitions
- *Extras* folder with
  - Demo filters
    CGM
    CHV Plugins
    G-Filters
    Lyric Drawing Plugins
  - Custom button bar
  - Four Photoshop preset images

Want to receive e-mail news updates for Final Cut Express 2 Editing Workshop?

Send a blank e-mail to:
fce2@news. cmpbooks.com.

We will do our best to keep you informed of software updates and enhancements, new tips, and other FCE-related resources.